To the most exe
and caring t.
met Peter Swales
to his wonderful wp
Ann . With all my warm
& friendly wishes.
Yis Pahmy .
S. Rawlings

C000020999

AROUND THE WORLD WITH ISIS

The family house of Isis Fahmy at Manshiet-el-Bakri near the entrance to the ancient city of Heliopolis on the outskirts of Cairo.

CONTENTS

AROUND THE WORLD WITH ISIS

Isis Fahmy

PAPADAKIS PUBLISHER

To my husband Peter

for persuading me to write my memoirs and for giving me so much support and help in preparing them.

I am indebted to my publisher, Andreas Papadakis, for his advice and encouragement, and to John Teague for his translations. My sincere thanks also to Gina Sedky, Beatrice Monsallier, Nigel and Marion Rawlings, and my dear friends Linda and Ray Freeman.

Cover: Photograph of Isis Fahmy by Bob Allen

Designed by Alexandra Papadakis

First published in Great Britain in 2003 by
PAPADAKIS PUBLISHER
16 Grosvenor Place
London SW1X 7HH

ISBN 1 901092 49 6

Copyright © 2003 Isis Fahmy
Isis Fahmy hereby asserts her moral right to be identified
as the author of this work

No part of this publication may be reproduced or transmitted in
any form or by any means whatsoever, whether electronic, by
photography, photocopying, recording or facsimile machine or
otherwise howsoever without permission in writing from the Publisher.

Printed and bound in Singapore

LIST OF ILLUSTRATIONS

Isis Fahmy

IN THE BEGINNING

At the beginning of the twentieth century, there was a young Egyptian doctor whose name was Ibrahim Fahmy. He wanted to find a wife for himself in the old traditional way. So he went to see Habachi bey Moftah, a close friend of his in whom he had the utmost confidence. Habachi, who was considerably older than Ibrahim and who already had a wife and family, listened to Ibrahim's request to help him to find a bride. He promised to do what he could and set about the task without further ado. He soon had a list of suitable young women. Alas! None of them would do for Ibrahim.

So Habachi said, "It is a pity my daughter Farida is too young; otherwise I would have suggested her." Ibrahim was delighted at Habachi's words. "I will wait," he said simply.

And so it came about. Farida was not only refined, pretty and intelligent; she belonged to an upper class Egyptian family. The Moftahs traced their descent from a line of prominent fourteenth-century figures in the Coptic community, starting with Raphael Mouftah, known at the time as the "Moallem," the Master. Habachi himself had the title "Bey" which was rare and bestowed only by the Khedive.

Ibrahim and Farida were duly married. Farida was just fourteen, Ibrahim in his late twenties. The marriage was a very happy one throughout their lives. When their family had increased to three sons and two daughters, Farida found herself with child again; but she was now middle aged, weary and unwell. Her doctor husband wanted above all else to ensure his wife's survival; he was in favour of terminating the pregnancy. Farida's mother thought otherwise. She fell to her knees before her son-in-law and begged him to save the child. "I want this child. I implore you with all my heart." Ibrahim listened to her pleas. They were so heart-felt that he gave way to her wishes. Fortune smiled. A girl was born, to great rejoicing.

And that was how I came into the world.

Everyone was happy to welcome a third daughter into the family. "There's no doubt about it," said uncle Ragheb Moftah. "We must give her a name from the time of the Pharaohs. Nefertiti! Now that's a name to conjure up the glory of the Pharaohs!"

At the registry office, Nefertiti was duly entered on my birth certificate. But after a few days everyone realised that Nefertiti was very long and cumbersome for everyday use, so my uncle suggested a shorter pharaonic name, which was Isis. But for the church christening I had to have a Christian name. What could have been more appropriate than Labiba, the name of my grandmother. Labiba means 'intelligent.' I hope I have been worthy of the name. Unhappily, grand-mother died shortly after I was born.

My godmother was a Miss Suzanne Fancourt, an English teacher from Derby. My father had engaged her to live with the family to teach his children English. Was it coincidence or was it fate which decreed that when I married many years later my husband should also come from Derby?

The family house was a large one, the first to be built at Manshiet-el-Bakri. We were on the edge of the desert, very near the entrance to the ancient city of Heliopolis about twelve miles outside Cairo. Behind us, about a mile away, were the British military camps. The house, built in the Victorian style, was imposing, luxurious and set in an extensive garden. A flight of marble steps led up to the main entrance door which was on the first floor. On this level there were two huge rooms with balconies supported on marble columns running round the outside.

The table in the dining room could seat sixty-five people. At the back of the house, father had seen to the building of individual rooms for the servants so that they could live on the premises where he could keep a friendly eye on their well-being. They were treated as part of the family. In this house we all enjoyed a happy, noisy, bustling family life.

A few months after I was born, my parents engaged a French nanny for me. Her name was Isabelle. She was a Parisian. Whereas my brothers and sisters had learnt English as their first language with Miss Fancourt, for me it was French. Isabelle stayed until it was time for me to start school when I was five. She taught me, under the active supervision of my parents, to walk, to be well mannered; in other words how to be a well-brought-up child.

Parting from Isabelle was very sad for me, but I was soon consoled. My Aunt Blanche had two daughters, Gina and Loulou Sedky who were the same age as me. It became a regular thing for Mother to send me to play with them, and sometimes they came to us. We became inseparable, so much so that we were called "the three sisters." The close relationship that grew up between us con-tinued throughout our lives, and still exists today.

Our cook was a Greek called Sawa. Whenever I felt like teasing him I would go into the kitchen. In those days girls were not allowed in kitchens and nor was I. Sawa would chase me out, shouting in Arabic "Emshi, emshi!" Go away! The kitchen was his private domain by right and in fact. Cooks in Egypt had short tempers for anyone trespassing on their territory! Sawa was our family cook for forty years; he was a continuous thread in all our lives, in good times and in dif-ficult times.

He finally left us when he was very old and became ill, asking us to arrange for him to be taken back to Greece so that he could die near his daughter. My brother Adib decided to accompany him back to his native country; but I was far too upset to go or to offer anything except my tears and emotion from knowing that I was unlikely to see him again. Sawa was with the family long before I came into the world.

MY FAMILY

My Mother

Apart from the two years I spent as a student in Paris, I lived at home alone with my mother as my brothers and sisters were all married. My life was obviously greatly influenced by this relationship, especially as mother was a woman of strong character and firm religious beliefs. She came from the Mouftah family, which since the fourteenth century has played an important rôle in the history and learning of the Coptic Church in Egypt. Of her six brothers, Aziz and Ragheb became learned ecclesiastics. Aziz wrote a four-thousand-page book about Saint Mark, and Ragheb devoted years of his life to studying and preserving the music of the Coptic liturgy.

My mother too devoted her life to serving the Coptic Church. Her great interest in charitable works was largely inspired by my father, as she always acknowledged. In 1912 she founded the first orphanage in Egypt for Coptic girls. The orphanage was called "The Coptic Ladies' Charitable Society." The orphanage still exists today. Its current president was my sister Aïda. I can still remember my mother taking me as a child to the orphanage to play with the little girls there. Every year two of them were invited to spend Christmas at our home. Out of the Christmas presents which were meant for me, I had to choose two to give to them. Once I organised a grand Charity Ball in aid of the orphanage, under the patronage of Lady Lampson, the wife of the British High Commissioner, Sir Miles Lampson. The event raised £3,000, a huge sum in those days.

Another of my mother's major occupations was the preservation and restoration of the Coptic Chapel of Jerusalem in the Church of the Holy Sepulchre. All the members of our family used to be given the task of collecting donations for the ornaments and decoration of the Chapel. Although Mother used to go every year with my father to various cities in Europe, especially London and Paris, to attend medical conferences, the visit that gave her the most pleasure was her annual pilgrimage to spend Holy Week in Jerusalem. Sometimes I would accompany her.

Mother practised her religion by the strict observance of rules which in some cases no longer generally applied. For example, she would fast for the fifty-five days of the Coptic Lent, eating and drinking each day only when the Evening Star appeared. Only Coptic Monks follow this austere practice. Even then, she would eat only traditionally prescribed foods. On more than one occasion I had to summon the priest because mother's fasting was making her ill. The argument he put forward to persuade her not to fast – "The sacrifice for you is not to fast" – always fell on deaf ears.

Just a week before she died in 1972, President Anwar El Saadat awarded her a special medal in recognition of a lifetime spent in the service of humanitarian and charitable causes. I treasure the medal to this day. On her death, the Patriarch of Jerusalem bestowed on her an ecclesiastical title of nobility – *Chamasa*.

At home, mother was strict with her children. Her stern views on their upbringing contrasted with father's more relaxed attitude. For me particularly this difference was very disturbing. As I was by far the youngest in a family of six, I was the apple of my father's eye. Mother thought that to counterbalance his indulgence it was her duty to be even stricter with me. My brothers and sisters had more or less grown up together; they had the benefit of each other's company. By the time I was growing up, they had all left home.

I was afraid of her. There were so many things I wanted to do; yet everything seemed to be forbidden. I wasn't allowed to have a bicycle; so from time to time I would use some of my pocket money to hire one. Eventually, mother came to hear about this, and that was the end of it. I wasn't supposed to speak to boy cousins over the phone. If mother thought she could hear a "non-female" voice at the other end of the phone she would enquire, "Is that a young man you're speaking to?" I would lie rather than say it was. Even when it was agreed that I was old enough to go with a chaperone to properly organised parties for young people, I wasn't allowed to talk to boys, let alone dance with them. Luckily for me, the lady who was my usual chaperone was Finnish. With her more tolerant European outlook, she turned a blind eye. When she brought me back home, she had to give my mother an account of my behaviour, so she told her what she wanted to hear: "Isis was very good; she stayed with me all the time". I never understood what fun my mother thought I could have at a party sitting still and silent, watching everybody else having a good time!

At the convent I was well behaved and obedient. At home I often rebelled against the constraints. In time the grief we both shared in our bereavement drew us closer together. As my adolescent years passed I came more and more to understand and admire this woman whose austere inflexibility concealed a heart full of sensitivity and compassion.

My Father

Father had a private clinic in the centre of Cairo. Helping the poor gave him great pleasure and satisfaction. He would often ring his pharmacy saying, "I am sending so-and-so to you with a prescription. Give him the medicine. I will pay." He had a love for humanity that enabled him to reach out to all kinds of people and that endeared him to everyone. He taught my mother to follow his example of caring for the poor.

I still remember from my childhood an incident that typified his attitude. Among his patients at the time was the Prime Minister, Yehia Pasha Ibrahim. He trusted my father implicitly and indeed the two were good friends. Whenever father visited him, Yehia Pasha always saw him back to his car. One day father had just returned home from the hospital. Before he had time to sit down, mother told him. "You have two urgent cases: the Prime Minister wants you to call on him as soon as possible; and your patient Tadros is getting much worse." I'll go to my poor patient first; he needs me more than the Prime Minister does."

Father's philosophy was to deal quietly and calmly with life's great problems. His manner was always assured and sympathetic. In addition, he was a handsome figure of a man. Tall, slim, elegant and fine-featured, he possessed an aristocratic air, which some said gave him the appearance of an English Lord.

But our home, to which his presence gave such special radiance, was struck by sudden tragedy. On 9th October, 1941, in the middle of the night, father was taken from us by a sudden fatal heart attack. The shock was overwhelming for all of us; our lives were thrown into total confusion and turmoil by the unexpected death of someone we loved so much. Many who had known his care and kindness shared our grief. On the day of the funeral, traffic was halted in the centre of Cairo for an hour. The whole city seemed to be walking in the cortege.

Family mourning was intense. Young as I was I wore black for two and a half years. Mother refused to leave the house, in which she had shrouded all the chandeliers in black net. For a year her grief kept her inside. Eventually my two brothers decided it was time she went into the outside world again. After trying without success to persuade her to go for a drive with them in the car, they attempted to carry her out by force. For half an hour she resisted; in the end they managed to get her into the car.

As for me, the benjamin of the family, my relationship with my father was a very special one. Although he was a busy man, he found ways of making time for me. When I was a small child, he would sit by me at my meal times while my nanny Isabelle, as always, was there to supervise. He would say, "My child, gently, eat gently." If I had been naughty or wilful, he explained calmly and patiently how I had been wrong and how I ought to behave. My love for him was something very special.

I was eleven when he died. I did not know how I was going to face life alone. My brother Adib, a doctor himself, assumed my father's role both at the hospital and in looking after me. He too had a calm, serene and patient temperament. I can remember him taking me to the cinema every Sunday and, when I was older, to have tea at the Mena House Hotel near the Pyramids. At the time this hotel was fashionable in high society as a place where friends met for tea on Sundays. There we would find hia friends, especially two brothers, Peter and Yousef Awad who were old school friends of his. Peter was a lawyer and Yousef an engineer; they were the sons of Elias Pasha Awad and belonged to Egyptian high society.

My Brothers and Sisters

I had three brothers and two sisters. As I was by far the youngest in the family they were all grown-up to me, or seemed so through my child's eyes.

My eldest brother, Mounir, was a jovial man, fond of good living and an enthusiastic cook himself. By profession, he was a career diplomat who, coming from a family of high social standing, was obliged, along with others like him, to transfer a few months after the Nasser-inspired revolution of 1952 from the Diplomatic Corps to a less important government ministry. Nasser thought it would be better for Egypt to be represented abroad by military personnel than by civilian diplomats. President Saadat later reversed this policy, but in my brother's case it was too late. Mounir's eldest son, Ibrahim, besides bearing a strong physical resemblance to his father, inherited his good humour, gourmet tastes and capacity for hard work. He made a career in hotel management and in June 2002 became Managing Director of Starwood Hotels & Resorts in Egypt and General Manager of El Geziah Sheraton Hotel, Towers & Casino. Fahmy, Mounir's younger son, entered the legal profession. At the early age of forty he occupied an important judicial post as Head of the Prosecution Department of the Egyptian High Court. He also had one daughter called Leila, who is bright and independent and speaks several languages. Leila has been working for many years as an international tourist guide.

My brother Adib qualified as a doctor, practising alongside my father in his clinic. Upon father's death, he inherited the clinic, spending all his working life there, a worthy successor in the family line of doctors. He had no children.

My youngest brother, Aziz, was not attracted to the professions. He left life in Cairo to become a gentleman farmer on the family lands.

Daisy, my eldest sister, was educated at the Cairo Convent of the Sacred Heart, as were her two sisters after her. When it became clear that in her teens she was contemplating taking up the religious life, my parents withdrew her from the convent. Shortly afterwards a marriage was arranged according to Coptic tradition with Heshmat Kirollos. She had two daughters, Hoda and Samira.

For my sister Aïda too there was an arranged marriage, to Boutros Sourial. Of their two boys, Fahmy left Egypt as a student to read medicine in Vienna. There he was spiritually adopted by the Dean of the Faculty of Medicine, Professor Felinger and enjoyed a brilliant medical career in Austria, carrying on for a fifth generation the medical tradition of the family. He is now married to an Austrian, Marie-Thérèse, and they have two lovely daughters Katharina and Stefanie.

My nephew, Georges, qualified as a chemical engineer but never pursued this profession. Tall, strong, athletic and fearless, he became a professional frogman, and was judo champion of Egypt for several years. He took part in both of Thor Heyerdahl's Ra expeditions. The part Georges played in the expeditions can be read in Heyerdahl's exciting story of the journey of these two papyrus boats, which crossed the Atlantic from Morocco to Barbados.[1]

Georges married a French woman, Marie-Eve and had one son called Adib thus carrying on a traditional family name. But Georges could not settle down in a day-to-day job and yearned for excitement. It was so sad when he died at the early age of thirty from a heart attack brought on by his diving activities.

Unfortunately, my surviving sister Aïda died on the 26th August 2002, so now I have no brothers or sisters left alive.

---

1 Thor Heyerdahl, "The Ra Expeditions," London, George Allen and Unwin. 1971.

CHILDHOOD AND ADOLESCENCE

I started school when I was five years old, at the Cairo French Convent of the Sacred Heart. The Convent was situated about twenty minutes' drive from our house on the road to Cairo. My father took me there every day on his way to the clinic. The car, driven by his chauffeur, was a Mercedes-Benz saloon and I still have vivid memories of it. It was huge, upholstered in red velvet. A glass screen separated the chauffeur from the passengers in the back. On one side of the passenger seats there was a speaking tube for communicating with the driver; on the other, a beauty case with brushes, combs and perfume. At four in the afternoon, mother, driven by her chauffeur in her car, arrived to take me home.

My schooldays slipped by as they do for everyone, from primary to junior to senior school, all of which were located within the same convent precincts. A few episodes and incidents from my teenage years are still fresh in my mind.

There was the case of the doorkeeper at the convent. In my day the nuns came, for the most part, from the French upper middle class. Indeed, some were from titled families. One such was the "portière" or doorkeeper, Mother de la Monneraye. I suppose I would have been about sixteen when this Mother asked another pupil and myself to go with her one day to the French Consulate. She wanted us to testify that she was indeed who she said she was. The reason for this was that she had just inherited a substantial fortune, including a large French country mansion. She was donating all her inheritance to the convent since she, like all the other nuns, had taken the vow of poverty. To satisfy the legal requirements, we two were needed as witnesses of her identity.

A regular feature in the half-hour after lunch was games supervised by the nuns. I used to think it odd that in this French convent in Egypt the game we usually played was American baseball!

I always looked forward to the Christmas religious services. There were three masses, one at nine o'clock on Christmas Eve, one at midnight and the third at eight o'clock on Christmas morning. I sang contralto in the choir and this was the one occasion in the year that I stayed overnight at the convent.

French literature was an important subject in the curriculum. All went smoothly in the lessons until the time came for the teacher to deal with Voltaire[1]. My sister Aïda who had been at the convent years before me had warned me what to expect. "Don't believe what the nuns tell you about Voltaire. They're biased because of his outspoken criticism of the church". The official line was still the same in my day.

---

1 *Voltaire (1694-1778), French satirist, historian, poet, dramatist, philosopher. Fierce critic of the intolerance, superstition, cruelty and fanaticism of the civil and ecclesiastical powers, especially the Catholic church and its priesthood.*

The lesson hadn't been going long before I decided it was time for someone to stand up for Voltaire. So I stood up and interrupting the full flow of the teacher's condemnation of Voltaire and all his works, I announced, "It's not true. You're prejudiced against Voltaire because he was against religion!" I wasn't quite sure what I was going to say next, but I did not get the chance. "Hold your tongue and sit down!" snapped the teacher. So Aïda had been right! Retribution, divine or otherwise, seemed certain to follow my outburst; surprisingly, none came. Perhaps Voltaire had put in a good word for me with the Almighty, in the name of religious tolerance!

On the subject of toleration, I have to give the convent full marks on another matter. Except when I sprang to the defence of Voltaire, I was always well behaved at school, so I was mystified one day to be called out of a lesson with a summons to the convent visiting room. Waiting for me there were the Mother Superior and my mother. At home in my handbag, Mother had found a powder compact. She had come to school to accuse me in the presence of the Mother Superior of this terrible crime. She was expecting the convent to punish me. However, the Mother Superior was more tolerant than my mother. She looked at me with raised eyebrows, but she kept her lips sealed; that was the end of the matter. I'm not sure I fancy Voltaire's chances against my mother.

We were taught two foreign languages, French and English. All our lessons were in French. The nuns were all French, except for Mother Anderson who was Scottish and Mother Child who was Irish. It was Mother Child who taught us English. She had a strong personality. When she wanted something from the government she went straight to the British Embassy, where her reputation was such that she always got a sympathetic ear. In a word, she was a character! She was the one who sent off to the Cambridge Examining Board for their School Certificate English syllabus. Armed with this she made sure we worked hard in our English lessons. Eventually examiners came out from Cambridge and put us through the English examination, written and oral. That is how, a few months later, I received my Cambridge certificate. I had passed with a credit.

Girls who liked acting could join the drama classes, learn about the stage and take part in school plays: classic Molière comedies and more modern ones. I had a part in Les Précieuses Ridicules and in Don Juan, where I played Monsieur Dimanche. In another play I took the part of an Englishwoman going to a market in France and speaking French with a very English accent. Our headmistress the Mother Superior was in fits of laughter. We only put the play on for the rest of the school and just one performance. What a pity that our parents were not invited. Happy days, long gone now!

I was good at literature, but I did not like maths. I did my best to be ill and stay away from school when the maths exams were on. Apart from this, my years at the convent were very happy ones, and I have pleasant memories of the friends I made there as well as of the nuns who gave us such a good education. The time came to say last farewells, I was now seventeen, and I had "distinctions" on my school-leaving certificate! My parents wanted me to have a very feminine education after watching my elder sister Aïda grow up to be a real tomboy. All she liked was sport. She was an Egyptian tennis champion while still young: she wasn't interested in cosmetics or fashions; any clothes would do.

Girls of twenty were supposed to get married but not Aïda. Customs and tradition were the last of her concerns. She used to spend her holidays travelling abroad with our brother Adib, especially to Greece. In the end, of course, Aïda did get married. Apart from sports and outdoor pursuits, music was one of her loves, and she did a lot to introduce me to the classical composers. She often took me to see Italian opera at the Cairo Opera House where my parents used to take a box. It was there that I wore my first evening dress, a beautiful one in blue taffeta. The Opera was patronised by all of Cairo high society, especially the royal princesses. It was the occasion for a glittering display of beautiful gowns and rich jewellery, where people went to be seen as well as to see.

By the time I was seventeen I was moving in society circles. This wasn't always fun. Some of the dinners were dull and boring affairs, but I used to make my own entertainment. From an early age I had made a serious hobby out of studying people, watching their behaviour, listening to their conversations and trying to assess their character. Quietly and without drawing attention to myself I used to take in all that was going on around me. Often I could feel things happening. Eventually, I asked mother if I could have private lessons in psychology. A tutor was found for me, a Jesuit schoolmaster called Stavros. For two years I went to his house once a week for my lessons. What I learnt about psychology from Monsieur Stavros was to be very useful to me in my future journalistic career.

EARLY ADVENTURES

A Driving Lesson

By the time I was sixteen, one of my consuming interests was learning to drive. This occupation had the added attraction of requiring deception on my part, since my mother would have certainly put her foot down, so to speak, on such an enterprise. It was an expensive as well as clandestine business, as it involved me parting with my limited amount of pocket money each week to bribe our chauffeur to teach me. Such lessons could only take place when the chauffeur was engaged in taking me on some approved journey. I was soon proficient enough for me to be able to change places with him and drive from our house in Heliopolis into Cairo and back – apart that is from the danger zone. This was of course the stretch of road visible from the house!

It was all perfectly simple, safe and straightforward, until disaster struck on the day I was being driven into Cairo to have a studio photograph taken by the famous practitioner who, for some strange reason, went under the name of Venus. This appointment with him was a special occasion for me; it was to capture me proudly wearing my first evening gown. I smiled for Venus and his camera and out I came, feeling very pleased with myself. I arranged myself in the driver's seat for the journey back home. The streets in the centre of Cairo were busy with slow-moving traffic at this time of day, about one o'clock in the afternoon, but on similar occasions in the past I had manipulated the controls perfectly well in such stop-go situations. The only difference this time was that I was wearing a long dress. The car in front came to a stop; I braked as well, or would have done if my shoe hadn't caught in my dress, causing my foot to miss its target! Our Mercedes-Benz bumped into the far less weighty car in front and shunted it into the one in front of that. Before the drivers emerged for the inevitable angry scenes, I rapidly changed places with the chauffeur. He was the one who had the driving licence. The damage to all three cars was very slight but the inhabitants of Cairo are very excitable people and the shouting, gesticulating and wrangling went on for some considerable time. I, of course, sat through it all, looking as if butter wouldn't melt in my mouth, but wondering anxiously all the same about the accident and the lengthy delay. How was it all going to be explained to my mother? I didn't want to admit that I had been driving; but nor did I want to get the chauffeur into trouble.

What we really needed was a witness who would tell my mother that neither of us had been to blame. Luckily, one was to hand. The car behind us was a Jeep driven by an English army officer. As he got out to try and persuade everyone to calm down and drive on, I jumped out also and asked him where he was going. I knew there were officers' quarters in Heliopolis; perhaps he might be going that way. He was. With no little pleading and wheedling from me, he agreed to follow us back home and tell my mother that the chauffeur and I were both innocent victims of somebody else's careless driving. In the end I think he was too intrigued, and too much of a gentleman, to refuse. After all, I was a pretty sixteen year old in evening dress in a traffic accident in the middle of Cairo in the middle of the day and in trouble! Mother, anxiously waiting on the steps of the house, accepted our concocted story the more readily perhaps because our witness had the respectability of age and position.

The photograph by Venus was perfect. As for my driving lessons, I had to wait another five years for my licence, twenty-one being the minimum age at that time in Egypt.

Disaster on the Nile

Our days in the house at Heliopolis came to an end soon after I left school. We were told that our home was going to be requisitioned for use as a 'public utility'. The government apparently had the right to do this with large houses, which had only a few occupants. We came into that category, being now just three – Mother, Adib and myself. We couldn't believe it. Nevertheless we received official written confirmation that the house was needed for a school, and we were given just a month to vacate it.

Finding suitable alternative accommodation in such a short time was impossible. Adib came up with a solution to the problem. He suggested that for the time being we could rent a houseboat on the banks of the river Nile at Zamalek.

Zamalek is an island in the river, not out in the country, but a suburb of Cairo itself and a desirable built-up residential area. The riverside banks of the island are a popular and crowded location for houseboats. I call them houseboats, but this term needs an explanation. Houseboats in the sense of river or sea-going craft serving as living accommodation are indeed to be found at Zamalek. Much of the space is however taken up by what should properly be called 'floating houses.' These are wooden structures built entirely above the water-line on the foundation of a raft, beneath which an arrangement of barrels keeps the whole edifice afloat, the house being secured to a permanent mooring against the river bank. These floating houses, of either one or two storeys, are often substantial affairs with spacious accommodation.

Adib's suggestion was adopted. We found a suitable two-storeyed house, quite large, with three good bedrooms and a huge sitting room. The move suited Adib; he was pleased to be living within easy reach of his hospital and the city centre where he had a flat which he used as his private clinic. For my part, I shrugged off the move as an inevitable decree of fate and was happy at the prospect of living on the Nile. For mother, it was a terrible wrench to take leave of the family home with its store of happy and sad memories built up over the years.

The biggest problem was our furniture, much of which was old, big and heavy. Nevertheless, even though this was a temporary move, we put 'on board' as much as we could, both for our own convenience and to make it possible for us to entertain friends in comfort – especially mine! I had visions of parties, and of impressing my friends with the novelty of the surroundings. The first party I organised was a great success. Unfortunately, it was also the last.

Within a week, catastrophe! It was three in the afternoon, siesta time for my mother and Adib, but I was up and about, luckily as it turned out. I was in the dressing room, changing to go to a friend's house for tea. Suddenly, 'crack', and the house started to sway. Nothing unusual about that; it happened whenever the raft was disturbed by the wake of some large passing boat. This time though, the house continued to tip further sideways and always in the same direction. The prolonged creaking and cracking noise was something new. "That's odd," I thought. "What's going on?" I soon discovered the answer when I went outside to investigate.

The whole house was continuing to list steeply; in fact, it was capsizing deeper and deeper into the Nile. It was a miracle it was tilting towards the bank, not in the opposite direction towards the open river. If it had gone that way, I think we would all have been drowned. I didn't stop to think, which was perhaps just as well. I jumped on to the grassy bank, ran to the next houseboat and banged on the door shouting, "Help! Help! We're sinking!" The surprised neighbours let me use their phone to ring Uncle Sedky, who managed to take in my sobbing explanation of what had happened and also the fact that my mother and brother were still in the house, possibly injured and with no way of escape. It took about twenty minutes for my uncle to arrive, along with the emergency rescue service. Out came ladders, planks, axes and ropes. It was not an easy operation. Both occupants, but especially Mother, were badly bruised, as well as dazed and shaken. Uncle Sedky took us all – 'the shipwrecked sailors', as he called us, to his large house by the Nile, and there we stayed for some weeks until everything was sorted out and we were able to move into a flat in Zamalek which was to be a permanent home for Mother and for me.

Salvage operations at the scene of the disaster did not get under way until the following morning. Our losses were heavy. Much of the furniture was ruined or lost in the waters of the Nile along with personal possessions, furs, clothes and valuables, including a diamond engagement ring Adib had just bought for his intended fiancée. Why had the house 'sunk'? We claimed that the owner had not done essential repairs, that the barrels and moorings were rotten with age. The owner maintained that we had overloaded the house with our heavy furniture. The courts decided in his favour

A Narrow Escape

I was seventeen at the time. A serious problem had arisen between the Coptic Church in Egypt and its Ethiopian counterpart. The head of both branches was the Patriarch of Alexandria who had been elected by the bishops, but as there were more Egyptian bishops than Ethiopian ones, the Patriarch was always an Egyptian Copt. The leaders of the church in Ethiopia were becoming increasingly reluctant to submit to the authority of the Egyptian Patriarch. In an effort to preserve the union of the two churches, the Emperor of Ethiopia, Haile Selassie, conceived the idea of arranging a marriage between his eldest son, the Crown Prince, and a young woman from the Coptic community in Egypt.

When the Prince came to Egypt, he stayed in a villa belonging to a cousin of mine.

Ten names of suitable young ladies from high society were chosen by the Coptic Church and approved by the Palace. I quickly discovered my name was included in the list when the Prince approached my family with a view to marriage. I was shown a photograph of him, which did not impress me.

I was talking about the proposal to one of the Turkish royal princesses, who said, "You mustn't refuse the Prince. The Ethiopian court is renowned for its collection of fabulous emeralds. Just close your eyes at night and think of all the emeralds." I replied, "Life at the Ethiopian court is terribly austere. I know a young Copt who was invited there, also with the aim of marriage, to one of the Emperor's daughters. He couldn't stand the stifling atmosphere. It terrified him, even though he's very fond of pomp and ceremony himself."

The Princess had an answer for that. "Look," she said, "Just put up with it for a few months, then say you want to visit your family back in Egypt. So you come home and you don't go back. That way, for the rest of your life you'll have the title of Her Highness the Imperial Princess, and the emeralds!"

The decisive moment came for me to give my reply, without even having met the Prince. My mother, who was always very strict with me, left the decision to me. At that point I told her about the advice of my Turkish friend. Mother, with her stern principles, was horrified, and absolutely furious. "It's out of the question, if you're going to say yes with that idea in your head. Just sit quietly and don't say another word."

After a long stay in Cairo the Prince returned to his native land, alone. No fiancée. King Farouk was extremely angry. He could see reprisals on the horizon. The Emperor, too, was furious at such an unbearable insult and loss of face. A few months later, the two churches separated. However, once the initial problems were overcome, a spirit of harmony was established between them that has existed ever since.

That was not quite the end of my involvement with the Prince. Some years afterwards, he was visiting Egypt as a tourist, with his wife (who was Ethiopian) and their two children. I was called into the office of my boss, Moustafa Amin. "You are well placed," he said, "to get an interview with the Prince. He's staying at the Mena House Hotel. Go and see him, and take a photographer with you."

I carried out the chief's orders. Seeing the Prince for the first time was an entertaining experience. Yet fate, once again, was waiting. If I had married him and stayed in Ethiopia, I would not now be writing this book. During the coup in Ethiopia in 1974 the Crown Prince, his father, the Emperor Haile Selassie, and their family were all assassinated.

SOCIETY LIFE IN EGYPT

By the time I was sixteen I had two best friends. One was Princess Khadija Hassan who was a first cousin of King Farouk; the other was Sherifa Hazma. All the descendants in direct line from the family of the Prophet Mohamed enjoy a title of nobility, Sherif for men, and Sherifa for women. In theory this title is equal in rank to Prince or Princess.

Sherifa Hazma was blonde and pretty. She had received a very Westernised European education. Princess Khadija had dark hair and was also pretty. She had a similar education in the tradition of the Egyptian royal family.

Both were twenty years old. I of course was still at school. There was no school on Thursdays, so the three of us used to meet for lunch, taking it in turns to visit each other. In addition, nearly every month we would organise an evening entertainment, either a ball or a dinner party. King Farouk, who spent every evening out at one party or another, paid us a surprise visit from time to time. If he found it boring, he did not stay long; if he was enjoying himself he would stay until the early hours. That meant everyone else stayed, for protocol decreed that nobody should leave before the King.

I remember especially one particular party as it was somewhat out of the ordinary. It was a kind of bal masqué: guests had to disguise just their heads. The General Administrator of the Cairo Opera House used to lend us costumes for our fancy dress parties and this particular evening my head was disguised as a Goddess of the Pharaohs. King Farouk's arrival at the party added to the excitement. As usual there was a lavish supper buffet. His Majesty came up to me, held out his plate and said, "Serve me." Somewhat taken aback, I offered him some meatballs. He shook his head, "I don't fancy that," he said very politely, "A King doesn't eat the food of a goddess." Then he broke into his usual booming laughter. This little incident became a subject of conversation. As my chaperone reported to me on the way home. Everyone was saying, "The King chatted to Isis for quite a while, and had a good laugh with her. What an honour!"

No description high society in Egypt some fifty years ago would be complete without a mention of the famous parties given by Princess Chevekiar. One such party in the late 1940s was never forgotten by those who enjoyed its wonderful moments. For the occasion, Prince Mehemet Ali had lent Chevekiar one of his palaces on the Nile at Choubra. The theme of the party was Turkey. Guests wore Turkish costumes and the decor was a faithful reproduction of a Turkish palace of the past. Exquisite gondolas glided over the Nile alongside the palace, taking guests for magical, fairy-like rides.

Several years later when King Farouk married Farida, Princess Chevekiar gave a fabulous Turkish soirée. It was held at her palace in Cairo and was unforgettable for me because Queen Farida was there. For me, so young, meeting the Queen was a dream come true. Many years later, when she was in exile in Paris we became friends. That evening the great attraction was the tableaux vivants. Nearly all the young girls of high society were brought in to be the statuettes, over a hundred in all, with twelve or so taking part in a series of scenes lasting nearly an hour. The girls were carefully chosen and I had the honour of being one of them. I was just fifteen and excited beyond words to be part of such extraordinary scenes depicting the history of Turkish palaces, the splendour of the costumes and the sheer magnificence of life in the harems of old.

Whenever Princess Chevekiar gave one of her incredible parties, there were coloured tents in her glorious park, with French, Italian and Russian food, pink champagne by the gallon, three orchestras and four hundred guests, the Four Hundred of Egypt. Her New Year's Eve parties were annual exercises in glamorous excess that neither Farouk nor anyone of importance dared to miss.

Princess Chevekiar was the fabulously rich grand-daughter of the eldest son of Ibrahim Pasha and therefore of the most senior line of the descendants of Mehemet Ali. She was married in 1895 at the age of nineteen to Prince Fuad (later King of Egypt) but they were divorced three years later after the death of their son, Ismaïl, and the near fatal shooting of her husband by her brother. At the time of their marriage the Princess was one of the richest women in Egypt whereas Prince Fuad's gambling debts had almost bankrupted him. Princess Chevekiar subsequently married four more distinguished men; the last of them, in 1927, was Elhamy Hussein Pasha.

Princess Chevekiar's tomb stands in a garden enclosure in Cairo. A double door gives access to the tomb chamber. In the centre stands the remarkable white Italian marble tomb of the Princess in the form of a directoire bed. There is a flowered bedspread and bowls of roses on each side. A coronet surmounts the ornate headboard. The sculptor was the Venetian Gabriella Donatelli.

Fashionable Cairo life was truly international. It was this that made it so interesting and fascinating. For their parties, rich aristocrats had tulips flown in from Holland; delicacies such as caviar, smoked salmon, foie gras, and sometimes a whole buffet were imported from Paris.

Shortly after returning home from my stay in Paris in 1949, I wanted to organise a party with a difference and came up with the idea of the Arabian Nights. I had a group of friends from many countries – France, England, the United States, the Far East. When I put the idea to them, all were in favour. George Atkinson, the American Vice-Consul, lent us his villa for the occasion. He had a soft spot for me and did not know how to refuse! We went to the Egyptian market of Khan Khalil and struck a bargain with a specialist in oriental furnishings who agreed to deck out George's villa in appropriate style. The alterations to his house were rather more than he bargained for: out went all the

Isis dancing at her Arabian Nights party given in Cairo in 1949 at the home of the American Vice-Consul, George Atkinson. Guests included the two Prince Romanoffs, and the spy Donald Maclean.

furniture from the ground floor. We thought it was great fun doing the removals but George stood there wringing his hands! We took it in turns to console him. In came richly upholstered sofas, low tables with copper tops, Persian rugs and carpets. Oriental tents sprang up round the walls.

There were over a hundred guests. All young and fashionable Alexandria came to join in the fun disguised in costumes that came straight from *The Thousand and One Nights*. A Pasha's wife, Madame Marie-Agathe Sidarous, had lent me a magnificent costume in Turkish Princess style, an authentic costume as worn by the ladies of the harem in those Turkish palaces of bygone days.

The two Prince Romanoffs, who lived in Alexandria, came as Maharajahs. Donald Maclean, the British diplomat and several other young diplomats were Arab princes for the night. Unfortunately, they entered into the role of Arabian princes straight from the days of Haroun El Rashid with excessive zeal behaving as if they were in a harem and going round making amorous approaches to guests whose own escorts took violent exception to these attempts at seduction. There were scenes of jealousy and angry confrontations. Nevertheless, the general setting with its exotic atmosphere generated a mood of euphoria that lasted until dawn.

Our American host was happy, considering the whole event to have been a great success and well worth all the upheaval. A score of local and foreign magazines reported the party, whilst *Akher Saa*, an Egyptian weekly magazine well known throughout the Middle East, gave it extensive coverage.

Fashionable life in Cairo was truly international. It was this that made it so interesting and fascinating. For years, writer after writer has described this life with its spectacular parties, lavish entertainment and displays of wealth and extravagance. Josette Alia, chief editor of *Le Nouvel Observateur* described the glittering scene in her book *Quand le soleil était chaud*, the 1992 French bestseller. Writing about the scale and opulence of the buffet at the Tegarts' winter ball, she says, "All Cairo was there…". Every year the Tegarts' ball brought a new surprise. That year everything had come by plane from Paris – from its most famous restaurant, Maxim's – that very morning. And the food was accompanied by a French maître-d'hotel.

In her account, she is kind enough to mention me, "Isis Fahmy was wearing a curious, straight-cut, embroidered tunic, with its belt high on the waist. Isis is a Copt and very proud of her line of descent from the Kings of Thebes, explaining to foreigners that the Copts were the only true inhabitants of the ancient kingdoms of Egypt. And that evening, with her fringe of short-cut dark hair above her straight nose, she did indeed resemble a Pharaoh's young queen."

Later in her book, Josette Alia recounts my own preparations for a more modest dinner party, preparations that were thrown into some confusion by an event which now has a place and name in the history of Egypt in the 1950s.

> "It was eight o'clock in the morning. Sitting in the kitchen of her
> flat in Zamalek, Isis was having an argument with Ahmed, her

Sudanese cook. Ahmed had been in service at the German
Embassy and still retained from his days there a liking for cabbage
soup; this irritated Isis. She was giving a grand dinner that evening
and everything had to be perfect: Moustafa Amin, the owner of
Akbar el Yom would be there; so would Hassanein Heykal, the chief
editor of *Akher Saa,* and the new press counsellor at the French
Embassy. In a word, the 'top' press people in Cairo. Isis was in the
early days of her career as a social columnist for Akbar el Yom.
Moustafa Amin was susceptible to the charm of this dark-haired
shapely young woman; he appreciated her young, well-bred style,
her ability to write amusing, airy, anecdote-sprinkled articles, her
gift for depicting the social scene whilst leaving reputations
unharmed. But Isis had other ambitions. In her sights she had the
front-page top spot *Le billet d'humour.* In this she could go further
than local gossip. Here she could indulge in occasional criticism,
or, more frequently, praise. It was a spot that bestowed undeniable
power upon its holder. The dinner that evening was meant to
prove to her guests that she was a woman who also knew how to
entertain.

"Why not ox-tail soup?"

Isis gave Ahmed a withering look.

"For heavens sake, no soup."

For the entrée she was considering, smoked salmon; that was in
fashion. Then roast pigeon, with saffron rice. A touch common
perhaps, but Moustafa Amin would like it. So, remember finger
bowls. Which table cloth? The white one. Mother's silver. The big
English candleholders. Don't forget the flowers. A few rose petals
to float in the finger bowls. For dessert? Mango sorbets from
Lappas, perhaps. To serve with the coffee, chocolates from
Groppi's, in a silver bowl. Right. So she would have to go to town
that morning. She went up to her room and ran the bath water.

Isis parked her car in Emad el Din Street, not far from Groppi's.
First she would buy the chocolates, then the sorbets at Lappas. Just
as she was shutting the car door a young man shouted at her as he
ran past, "Go back, right away." "Why?" "Can't you see the Rivoli
cinema is on fire?" Thick black smoke was indeed billowing up at
the street corner. Isis went to have a closer look. Long, orange
flames were coming from the front of the cinema. On the pave-
ment, a milling, yelling crowd. No fire engine was in sight to put
out the blaze. Isis hesitated. She would need ice cream at least; perhaps if she made a detour via Kasr el Nil Street.... An old woman
shouted to her from her window, "You there, be off with you!
They are starting fires everywhere." When Isis, whose mind was on
her dinner, did not move, the old lady began to shout in Arabic,

"Do you want to die? Go home. The streets are no place for a woman today." Isis got back into her car, turned round and set off back to Zamalek. For dessert, she would think of something else!"

I had been caught up in the events of 'Black Saturday.'[1]

Involvement in society life required stamina. It was a strenuous pastime with parties one after another in quick succession. The same still holds true today. On occasions, the parties could be boring and monotonous – the same people all the time, with nothing left to say to each other apart from polite banalities. Madame de la Fayette had the same to say, very succinctly at Versailles when she wrote in the seventeenth century about life at the court of Louis XIV, "Always the same pleasures, always the same hours and always with the same people." (*Mémoires de la Cour de France*). On the other hand there were times when suddenly one struck up an understanding with someone, became interested in them as people and developed unexpected friendships as a result. In my case this happened from my contact with Donald Maclean and his wife Melinda. Who at the time knew what he was really doing in Egypt?

I lived in the residential district of Zamalek, close to the houses of the senior British diplomats. Maclean was the political counsellor at the Embassy and consequently entitled there. We were neighbours; we became friends and paid frequent visits to each other's houses, especially Melinda and I. We got on very well and I became more or less her confidante, a shoulder to cry on. Cry, she frequently did, as she recounted how her husband went out every evening and did not return until the early hours. She said that his excuse was that he spent his evenings at the palace of her Royal Highness Princess Fayza who was one of Farouk's four sisters. She was married to a tolerant Turkish prince, Ali Raouf and liked her friends to organise parties and dances for her on an almost daily basis.

Most of the foreign diplomats who enjoyed night-life were invited, bachelors mostly, but some couples. To be admitted into this exclusive circle one had to be refined, handsome and charming. Maclean had all the qualifications. No one could dispute that he was smart, tall, and slender, with delicate features; the man-about-town par excellence. Thanks to his physical qualifications, his

1 *Egyptian guerrillas and saboteurs were carrying on a campaign against British bases in the Canal Zone. The British hit back and on 25 January 1952 surrounded a police station in Ismailia which was thought to be harbouring guerrillas. Following government orders, the police refused to surrender. The British attacked. By the time the police ran out of ammunition and finally surrendered, forty-three had been killed and seventy-two wounded. When the news was broadcast the following day, the Cairo populace went on the rampage. Mothers burned down and looted British-owned businesses, properties, department stores and clubs. The Turf Club, Sheperd's Hotel and nearly every bar, cinema and restaurant in the centre of Cairo were destroyed, as well as property belonging to other foreigners. Clouds of black smoke hung over the capital, as ordinary citizens stayed behind closed doors, too afraid to go out. By the time order was restored in the afternoon, some seventy people, including nine Britons, had been killed and much of central Cairo had been devastated. Who co-ordinated and encouraged the riots has never been clearly established, but the event was a landmark in Egyptian history. The days of King Farouk and his successive governments were numbered. Six months later came the army coup d'etat, the overthrow of the monarchy and the beginning of the Nasser years.*

approachable nature and ease in conversation, he had no difficulty in gaining access to the best circles. All fell under the spell of his charm.

Work over for the day Maclean, who was a keen tennis player and swimmer, would be off in the afternoons to the Guezireh Sporting Club. This club was founded by the British some fifty years ago. Egyptians wishing to become members had to be of superior social status and even then sometimes had to wait years before being accepted. (Nasser nationalised it and opened its doors to all.) Naturally the club was a favourite meeting place for its members. Maclean began to invite his Soviet counterparts and went on to meet them more and more often, quite openly. In addition his secret night meetings with the Russians became more frequent. He used Princess Fayza's parties as a cover, going on from them late at night to meet the Russian diplomats. Melinda, who was still in love with him, cried because she was convinced he was seeing another woman. I did what I could to calm her down, but to no avail, because it was true that Fayza was attracted to him and danced regularly with him at her parties.

I talked with Maclean on several occasions; we used to exchange ideas, especially about politics. Despite our friendship we never agreed. More than once our 'discussions' ended in violent political slanging matches. One particular argument went on for a solid two hours. I went home feeling shocked that a British diplomat should have such left-wing leanings that I kept asking myself, "Is he a Communist? He can't be. He's too much of an aristocrat". So much for my opinion!

In June 1958, I made my first trip to Tunisia. In the hotel I asked for a newspaper and took it with me into the restaurant to glance at over dinner. There, on the front page, was a photo of Maclean with the headline, "English Spy flees to Russia." I was dumbfounded. I just could not imagine him as a spy, a traitor to his country. It took me a long while to take it in.

It's the same the world over. In the circles variously called High Society and Cafe Society, there are and always will be, infiltrations by gigolos, rogues, cheats and spies, male and female. As the Duchess de La Rochefoucauld put it to me, "The important thing is to know who is not who he pretends to be. It's pointless to try and avoid such people and sometimes there are interesting situations."

In fact, there are still parties in Cairo every night. During our visits, my husband and I have attended many of them. My cousin Yvonne is a perfect hostess. She and her husband Youssef Gaffar are known for their fabulous buffets.

I must not forget Ihab Shafik, an old family friend, a handsome bachelor who has many well-known international contacts, he entertains exceptionally well.

Then there is Hassan Moumtaz and his wife who live on the banks of the river Nile. He is related to the ex royal family. Sometimes black tie and evening dress is required for these functions.

There are others, too many to mention, all who entertain very well. The atmosphere and cross section of interesting people together with the varying topics of conversation make these soirées enjoyable and relaxing events.

MARRIAGES

In Egypt, at the beginning of the twentieth century, in the days of our grand-mothers, or more likely great-grandmothers, marriage customs still decreed that marriages should be arranged by the choice of the respective families. This practice held good in all classes of society. The prospective bride had no say in the matter and would meet her future husband for the first time on the wedding day, whereas the man had the right to ask for a photograph of all eligible girls, and then make his choice. Once he had made up his mind, he was always accompanied by his parents when he went to the family of his choice to ask for the hand of their daughter.

One of my aunts used to tell a story about her marriage. On the day of her wedding, the male guests were gathered in a room with the bridegroom. A cousin of my aunt said to her, "Come on, let's peep through the keyhole". The cousin looked first, located the bridegroom and described him to my aunt who burst into tears when she had her turn to look. "He's too ugly. I won't have him." But her cousin had identified the wrong man as the bridegroom and my aunt ended up with a much more handsome husband.

By the 1930s, a change was taking place in these practices. The girl was allowed to meet her 'fiancé' before the wedding, perhaps over a period of weeks or months but chaperoned, of course. However, if the girl was reluctant to accept her parents' choice, her mother would always try to persuade her, saying, "He is rich, he comes from a good family, he is very presentable." Even in cases where the girl felt no inclination at all, she would often accept from a sense of duty towards her parents – the duty to get married. Naturally enough, when such a marriage did not work out well, the girl blamed her mother.

Recent years have seen more changes. Young people's lives today are more influenced by western European patterns. Young women go out to work; they have more independence and insist on choosing a husband for themselves. Where parents disapprove, there can be serious arguments, and even complete family breaks. Marriages of convenience are nevertheless still frequent, in both Moslem and Coptic families. In the case of Copts, it is still not unusual for a son, accompanied by his mother, to go to the parish priest and receive from him a list of marriageable girls. In the provinces and the countryside, workmen and peasants still hasten to marry off their daughters as soon as they reach the age of puberty, even to much older men. This is the safest and easiest way of ensuring that the girl does not lose her essential virginity outside of marriage.

On frequent visits to Egypt I still hear of grand weddings in what is called 'the New Society' costing anything from 60,000 to 100,000 Egyptian pounds,

occasionally more. In families of more modest means, the money given to the
bride and groom by parents is often spent on a honeymoon to remember, rather
than an expensive wedding reception.

To give an example of the lavish society weddings of an earlier day, let me
describe the ceremony involved in the marriage of my friend Nadia El Gamal
to Tewfick Badraoui in 1938. In this instance the marriage was a marriage of
convenience. Nadia told me, "I listened to my mother's advice, and then after the
engagement I met my fiancé several times over a period of months before the
Katb El Ketab."[1] For the wedding itself Nadia wanted to order two specially
made dresses from Paris but her future mother-in-law said she needed three, one
exclusively for the car. This she wore when she left her grandfather's house in
the car to go to the home of her fiancé where all the ladies were waiting. The
dress was in white satin with long sleeves, white veil and a crown of white lilies.
For the Zafa, the traditional wedding procession, Nadia wore a second dress, in
silver brocade with a long train. During this procession, the mother of the bride
and groom showered the lined-up guests with the customary little gold sequins
for which the guests scrambled excitedly.

For the wedding feast that followed, Nadia changed into her third dress, this
time a close fitting matt silver lamé dress, with a high bust in light blue tulle
embroidered with dark blue spangles.

The buffet was in the hands of Azouz, the most famous caterer of the day.
Whole sheep, turkeys, pigeons, and sides of stuffed veal were laid out on crystal
tables illuminated from below. Other tables carried a dozen or so cakes of huge
proportions. All night long there were entertainments in Egyptian style with bal-
lets featuring the most celebrated oriental dancers of the time. When the party
came to an end, the newly-weds were driven to their home in an apartment
building belonging to the groom's family.

---

1 *The Moslem religion requires marriage to be arranged by a contract, drawn up perhaps weeks or even months before
the wedding ceremony. If, during the intervening period, there is a breakdown between the two parties, a divorce
becomes necessary to end the relationship and annul the contract.*

PARIS DAYS

In 1946, after completing my studies in Egypt, I was very keen to continue my education in post-war Paris. Family contacts gave me the opportunity to do so and to spend two years there in the most favourable conditions imaginable.

The Egyptian Ambassador in Paris, His Excellency Ahmed Sarwat, was a family friend. He introduced me to Madame Chauvel, whose husband was the Secretary of State at the Quai d'Orsay, the French Foreign Office. Madame Chauvel had recently formed the Lyceum Ladies' Club in Paris, and become its President. Lyceum Ladies' Clubs were eventually started in many capital cities inspired by the London Club founded by Constance Smedley. In Paris the club was established in a magnificent private mansion in the heart of the Champs-Elysées district. It belonged to the Duc de Nekelgen, who had very generously made it available for Madame Chauvel and her group.

It was in this mansion that I was privileged to live for the two years I stayed in Paris. The General Secretary of this highly exclusive centre for social and cultural gatherings was Countess Edith de Poligny. She took a great interest in me, looking after me as if she was my elder sister. We were the only two permanent residents. From time to time it had temporary residents – ladies from many parts of the world staying perhaps a few weeks or just for a few days.

I duly enrolled to study the History of Art at the Ecole du Louvre, which has an international reputation for academic excellence in many fields of study. Regrettably, I was not to add lustre to its roll of honour. Music, especially the piano that I had studied for some years, was another subject that greatly interested me. I happened to mention this at the Lyceum to Madame de Lestapis. who had a lively personality and tremendous enthusiasm. "If you are really serious about wanting to continue with your piano studies in Paris, I can have a word for you with Soulima Stravinsky." I jumped for joy. Thus it was that I enjoyed the extraordinary privilege of being one of the ten pupils of this famous pianist, the son of the even more celebrated Igor. For two years I had a private lesson every week at his home. Soulima's personality made a strong impression on me. He was a modest man, shy and reserved; in his teaching he was strict, over serious even, qualities determined perhaps by his upbringing.

The main reception room in the Lyceum was large, magnificent, and sumptuously decorated. What a wonderful setting for a concert! I asked the President if she thought it would be interesting to invite Stravinsky to give an afternoon recital for the members. She was enthusiastic. Soulima was asked and he agreed. Madame Chauvel had also given me permission to invite well-known society personalities I had met through the Duchess Edmée de La Rochefoucauld. I had been introduced to the Duchess at the Egyptian Embassy. She was famous for her salons, where she entertained many eminent guests drawn from the worlds of society, diplomacy and the arts. I was now eighteen years old and felt rather daring to be inviting people so much older than myself – the Duchess de La Rochefoucauld, the Duchess de Clermont-Tonnerre, the Egyptian Ambassador, the Embassy Counsellor and other personal friends.

The afternoon was a great success. Soulima was loudly applauded and fêted by all. Socially, too, the event was memorable. There was, though, one note of disharmony. I had invited the Begum Aga Khan – Begum being the title given to the wife of the Aga Khan. I had known her from early days in Egypt. At the party after the concert none of the titled ladies present would speak to her. French she may have been, but she was certainly not of the French aristocracy. The Egyptian Ambassador noticed her isolation. He stayed with her for a while and asked my other friends to keep her company. In later years I interviewed her several times. She had a strong personality and was very courteous to all her entourage. Before leaving the party, the Egyptian Political Counsellor came up to me with his wife and said, "You are our Ambassador in Paris". This remark was prompted by the fact that the actual Ambassador, whilst being a brilliant diplomat, was an old bachelor who never did any entertaining.

The château of Vaux-le-Vicomte, situated near Melun, about twenty-five miles from Paris, is a magnificent example of seventeenth-century architecture, not as splendid as Versailles, but the inspiration for it. Its owner invited the Lyceum Club in 1947 to a grand reception there. Some Ambassadors were also invited. Edith and I were taken to the party in the car of the Ambassador for the Vatican whose name was Roncalli. He later became Patriarch of Venice and in 1953 was elected Pope upon the death of Pope Pius XII. So that day we were driven by the future much-loved Pope John XXIII. It is not surprising that I remember the event now as one to treasure. The château was for a long time in the hands of the Sommier family but had been sold in 1945 to Count Jean de Vogüé, whose son Patrice is the present custodian.

During my stay in Paris I led an intellectually and socially stimulating life. I was surrounded by older friends who took me to lectures, theatres, concerts, the Opera and important social events where I met famous figures of the time, including the Prince and Princess Guy de Polignac, Edith Piaf and Yves Montand. At Madame Abrami's influential political salon I met well-known politicians and especially the Count of Paris, of whose presence she was very proud. But all good things, all wonderful moments come to an end. So it was that one day I made up my mind to return to the fold to live with my mother. She was alone, because all my brothers and sisters were married and living their separate lives. Although I left Paris with such happy memories, I had one great regret. I had lived in the company of older people. Unlike my cousins, Gina and Loulou, who were students in Paris whilst I was there, I had not known what it was like to be a real student, to savour all the life and atmosphere of the university quarter, home to students since medieval times – the 'Quartier Latin.'

HOW I BECAME A JOURNALIST

When I finished my studies in Paris and returned home to Egypt in 1948, I was bored doing nothing but attending social functions. Life was empty. I wanted to have an aim in life and the following events gave me this opportunity. At that time, my brother Dr. Adib Fahmy bought a building in Garden City, which is a refined area of Cairo, and there created his private hospital which he called Garden City Hospital.

He took, as partners, several well-known and very experienced doctors. He held ninety per cent of the shares and the other doctors had various percentages. One day my brother said to me. "If you want an occupation, come and supervise the hospital." I accepted the offer and started immediately. All the partners thought that I was working as a volunteer but in fact my brother was very discreet and at Christmas gave me a large cheque as my present.

Some time later, two of the doctors noticed that I had become interested in medicine and suggested that I attend and assist them in the operating theatre. I was very happy about the proposal and accepted. At that time we had an Irish Matron, Mrs Falkson who was a dictator and very strict. She used to wake me at home with a phone call at 5.30 am and say, "Miss Fahmy, you have to be ready in the operating theatre by 6.30. The operations are due to start at seven." I took my job very seriously and was fascinated by medicine. It must have been in my blood as father's family had been in the profession for five generations.

Matron attended my first day in the operating theatre and watched with interest every move I made. When the operation was over she left without comment. Knowing Matron this meant she had approved of my performance.

At this time in Egypt women doctors were only allowed to practise in gynaecology. The main reason for this was that many conservative traditional families had to have a woman doctor at the delivery and not a male doctor. They only called a male practitioner in an emergency if there were complications.

There was a well-known humorous story in Egypt that involved one of my uncles, Professor Naguib Mahfouz Pasha. One day the wife of a wealthy provincial mayor had a serious vaginal problem so exceptional that he took her to consult my uncle, who was known to be strict and serious. In his consulting room he asked her, "Would you please undress?" She replied, "No doctor! You first."

I could not in any circumstances become interested in gynaecology, but was very fond of surgery, so Professor Abou Zikri, who was a noted surgeon asked me if I would be interested in helping in the theatre. I found it fascinating to be his assistant. It was very demanding work and he saw that my hands were gifted enough for me to become a surgeon, should I choose to do so.

I was also working in the operating theatre with a famous laryngologist, Professor Abd El Salam El Barbary. Each morning he would carry out five to seven operations. After I had been assisting him for several months, he said with a laugh: "Now you can take out tonsils on your own as you have become an expert." Needless to say, I never did.

My brother was not happy that I was assisting two surgeons and neglecting him, but as he specialised in gynaecology I was really not interested. I felt rather guilty, as my brother had helped me so much in the past, so I decided to attend the next emergency delivery that required my brother to be present. This I did, but I ran out in the middle of the proceedings. I could not bear to see the spectacle of a woman suffering, surrounded by nurses and doctors trying to help her, as in those days they did not give anaesthetic unless there were severe complications. I never again attended a delivery. I was thankful that my brother was sympathetic to my feelings.

I had been working in the hospital nearly three years and had started to think about a career in medicine but I would have to specialise and surgery was what interested me most. Many thoughts passed through my mind. Would patients one day be operated on by a woman doctor? Thirty years ago the answer was certainly not.

While I was turning over such thoughts in my mind and wondering what would be my best course of action, within the space of a few months two events occurred that changed my way of life and gave it a new direction. To some extent these events were interconnected and for a time led me along two parallel, compatible paths. Eventually one path became blocked; all my energies were turned to following the other, with profound implications for my future.

One morning, Professor Abou Zikri said to me, "Today it is better for you not to assist me with this operation because the father of a well-known newspaper editor, Hassanein Heykal, is having a hernia operation and it will be safer if you are not involved in case any complications occur." It was a wise decision because I was not qualified as an assistant surgeon, so I stayed in the doctor's office.

In the hall adjacent to the operating room Hassanein Heykal was anxiously pacing up and down while his father was in the operating theatre. Eventually he saw me and started to talk. I think it was a journalist's curiosity that prompted him to make conversation. He asked me politely who I was, so I introduced myself. He then asked, "What other interests do you have besides medicine?" I replied, "I have a social life which is interesting as well as being very entertaining." He became more and more interested in me and my social activities because he was the Chief Editor of one of the most famous Egyptian magazines Akher-Saa, which can be compared with Paris Match and was sold all over the Middle East. One of his weekly jobs was to produce at least four or five columns exclusively devoted to social events.

Since his father stayed in The Garden City hospital for three weeks, Heykal and I established an interesting friendship discussing the social calendar. Heykal was short of news for his social columns; but his consuming interest was politics, and it was on this subject that he wanted to concentrate his time. Naïvely and without thinking about his magazine, I was giving him enough information for its coverage of social events. When his father was discharged from the hospital, Heykal used to call me each week asking for all the social news. In his articles he would mention that I had been present at various parties and receptions. As I did not read Akher-Saa, it was only when friends started calling me to tell me that my name had been mentioned that I began to take an interest in it. I soon realised that all the news on its social pages was being supplied by me. That was the start of my interest in the press and in journalism. I was in my twenties and thought it was fun to be in the news. After a while my mother became furious. She was very "old school" and traditional and objected strongly to my name appearing in the press.

Some weeks after my chance meeting with Heykal, fate again took a hand. At a French Embassy party a young very attractive fellow came up to me and introduced himself. For me it was love at first sight with Serge de Tchaikovsky, a descendant of the famous Russian composer. We were soon going everywhere together. Naturally I used to talk to him about the various people I knew, including Hassanein Heykal. Serge, who was the Commercial Counsellor at the French Embassy, said he would like to see round his newspaper offices. By now I knew Heykal quite well and it was relatively easy to arrange a visit. Throughout I was enchanted by the whole atmosphere and the work of the journalists who appeared so creative and full of life.

Hassanein saw how enthusiastic I was and said, "Why don't you come and work with us?" I laughed and replied, "Me? I don't think so; it's impossible." When I told Serge about Heykal's invitation, his comment was, "You? Work for a magazine? Out of the question!"

A few months after this visit, while I was still working at the hospital, Serge and I became unofficially engaged. Alas, the romance did not last long. Women found Serge irresistible. He was handsome, elegant and refined, with a captivating Slavonic charm. He was also without money of his own, so he was on the lookout for a woman who was rich. Private fortunes were far from rare at that time. One day the blow fell. Serge came and told me that he had met someone at a party, a Copt who was separated from her husband. She was one of the richest landowners in the country, with about five thousand acres of prime farming land. Serge had decided to leave me. He was as happy as could be. He had won the lottery!

As for me, I was inconsolable. To try and forget my griefstricken love, I took a momentous decision. I would start to work immediately as a journalist on Akher-Saa. This was more easily said than done. A young woman from a well-connected Coptic family was expected to get married when she had finished her education. She did not have the right to go out to work. Already I had received several proposals of marriage. I had refused them all, from young and old. I was a romantic, a dreamer seeking an all-embracing love and above all someone who had made his own way in the world. A marriage of convenience was not for me.

I said not a word to anyone in the family, especially not to my mother. I went to Hassanein Heykal and announced, "I want to take you up on the offer you made a while ago, and I have come to work with you." He was very pleased. On the spot he put me in charge of the social column. For several weeks I told no one what I was doing, keeping up my work at the hospital as well. Eventually, Heykal came up to me and said, "With all the contacts you have, it's time for you to start doing interviews and reporting them as your own articles."

My first article appeared in the spring of 1950, signed Isis Fahmy. It gave my mother a terrible shock, but this was soon soothed away by numerous phone calls from leading members of Coptic society. "Congratulations, Madame Farida. What glory this brings upon us. You must be proud of your daughter. Not only has she become a journalist. She has become the first one ever in the history of the Copts." Conversations like this calmed my mother's fears of family scandal.

I now began a life of constant work, with not a moment's respite, even when I was officially on holiday. Of course I had to give up my work at the hospital. Although my brother and the other doctors along with the hospital staff in general were sad to be losing me, I left with their best wishes for success in my new career.

Two years later, the Revolution brought Nasser to power. One of his main policies was agrarian reform. This involved taking the land from the rich and distributing it to the peasants. Serge's wealthy lady friend had her lands sequestrated. They left Egypt to live in Paris, and after a while they parted.

Not long after I had started work, I attended a private reception at which I met Hussein Serry Pasha, who was at the time Egyptian Prime Minister. His youngest daughter, Nevine, was the owner of a shop in Kasr-El-Nil, one of the most fashionable streets in Cairo. Here she sold elegant handbags made of high quality Egyptian leather, all based on models she brought back from famous Paris fashion houses, such as Christian Dior, Lanvin, Chanel. I asked her father what he thought about his daughter's commercial undertaking because she was the first young woman to open a shop. Hussein Serry replied, "My child, just remember this. In life there are many professions. So no profession is dishonourable." This remark helped to give me the enthusiasm and courage to continue with the career upon which I had so recently embarked.

MY EARLY DAYS IN JOURNALISM

When I started my career as a journalist, twin brothers Moustafa and Ali Amin owned the newspaper group I was writing for. Journalism was their passion. They spent most of their time writing, putting in long hours at their newspaper office. Each morning they would arrive at ten and stay until three in the afternoon. After two hours for lunch, they continued to work till midnight. Every evening they would be at the printing presses in the basement supervising the production of the next day's edition. This was their daily routine throughout their working lives. They had little time to spare for their friends who had to make do with short visits when they called at their offices.

In a country where there was press censorship, the brothers were quite fearless, publishing political news however sensitive or sensational, utterly regardless of the consequences. They defied government threats of confiscation or suppression of whole editions, court proceedings and even imprisonment. Their newspapers gained an international reputation; their scoops were often quoted in the English and particularly American press. After a few years in their employment I accepted an offer to work for a different newspaper. I was not really happy in my new job; the atmosphere was completely different from what I had been used to. I had always remained on very friendly terms with the Amins, and was lucky to have worked for owners who willingly taught me what journalism was all about when I was new to the profession. They had asked me several times to go back and work for them, so eventually I did.

Every Saturday Moustafa brought out a special edition of their paper *Akhbar el Yom* (*The Weekly News*). In this edition Moustafa had created a column for me called, as near as the Arabic will translate, *Salon Talk*. On one occasion I wrote in detail about the first afternoon tea given for the Diplomatic Corps by Queen Narriman. The event, held in the Abdin Palace, was exclusively for Ambassadors' wives in Cairo. Now many of the wives liked seeing their names in print in my column and would often give me details about parties they had attended where the press was excluded. The wife of the ambassador of one of the Scandinavian countries was a particularly generous source of information in this respect. She enjoyed ringing me up every morning with some item or other especially if the news was about something out of the ordinary. So I soon had the inside story of the Queen's tea in good time for my Saturday column. When King Farouk read it on the Saturday evening, he was absolutely furious about the leak and immediately ordered a stop to the distribution and sale of the paper. It was far too late for that. The paper had been on the streets since eight in the morning! The King was not an early riser.

ONE OF MY FIRST NEWSPAPER STORIES

Madame de Fisher, the wife of the Swiss Ambassador in Cairo, said to me one day, "Did you know that twice a week I go to the American University for lessons in Arabic?" It's a special course for members of the Diplomatic Corps. There are quite a few of us attending from different embassies." "It sounds very interesting," I replied, "I would like to make it a feature for my newspaper." "Well if it really appeals to you would you like to come with me and I will introduce you to the course lecturer?" I said I would be glad to; so the next time there was a lesson I went, taking the newspaper photographer with me. He took several photographs of the "pupils." When their lessons were over I interviewed ten or so of the diplomats, asking them who they were, which embassy they came from and especially why they were having lessons. Some said they were learning the language to improve their ability to understand and communicate with the Egyptian people; others were doing it just for the pleasure of learning.

I made the interviews into a long article which was a big success because it was an original subject and highlighted the interest shown in Arabic by foreigners like the British, American, German and Swiss. Two days after the article appeared in the paper I was summoned to the office of the big boss, Moustafa Amin, the newspaper proprietor. This was the first time he had called me in to see him. He told me to sit down and started to read out a letter, which I later discovered had been addressed to me but delivered on purpose to his office.

The writer of the letter was Professor Bado, the Dean of the American University. The professor was an eminent American orientalist with a perfect knowledge of Arabic. He later became the American Ambassador in Egypt.

"Dear Miss Fahmy," read Moustafa Amin, "You came like a thief into my house without permission. For the last six months I have been working on a feature for publication in our magazine, and now you have ruined it. Congratulations. But don't do anything like this again."

I looked at Amin and said in a trembling voice, "Oh dear, I didn't mean to offend him. How am I going to put things right?" "There's no need to do anything at all. Here, take your letter and look after it. Your article was an excellent piece of work. And always remember, in journalism it's essential to be the first with the news and to have exclusive coverage of it.

And so it has been throughout my career: always a race to be first and to secure exclusives with interviews, news and any other subject that would make the headlines.

MATCHMAKER – UNINTENTIONAL

When I first started work at *Akhbar El Yom*, the chief editor Hassanein Heykal allowed me the freedom to choose my own assignments. This gave him the opportunity to see what would eventually be the best area for me to specialise in. However, I had to have his prior approval for my plans, so I would put forward my ideas about the subjects I wanted to cover and the people I hoped to interview. Occasionally, Heykal would have some project of his own for me, as was the case when he suggested that I should see if I could obtain an interview with a young woman from exclusive society circles. No journalist had managed it so far. I responded by saying that I thought I would be able to do better, because I belonged to that society. Back in my office I rang one of my friends, the eighteen-year-old Baheya Izzet, daughter of Abdullah Izzet Pasha.[1] Baheya liked the idea of an interview and obtained permission from her father for it to take place. I came away with enough material for a two-page feature, including photographs taken by the staff photographer who accompanied me.

My article about Baheya and the life she led in society caused quite a stir. The view in certain artistocratic quarters was that the publication of such details and photographs was a scandal; those with a more modern outlook thought it perfectly acceptable. One consequence of the article was entirely unexpected.

Five days after its appearance I received a phone call at work from someone I did not know at all. "Am I talking to the journalist Isis Fahmy?" "Yes." "Well, my name is Zaki Serag El Din. My elder brother is the Minister of the Interior, Fuad Serag El Din Pasha. May I come to see you and bring one of my brother's friends? It's a very personal matter." I said I would be pleased to meet them. So along they came. I was somewhat curious, to say the least.

"Before I explain," said Zaki, "All the things you wrote in your article about Baheya Izzet are they true and accurate?" I assured him they were. "In that case," he continued, "I want to marry her. Do you think you could arrange a meeting?" He certainly did not beat about the bush. I was taken completely by surprise and found myself at a loss for words. What could I say? In the end I managed to suggest that all I could do would be to make enquiries and let him know the outcome. "Good," he replied, "I look forward to hearing from you." And out he went followed by his friend and moral support!

Visitors safely out of the way, I shook with laughter at the idea that the journalist had suddenly become a marriage broker! The whole thing was comical. I

1 *When Farouk was forced into exile in 1952 at the start of the Nasser Revolution the new government appointed Abdullah Izzet as one of the three regents of his baby son, Ahmed Fuad II. The monarchy was formally abolished a year later.*

told Heykal the story. He was highly amused as well but thought I should treat it seriously enough to make the promised enquiries. I explained it all to Baheya over the phone. There was silence for a few moments, then she too burst out laughing but rather surprised me by saying, "Well why not? But I'll have to see what my father thinks about it first." (Baheya was his daughter from his first marriage). I thought that would be the end of the matter, but no. Baheya rang back. Her father had told her that she was free to marry the young man and to go and see him if she wished. Well, of course she wanted to. So the journalist-become-matchmaker got the job of arranging things.

Chaperoned by her stepmother, Baheya went daily to the Guezireh Sporting Club. I arranged for Zaki to be there. Introductions made, Baheya and Zaki were soon deep in animated conversation. At a discreet distance stepmother and I discussed the developments. We were in agreement. Zaki came from an extremely rich family. He did not share the same culture, and especially education as Baheya, who had a very westernised European mentality. Zaki was the embodiment of the traditional Egyptian gentleman farmer.

We felt that Baheya would turn him down but after chatting with him for the best part of an hour Baheya came over to us. "He's very nice. I want to marry him. Why not?" Zaki had fallen madly in love with her on the spot. However, out of respect for her father, she told him she would not give him her final answer until her father had had the opportunity to meet his prospective son-in-law.

Once more I was the arranger. The coffee room at Groppi's pastry shop[1] was the daily meeting place where Baheya's father Abdullah took coffee with his friends. It was agreed that I should escort Zaki there to meet him. As we walked in, Abdullah came forward and I made the introductions. The two of them shook hands, exchanged a few words. Mission accomplished. Father's verdict was approval of his daughter's choice.

The marriage took place a few weeks later, with Zaki worrying all the time in case Baheya changed her mind. The wedding was held in Abdullah Izzet Pasha's splendid mansion on the banks of the Nile in Zamalek. The guests, about two hundred in all, were very select. Most of the Egyptian royal family were present, including two of the King's sisters.

The marriage that started so auspiciously became over the years more and more unhappy for both parties. They had nothing in common. Why had Baheya married Zaki? In those days, family upbringing was so strict that unmarried girls even at the age of eighteen were not allowed to go out alone. So it was not uncommon for a girl to accept the first suitor to gain her parents' approval, even if she did not care for him, just to get away from the family home and be free to lead an independent life. Such marriages of convenience sometimes worked. Sometimes they ended in divorce, as in Baheya's case.

---

1 *Groppi's Pastry Shop at that time was a well-known meeting place where many Pashas met for morning coffee and discussed general topics of the day.*

A SLIP OF THE TONGUE WITH NASSER

Not many days after the coup d'état, which in July 1952 brought an end to the monarchy in Egypt, I came into contact with General Neguib's aide-de-camp Ismaïl Farid. His brother was a friend of mine and introduced me to him. When Ismaïl knew I was beginning a career in journalism, he asked, "Would you like to interview Colonel Nasser? I am sure I can arrange it." It was a fantastic opportunity for me, so naturally I jumped at the offer. Although Neguib was a figurehead of the new régime, the real leader of the group of "free officers" as they were known, was Nasser. For the time being, however, he was content to remain the *éminence grise*, wielding power from behind the scenes.

Having received an appointment, which gave me authority to enter the military headquarters where Nasser had his office, I reported there on Monday at 10am. A junior officer showed me into an empty room and closed the door. I could hear noises outside, raised voices, and footsteps. Feeling somewhat apprehensive in this military atmosphere, all I could do was to sit there and wait. Two o'clock came and went. At about three o'clock the door opened, a different officer came in and said, "It won't be today. Come back tomorrow." This I did, but Tuesday was a repeat of Monday. So were Wednesday, Thursday and Friday.

When I arrived on the sixth day I was taken up to the first floor where Nasser's cabinet secretary, Amin Chaker was waiting for me. He told me that Nasser would see me some time that day and put me in an office leaving the door half-open. After a while it became clear to me that this room was situated between Chaker's office on one side and Nasser's on the other, so I was able to get a good idea of what was going on. In fact, Chaker had arranged a sort of international women journalists' day for his boss. There were reporters from the USA, Germany, Britain, France and, of course, Egypt, represented by me. Again, I was kept waiting and wondering whether my turn would ever come. At about three o'clock I caught a glimpse of Nasser as he came out of his office dressed in his colonel's uniform, and heard him say, "Amin, have we got to the end now?" "Well, no sir; there's an Egyptian reporter. She's been waiting quite a while." I heard Nasser grumble, "Another woman. Bring her in then."

More than a little overawed, I found myself face to face with the man who destined to rule Egypt for the next eighteen years, the first native Egyptian ruler for almost two thousand years. I shall never forget his first remark to me. It was a question: "There are some well known people from the old régime who want to join me and serve our cause. What's your view on that?" I paused, and then said nervously, "No. Your ways of thinking and doing things are too different from theirs." "That's just what I think too," was Nasser's comment.

As my interview was obviously of the greatest importance to my paper, the editor had helped me prepare my questions. He was mainly interested in the military side of things, so all my questions except one were on that subject. All nine of them went well. The problem was the tenth, the one that for me was the whole point of the interview, the really essential question. The old régime had done little if anything on the matter of women's rights. I had been quite active in the campaign to obtain social justice for women and was anxious now to find out what their position would be in the eyes of a government committed to sweeping changes in the way the country was run. I had been warned that Nasser was an anti-feminist. I hesitated. Nasser asked me if I had any more questions. "Yes," I said, but now I was flustered and continued very clumsily, "It seems you don't like women." Nasser gave a start. A look of shock came over his face. "What did you say?" He bellowed. I managed to gather my wits and rephrase my question, "What will be the role of women in our new society?" "They should stay at home and look after their husbands and children. Nothing else." I wanted to make my escape, but Nasser went on, "And what do you think about it?" All I could do was mumble, "Yes, of course. Thank you." and make for the door.

I had not been home long when the telephone rang. It was Neguib's aide-de-camp. "I've had Nasser on the line. Do you know what he said? Well I'll tell you. 'You've just sent me a young woman who told me I didn't like women. If I wasn't so busy I'd have shown her whether I like women or not!'" The aide-de-camp laughed.. And that was the end of the matter.

With the passage of time, Nasser's attitude towards women's rights and their role in society was to undergo a considerable change. In the spring of 1955, he travelled to Indonesia to attend the Bandung Conference, the first gathering of the heads of thirty newly independent African and Asian states, including Pakistan and India. Pandit Nehru, the Prime Minister of India, had played a large part in bringing about the conference, and having met Nasser for the first time in Egypt the previous year, was anxious for the Egyptian leader to attend.

My chief editor, Hassanein Heykal, was a close friend and confidant of Nasser and accompanied him to the conference. On the way, Nasser paid brief visits to both Pakistan and India. Heykal later related his experiences there to me. When Nasser met President Ayub Khan of Pakistan for political talks, he was amazed not only by the presence of the President's wife but also by her participation in all their discussions. A further surprise awaited Nasser on his visit to the Pakistan Parliament. Fifty percent of the MPs were women. Nasser experienced a similar situation in India, where Nehru's daughter, Indira Gandhi, took part in all the private discussions between the two leaders. When Nasser addressed the Indian Parliament, women made up half his audience.

Nasser told Heykal, "As soon as we are back in Egypt, I will give our women political and social rights." He began by appointing eight women to sit in Parliament. To say that he immediately carried out his intentions would be a gross exaggeration, but the process had begun. His change of heart was further reflected when a code of women's rights was included in the 1962 National Charter.

A TYPICAL DAY

My work as a social and diplomatic journalist was never governed by office hours. My usual routine was to wake up at eight-thirty and have breakfast brought to me in bed – an enjoyable start to the day in Egypt, where one would have a chambermaid and a butler. From about nine o'clock onwards I could expect telephone calls from ambassadors' wives ringing to give me the latest news about social events at which I had not been present. At certain functions, I was invited as a friend and was told that they were off the record; consequently I wrote nothing about them. There were many families who just did not want their parties mentioned in the press. If nothing was said, however, I knew I was free to publish. The social season was at its busiest in autumn, winter and spring. Invitations came thick and fast in this peak period of the year.

I spent much of the morning at home compiling my articles based on events I had attended and on the news I had received over the phone. I would then go to my office in the newspaper building, hand in my copy and discuss matters with my editor and colleagues.

At lunchtime, during the height of the season there would frequently be an official embassy engagement for me; my afternoons were partly taken up attending tea parties given by ambassadors' wives. If I had no invitations, I was free to relax, often going horse riding at a club near the pyramids; membership of this club was reserved for diplomats who owned horses. A Brazilian couple who were friends of mine owned three horses and offered me one to ride whenever I wished.

Between six o'clock and eight o'clock, there would be cocktail parties to attend, going from one to another. At the height of the season, it was not unusual for me to visit five in an evening. I often went to them in a long evening dress to make sure I would be on time for a dinner invitation later on.

These dinner parties started at eight-thirty; punctuality was essential. At eight-fifteen, nobody would have arrived; ten minutes later, all the guests were queuing up to go in. I remember on one occasion I arrived a quarter of an hour late for a dinner at the Spanish Embassy. I had been interviewing a government minister at a cocktail party earlier in the evening. The minister concerned was very talkative; obviously I was not in a position to interrupt him and take my leave. Arriving late for the dinner engagement, I apologised to the Spanish Ambassador who, despite being a friend, made it clear that he was considerably displeased.

A fortnight or so later, the Spanish Ambassador invited me again. His secretary rang me to say the dinner began at eight o'clock. I made sure I was on time, only to find that I was the only one there. I was kept waiting in the reception room for ten minutes before the Ambassador appeared. Good friend that he was, and of course much older than me, he said with a smile, "Young lady, I have made you wait on purpose to teach you a lesson on the importance of being punctual." He had instructed his secretary to give me an incorrect time.

At all these functions I had to observe everything – who the guests were, the menus, the ladies' dresses, those whose elegance, beauty or personality made them the centre of attention. I also noted amusing or interesting anecdotes. Unpleasant incidents were rare but did sometimes occur. On one occasion, I arrived to find the guests searching everywhere in the reception rooms, but in vain, for a valuable earring, which one of the ladies had lost. The atmosphere at the party was decidedly uncomfortable. Was it possible that some one had found the diamond and said nothing? The owner of the earring found it when she returned home. Being of ample proportions, she required considerable support for her bosom, and that is where her diamond was!

Chantilly cream is very nice, but not as a substitute for shampoo. During one of my diplomatic visits to Paris I attended a dinner given by the Swiss Ambassador, the headwaiter accidentally dropped a large spoonful of cream on my head. Sitting on my left was a Count. His wife, who sat opposite to me, seemed to be jealous of the interest her husband was showing in my conversation, said with a loud laugh, "Oh, look! You have a daisy in your hair!" I sat still, without saying a word. The German Ambassador sitting on my right coolly picked up his napkin and without any fuss wiped away my daisy. I continued to smile, resisting any desire to reply to the Countess's remark.

When the meal was over, the hostess came up to me and offered to send her chauffeur round the following day to take my dress to the best cleaners'. Although a few drops of cream had fallen on the dress, I declined the offer saying that no harm had been done. As far as the dress was concerned I had been lucky. It was the latest model from Carven, a well-known Parisian fashion house, a black velvet sheath dress with a little black heavily sequinned jacket; and it was not mine. The day before the dinner I had gone to the fashion house hoping to find something suitable to wear. I had been offered this particular dress at a reduced price that was very tempting, but I hesitated. Frankie the manager, offered me a deal. "Look," she said, "I will lend you the dress for your dinner at the embassy. Think about it; if you decide you don't want it, bring it back afterwards." And the spots of cream? They had landed on the sequins of the jacket and trickled down them, but wiped away before they reached the dress. Nevertheless, there was one tiny speck left on the black velvet. I felt obliged to buy the dress. It was a classic creation. I still wear it, so I have no complaints. It was fate I suppose.

My personal friends often envied my job, with its round of parties and receptions. However, those who have not experienced such a hectic way of life cannot understand how tiring it was. It sounds fun, and of course I enjoyed it, but not in the same way as the ordinary guests were able to. For me it was work.

Concentration was essential. I had to practice rigid self-discipline day after day, as if I was acting in a play. I had to think constantly about the clothes I should wear – it was essential to be impeccably dressed. One had to think carefully before speaking, know how to choose one's words and learn the art of suiting one's conversation to the occasion and to the people around one, applying as much psychological insight as one could command.

In my articles and in my personal relationships, discretion was all-important. Without it, there would be no trust. If I lost people's confidence, doors would start to close. It would be a mistake to think that the frivolous, light-hearted incidents I have described made up the major part of my articles. It was at such functions that I could most easily obtain serious interviews with diplomats, government ministers and important personalities from both home and abroad. For them, the atmosphere was relaxed; for me, these people were there and available. Trying to arrange daytime interviews via their secretaries was much more difficult. Their engagement diaries were full. One could wait weeks for appointments arranged through official channels. Much of the material I obtained appeared in my own columns, but important interviews I had conducted at parties, receptions and dinners were given the front-page treatment.

When the weekend came, I was exhausted. For relaxation I enjoyed nothing more than being with my mother and family, spending time with a little nephew, going for walks in the fresh air and especially being able to wear casual clothes.

Diplomats themselves fell into two categories. There were those who were never tired and who enjoyed every minute of the hectic social round; South American diplomats especially relished it all. For them it just seemed part of their ordinary daily life. Then there were the others, those for whom weekends and holidays could not come soon enough, who were glad to be able relax away from the merry-go-round.

In my day, few diplomats kept up with this social life when they reached retirement age. Nine out of ten withdrew from it completely. The others still went on and on. In my case, I tried to disengage myself when I gave up my journalistic career after twenty years in the profession, but the life I had led seemed to pursue me and, I must admit, had a fascination for me in Paris and London which was hard to resist. Of course, there were no longer articles to write and deadlines to meet, no longer the necessity to be present day after day the at every important gathering. But an occasional ladies' lunch or an embassy dinner was something I could continue to enjoy.

Isis with President Gamal Abdel Nasser of Egypt

A SLAP IN THE FACE FOR NASSER

One of the most important political and economic issues at the outset of Nasser's reign was agrarian reform. The Turkish ambassador to Egypt at the time was Mr Fuad Toughaï, whose wife was Amina Toughaï, one of the wealthiest Princesses of the Egyptian royal family. She owned estates extending over thousands of acres but lost everything in the reforms, which sequestrated all her land and distributed it to the peasants.

Her husband was very angry. Despite the fact that he was the highest official representative of Turkey in Egypt, he completely failed to keep his personal feelings under control and indeed behaved as if he had taken leave of his senses. He invited to dinner some of Nasser's staff officers, the very people who were part of the new ruling group. He treated his guests not only to a lavish meal but also to a bitter denunciation of the government and its land policy in particular.

There was more to come. The Cairo Opera House was the scene for his most scandalous outburst. The occasion was a gala performance of the visiting Russian Bolshoï Ballet. Nasser was present, as were all the Diplomatic Corps Heads of Mission, including of course the Turkish ambassador. I was there also, in my capacity as social press correspondent. During the interval, Nasser left his box to greet the foreign ambassadors in the lounge. I slipped in with my photographer. Standing in a corner we chatted with Nasser's aide-de-camp, who kept glancing over in Nasser's direction in case he was needed, suddenly he said, "Something is going on," and he hurriedly made his way over to where Nasser was standing. Something was indeed going on! The Turkish ambassador was gesticulating wildly and shouting a torrent of abuse at Nasser. A moment later the demented Turk raised his hand as if to strike him in the face. Nasser's bodyguards grabbed hold of him, but Nasser motioned them to let him go. My photographer had been smart. His camera had clicked at the very moment the ambassador had raised his arm. The photograph made the front page, along with my exclusive account of this extraordinary diplomatic incident, which could not have been more undiplomatic.

That was the end for Ambassador Toughaï who was immediately recalled, and for a time relations between the two countries were very strained. As for me, well, I should not have been in the lounge at all, but in the event, Nasser's press office was glad to clear my article and its damning photograph, which helped them to get rid of the troublesome man.

This goes to illustrate that the most important assets for a journalist are cheek, nerve, timing and luck; and also, perhaps, the hand of fate.

UNDER SUSPICION

Not long after Nasser came to power, a few months perhaps, I realised that my movements were being watched and I was being followed. Every day, a man arrived early in the morning and took up position more or less in front of the door of the block of flats where I lived in Zamalek. As soon as I came out to drive to work, he jumped into a taxi obviously waiting for him, and followed me wherever I went.

To start with, I was quite amused by all this attention. I saw myself as somebody important enough to have a protective escort. After a few days my amusement began to be replaced by annoyance. My unknown shadow was getting on my nerves. From time to time my work took me to the Egyptian Foreign Office. When the security staff at the door asked my "escort" what he was doing there, he replied, "I'm following that Communist newspaper reporter." Everybody who knew me, including the Ministry security personnel, knew well enough that I wasn't a Communist. One of the ministry men informed me discreetly, "Miss Fahmy, you have a plain-clothes man following you. You are suspected of Communist activities."

At the time, Nasser was rounding up the Egyptian communists en masse and throwing them in gaol, so any accusation against me, false though it might be, was a dangerous and frightening one. I had a friend whose daughter was already in prison because she was a Communist. However, I carried on with my life as normally as possible, though one morning when I came out of work I went up to my waiting escort and said politely, "Instead of spending so much of the government's money on taxis, why don't you just get in my car with me? It would be much simpler." "Yes," he replied, "It would be a lot easier but I have my orders." Those orders took him to the Guezireh Club where I went regularly to meet my friends. The security man there, who had known me for a long time, said, "Excuse me, Miss, but take care. You're being followed by the secret police."

The last straw was when I went to the cinema with some friends. There is no need to tell you who found a seat behind mine. I was so fed up with the whole business that I made up my mind to do something about it. I telephoned Nasser's headquarters. "I don't know why you are having me followed. All I know is that I am being spied on and you have put someone on the job who isn't doing it properly because I have known from the beginning what's been going on." After a few moments, I had the reply, "We'll take our man off straight away." End of conversation.

This story illustrates the fact that being a diplomatic or even a social journalist in Nasser's early days was a hazardous occupation. The police did not seem to understand why I kept on visiting the various foreign embassies to which my work took me every day.

I was unaware that to be a journalist officially, I was required to be a member of the Union of Journalists. My boss had never mentioned it to me. So when a law was announced making it quite clear that no one could practise as a journalist without an official press card, I had to apply for one. This was not just a matter of routine.

I was summoned to attend an interview before a tribunal that was to determine whether I was a suitable candidate to be accepted as a member of the union. I duly arrived at the appointed time and was taken into a room where I was questioned by three judges. The senior judge asked all the questions while the other two took notes. The interview went as follows:

"I have your files in front of me. Look at all these dossiers. They appear to be contradictory. You are reported to be a multi-spy for the USA, the USSR, France and Great Britain. Who are you? What are you? Why all these files?"

Such statements did not disconcert me because nothing surprised me about the present political regime. "Who are you? Why all these files?" I replied, "Sir, I am just doing my job correctly. My work requires me to visit embassies, conduct interviews, and obtain as much information and news as possible. I do indeed visit the Russians and the Americans, and I frequent the diplomatic circles of various political regimes. Above all I am an objective reporter and an Egyptian patriot. The fact of the matter is that I am nothing more nor less than a diplomatic journalist."

The three judges conferred seriously between themselves in a conversation I could not hear. I waited, wondering what my fate would be. Would they believe me, or decide that I was a spy? What was only a few minutes seemed like hours before the senior judge delivered the verdict. I gave a sigh of relief when he announced that they understood my position and agreed to my application for membership of the union.

That, however, was not the end of the surveillance by the secret police. Whenever there were receptions at foreign embassies, two or three plain-clothes men were invariably to be seen taking down the registration numbers of the parked cars to trace their occupants. Everybody knew, despite the rather futile attempts by the police to hide behind trees or bushes. On one particular occasion the press attaché at the Austrian Embassy called a press conference to which I was invited, to release news of an archaeological discovery made in Egypt by an Austrian. At the end of the conference, as I was about to get into my car, I was approached by one of the policemen. "Excuse me Madam, what were you doing at this meeting?" "We have just been informed that the Austrians have discovered an archaeological site of interest and importance to Egypt," I replied.

There were many similar incidents, all illustrating the degree of which Egypt at that time had become a police state.

Isis with Josephine Baker in the 1950s.

JOSEPHINE BAKER

One of the famous personalities I met in the 1950s was Josephine Baker, the "Black Goddess of Cabaret." Originally from St. Louis, Missouri, she had trained as a dancer in New York and sang in Harlem nightclubs before appearing in Paris in 1925 at the age of nineteen with the *Revue Nègre* at the Théâtre des Champs-Elysées. This show was the starting point of a long international career, based in Paris, which embraced starring in variety, reviews, operettas and films. Audiences at the Folies-Bergères and the Casino de Paris were tantalised by her sensual and spectacular performances – dancing on a mirror wearing nothing but a bunch of bananas around her waist, or swinging from a trapeze and throwing roses to her excited admirers. The seductive rhythms and originality of her exotic dances made her famous in theatres throughout the world, as did her many captivating songs, especially *J'ai deux amours, mon pays et Paris*.[1] This is the song I find myself singing whenever I hear her name. Behind her outwardly public image of sophisticated and seductive glamour, the Black Goddess nurtured very strong humanitarian instincts.

When I interviewed Josephine in Cairo, her variety show running there was part of an international tour of cabaret performances. She had come out of retirement to raise money for her charitable enterprise. Josephine asked me if I would be willing to act as her public relations officer and guide during her stay in Cairo. Although she had been given a warm and enthusiastic reception in Cairo where her show played to full houses, she said she still felt the need for someone with local knowledge and social contacts to help her in her efforts. I was only too willing to be of assistance.

On the social side, I arranged an invitation for her to a private soirée given by one of the counsellors at the British Embassy. She was made very welcome and delighted the guests with her charm and personality, whilst also not failing to publicise her charitable cause. The party did not break up until dawn. A small group of French diplomats thought it was too hot and too late to go home and sleep, and suggested they go straight on to spend a day by the Red Sea at the fashionable resort of Sokna. Josephine and I were invited to join the party. It was a day spent lazing and bathing and enjoying a restaurant meal of renowned local seafood.

By 1948, Josephine, to whom a glittering stage career had brought considerable wealth, bought the Château de Milande in the village of Bergerac, in the Dordogne. This was to be a home for her and also for what became her adopted

1 *I have two loves, my country and Paris.*

family, her 'rainbow tribe' as it was called: twelve orphaned children from ten different countries. At the château a truly multi-racial orphanage developed.

Josephine employed a staff of seventy, dedicated to her purpose of bringing up and educating her family of abandoned children in an atmosphere of happiness and peaceful luxury. However, for this courageous enterprise in generosity of spirit the cost was enormous, too high to be sustained by Josephine's accumulated wealth alone. Her stage tours gave her the means to keep the orphanage going for a little longer. It was her concern for her 'children' rather than any irresistible call to the stage that motivated her return in October 1959 at the Paris Olympia and her appearances, at the age of sixty-eight, in the London Palladium show in 1974 – wearing a skin-tight cat-suit and head-dress of huge feathers.

She died in Paris in 1975, a few days after appearing at a gala performance of a review to celebrate her fiftieth year in show business. In the audience, which gave her a standing ovation, were such famous names as Sophia Loren, Alain Delon, Jeanne Moreau and Princess Grace of Monaco. They were applauding her for more than her stage success. They were applauding her also for her 'rainbow tribe', for her campaigning for Civil Rights in the United States and for her work as a member of the French Resistance during the second world war, for which she was decorated with the *Croix de Guerre*, the *Légion d'Honneur* and the *Rosette de la Résistance*.

CAIRO TO PARIS – VIA TUNIS

In June 1951, a fortnight before I was due to leave Cairo for a holiday in Paris, I attended an evening concert where I met the press attaché of the French Embassy and his wife, Monsieur and Madame Fleurie. During our conversation I mentioned that I would shortly be going to Paris to visit my relations. "Well", said Madame. Fleurie, "What a coincidence! We are also going to Paris, why don't you travel with us? We're travelling by car from Cairo to Tunis. Then we shall take the boat from Tunis to Marseilles and finish the journey to Paris by train." The prospect sounded very exciting, so I jumped at the chance, offering of course to share all the expenses of the trip.

As the press attaché and his wife both came from French North Africa, they intended spending two days in Tunis seeing family and friends before continuing their journey. I now had two problems facing me. Firstly, they were starting out in a week's time but my own holiday was not due to start until a week later. Telling myself that everything was possible, I reckoned that although it would be a bit of a rush, I had enough time to make all the necessary arrangements and preparations. Before me was an opportunity to turn my holiday into an adventure, an expedition! It was too good to miss. Secondly, would my editor, Hassanein Heykal allow me to bring forward my holiday?

The next day, I made my request. Heykal made a few objections but eventually agreed. However, being a newspaper editor, he had his terms. "OK, but I've a couple of suggestions for you. Whilst you're in Tunis it would be a real scoop if you could manage to cover the political situation there, see what the atmosphere is like in the city and above all try your luck at making contact with Farahet Hachet.[1] "What! Me! Politics! I've never done any political reporting!" "Well, there's a first time for everything. It's time you began to broaden your experience. Come to think of it, there's something you can do in Paris as well: find out about a famous French writer called John-Paul Sartre and existentialism. You have good contacts in Paris, haven't you? See if you can interview him!"

My 'holiday' was becoming not only an expedition but also a young journalist's initiative test! I agreed these arrangements with Heykal, accepted the invitation from the Fleuries and spent a hectic week in a state of some excitement discussing arrangements and packing everything I was going to need.

We duly left Cairo by the coastal road, which passes through desert terrain for most of the way to Tunis. We expected the journey to take six days and

---

1 *Farahet Hachet was head of the workers' union and also one of the leaders of the Tunisian resistance movement. In 1951 Tunisia was still a French colony; the Tunisians were fighting for their independence and the political atmosphere became extremely tense.*

planned to stop overnight in villages or small towns. Our daily routine was to wake early, at five-thirty to be ready to leave by six-thirty, then to travel for at least six hours with occasional stops to relax, have a snack and visit any interesting places en route. In the early evening we would stop, enjoy a meal and sleep. (We kept to this plan until we arrived in Tunis, some 1,800 miles from Cairo).

We saw very little traffic on the desert roads, so we were able to make good progress. The roads were narrow and in some areas the surface was very uneven, a legacy of tank-tracks from the Second World War, but as our transport was a large, strong stationwagon type of vehicle, we were not too uncomfortable.

To ensure that obtaining gasoline and drinking water during our journey was not a problem, we carried a good supply in cans. Fortunately we had no difficulties with either, and the stationwagon stood up very well to the sometimes difficult conditions, causing us no anxieties.

During our first day we passed several lovely summer beaches. Our road took us past El Alamein. We decided to stop and visit the different cemeteries; it was quite a long walk to see the Allied and German graves.

The first night we slept in a hotel at Marsa-Matrouh. The beach there was and still is one of the loveliest beaches in the world. The sand is so white and smooth, the sea like green crystal, phosphorescent at night.

Early the next morning we left to cross into Libya. All was peaceful now, but during the second world war the opposing armies had fought along this coast and in the adjacent desert, advancing and retreating in successive campaigns. Our road took us through Tobruk, which fell to Rommel in 1942, a severe blow to the British. We travelled on to Benghazi, another port that saw bitter fighting and changing ownership. Stopping for a break and a picnic, we were warned by the local inhabitants to stay on the road and not to walk on the sand because the desert was still full of landmines planted during the war. Many Bedouins died or were maimed while going about their daily business in the desert.

One of the villages where we stayed for a night was called Adjedabia; it is situated just inland about a hundred kilometres along the coast after it turns south from Benghazi. It was here that General Rommel[1] had his headquarters during the desert campaign. I must confess I could hardly sleep, and as the Bedouins tend to stay up late, I heard all sorts of noises. My imagination seemed to be weaving them all together to create the atmosphere and excitement of the German HQ in action; for me the night did not pass without nightmares.

The next day saw us on the first stage of the long journey to Tripoli, situated some eight hundred kilometres to the west. Flat monotonous country, with the Gulf of Sirte on our right and uninteresting desert inland. Another night, and then with Tripoli still eighty kilometres away, we stopped to marvel at the spectacular Roman remains of Leptis Magna, trying to imagine it set in fertile land, as it was in its long-gone glory days when together with the two other

---

1 *During the 1950s, Mrs. Rommel made an official visit to Egypt and I was appointed as her escort. She was a calm pleasant lady, always smiling, apparently in complete contrast to her husband.*

cities – Oea, now Tripoli, and Sabratha of Tripolitania. The three cities supplied the Roman Empire with grain, slaves and wild animals in a never-ending stream from the African interior for the arenas. We tried in vain to conjure up the scale of the operation needed to keep the entertainments and gladiatorial combats supplied. To give but two examples: lions were practically two a penny, with as many as six hundred appearing in a single show; one gladiator, who prided himself on his marksmanship, is recorded as having killed five hippopotamuses in a single performance.

Sabratha is some seventy kilometres west of Tripoli. Here we lingered, admiring the Roman ruins, not as extensive as Leptis Magna, but on an attractive site overlooking the sea. Unlike Leptis Magna, which is uninhabited, the Roman remains of Sabratha have seen a modern town grow up around them.

At a desert crossroads as we approached Tripoli, we came across a stationary car with a young man standing near it. Thinking he may have broken down, we stopped and spoke to him. Surprisingly he turned out to be one of the royal princes, a son of King Idris Senussi. As a matter of interest, in December 1951, just months after our journey, the French and British control of Libya came to an end and the country became an independent Kingdom under King Idris I. He was overthrown in 1969 in a military coup d'état led by Colonel Muammar Gaddafi, who proclaimed Libya a Republic.

On to Tripoli the Libyan capital. In olden times it bore the rather seductive nickname 'The White Bride of the Mediterranean' and is the only one of the three ancient cities of Libya to have been continuously occupied since Phoenician times. Here stands the huge royal palace (now the People's Palace), the vast castle and citadel, mosques, colonial buildings and the busy animated souk.

Eventually we reached Tunisia, with the road turning due north to follow the coastline and take us on the last leg of our journey to Tunis.

My friends drove me to my hotel and there we parted company. They were to call and collect me again two days later to complete our journey to Paris. I had thoroughly enjoyed their company and friendship on our long drive from Cairo, but now I was happy to feel independent again.

There was not a great deal of time left for me to try to fulfil the first of my editor's requests. It was afternoon when I booked into my hotel and without wasting any time I asked the receptionist if he could do anything to help me in my search for Farahet Hashed. I explained that I was an Egyptian journalist and how Egypt was always interested in the current affairs of North Africa. It may seem strange that I should approach a hotel receptionist, but people like Farahet Hashed kept their whereabouts secret. Tunisian nationals working in hotels were a useful go-between for receiving and passing on information. That was one of the ways it was done. In my case the system seemed to be working.

"I think it might be possible to fix something. Leave it to me, I will contact you later."

I had made a start. I sat quietly in the hotel, not risking to venture out. I was afraid of being attacked, as I had been told that my appearance was definitely

French! Picking up a local newspaper I went into the dining room for dinner.
While waiting to be served, I opened the paper and what I saw gave me a terrible shock. There on the front page was a photograph of an English diplomat
who had been a friend of mine during his posting in Cairo. It was Donald
Maclean, now revealed as a spy for the Russians. Such was my surprise I did not
realise that I was talking out loud to myself. I just could not believe it. I became
aware of other diners looking at me, probably thinking I was crazy. After dinner
the receptionist came and whispered very discreetly. "Everything is OK, I have
arranged for you to meet Farahet Hachet. Tomorrow morning at nine o'clock
someone will come to collect you." I was feeling quite pleased with myself.
Heykal would be delighted.

Next morning, ready and waiting, I watched three men enter the hotel and
talk briefly to the receptionist. He nodded in my direction. One of the men
came over and announced, "We have come to take you." Thus started what
turned out to be quite an adventure. The drive was a long one, out into the
country. We passed through many small villages. I dare not ask where we were
going and nobody told me. Eventually we arrived in a small village. I was taken
to a decrepit building and up to the third floor where, in a small poorly furnished room, I was introduced to Farahet Hachet. During the course of our
conversation, he repeated to me three times. "We want our independence and
that's all. Personally I have nothing against France or the French people. We only
want France to give us our independence." All through our meeting he was surrounded by men dressed like commandos. Also present were the three men who
had brought me to him. I never gave a thought to the possible danger I had put
myself in, allowing three strange men to take me to an unknown destination. I
was fascinated by the whole affair. (When the adrenalin is high, danger is part of
the excitement).

After the interview was over, the same three men took me back to my hotel;
again in silence for the whole journey. On getting out of the car I saw the press
attaché and French security police standing impatiently on the steps of the
hotel. They had apparently been waiting there a long time! They were very concerned to know where I had been all day from early morning, as it was now
early evening. I replied calmly, "I just went for a sight-seeing tour around the
city." Mr. Fleurie was not amused.

On 5th December 1952, some twelve months after my interview, Farahet
Hachet was assassinated and never saw his country achieve (in March 1956) the
independence that he had fought so hard to obtain.

Two days later we left Tunis, taking the boat to Marseilles and then the train
to Paris. I thanked my travelling companions for giving me the opportunity to
have such an unusual and fascinating trip. I was so happy to be in Paris and to
be reunited with my cousins Gina and Loulou who were at that time studying
at the Sorbonne. Although I was on holiday, I intended to do some journalistic
work and of course try to fulfil the second of my editor's requests, to find out
about Existentialism.

In 1951 the philosophy of Existentialism as expounded by Jean-Paul Sartre and collaborators, including his partner the well-known writer Simone de Beauvoir, was at the height of its popularity in intellectual and fashionable circles. An interview with Sartre would be a feather in my cap. I called a colleague of mine, a French editor by the name of Pierre de Bethman, to ask if he could help me. He promised to see what he could do and a few minutes later rang me back. "I have managed to arrange an 'existential night out' for you with Sartre's private secretary and his press agent. Come tomorrow evening to the Alexandre bar on the Champs-Elysées at seven o' clock. We'll see you there. I will introduce you to them but it will be up to you to do a deal. It will not be easy and don't expect me to be responsible for the way things turn out."

Excited and intrigued, I arrived exactly on time at our meeting place, which was a favourite haunt of journalists. Pierre and the other two were waiting for me. I thought they would be dressed casually, so I had done the same. To my surprise, they were rather elegant and smart. I apologised for my own appearance. Sartre's agent replied, "Yes, just look how properly dressed we are, with ties as well. Just because we are existentialists does not mean that we dress scruffy, like many things we do. Anyway, we would like to explain what the philosophy of existentialism means. What are you doing tonight? Are you free to come and have dinner with us?" Naturally I was.

Pierre took us in his car to a bar in St. Germain-des-Prés, the district that was the fashionable gathering place for those with professed existentialist leanings. We then moved on to dine at one of the area's most famous nightclubs, the *Montagne St. Geneviève*. After the meal a man approached our table and asked Pierre to dance. Pierre turned to me and said, somewhat nervously, "You go and dance with him!" While I was dancing, our stranger remarked, "It isn't you I wanted to dance with, it's your partner. He looks distinguished and refined to me." "I'm dancing with you," I replied, "because he asked me to. Dancing with men does not appeal to him. He is the editor-in-chief of a very conservative newspaper!" That was that. The stranger went off to try his luck elsewhere.

Sartre's press agent had been trying to flatter me all evening. I wasn't interested. I was there, so I thought, to learn about existentialism and try to arrange a meeting with Sartre. Eventually he gave up, lost interest and left. Now Sartre's secretary started flirting. I had felt protected so far by Pierre's presence; when he whispered, "Can I leave you alone now. You won't come to any harm," I agreed. It was well known that the man was not interested in women. Later, the secretary suggested we move on to a discothèque. Here my problems started. The secretary proposed that I should spend the whole night with him. I tried to be diplomatic, saying, "Not tonight, perhaps another evening," but he persevered. "It is tonight or never, that's what existentialism means!" He kept on in the same vein. Now I was beginning to feel rather scared, and started to think of a way to make my escape. I picked up my handbag and made the excuse of wanting to visit the ladies. From there I made for the exit and ran into the street at two o'clock in the morning, desperately looking for a taxi. Luckily I found one, but the secretary came running close behind! As I was closing the door, he tried to stop me by pulling it open. I was now extremely scared. The situation was saved by the taxi-driver. "Why don't you understand," he shouted, "You can see the lady doesn't want you. She doesn't fancy you. Clear off and leave her in peace!"

Back in my hotel I laughed and laughed, telling myself what an adventure I had had, but relieved all the same to be safe behind locked doors.

A few days later I tried to contact Sartre's secretary. As soon as he heard my voice on the phone he reacted furiously, shouted abuse and slammed down the receiver. When eventually I met Pierre de Bethman again, he asked if I had succeeded in obtaining an interview. I told him my story. He was highly amused and surprised, because the secretary was a well known homosexual. "What a pity," he remarked. "Well, that's one interview you won't have!" He was right. Nothing this time for Heykal back in Cairo.

I was so intrigued by my recent experience, that I wanted to know more about this philosophy. So what is existentialism? Existentialism is a philosophical doctrine according to which man, who exists primarily in a quasi-metaphysical state, creates himself and forms his own destiny by his actions.

There are different types of existentialism developed by various philosophers, each based upon a different concept of reality. Atheistic existentialism, created by Heidegger and Jean-Paul Sartre, argued that there was no God and that human nature was infinitely variable: humans were free to make their own destiny and were therefore responsible for their own lives.

Religious existentialism, propounded by Kirkegaard, Jaspers and Gabriel Marcel held that one's sense of dread and despair arose from one's responsibility for one's own decisions and for one's relationship with God. In general existentialism emphasises the fear and despair felt by isolated individuals. The fundamental feature of every philosophy of existence is that it is a philosophy of absolute freedom.

Who is Jean-Paul Sartre? He was the first representative of existentialism in France. He was by far the most famous and most popular existentialist and during the fifties he figured constantly in the press. Various schools promoted his philosophy. However, existentialism has had its day. It is now completely outmoded. But Sartre's plays are still performed today, and his works are still much appreciated for their literary value.

A DIPLOMATIC INCIDENT

In Egypt the month of May can be warm during the day but the evenings are very cool. The Republic of Argentina celebrates its National Day on 25 May.

One particular Argentinian Ambassador to Egypt and his wife were fond of giving frequent balls that often carried on into the small hours. So naturally, they organised one for their National Day, inviting all the government officials, heads of diplomatic missions and, of course, all their friends.

The Argentinian Ambassador's residence is situated on the banks of the Nile, surrounded by a beautiful garden, as are most of the houses along the Nile. The Ambassador and his wife decided to have the reception in the garden. They were strongly advised to do no such thing, since evenings could become very cool if not cold. However, they persisted; even dinner was to be held in the garden, with the guests seated at tables.

As fate, or luck would have it, I was at the table directly behind the official one where the important guests were seated, among them the Egyptian Foreign Minister, his Chief of Protocol and, representing the Shah of Iran, the Iranian Ambassador, M. Sepahbodi, who was elderly, very elegant and distinguished.

As the evening progressed, the temperature dropped. Everyone in the garden started to shiver. The ladies put their fur stoles around them. Mr Sepahbodi had recently been unwell and found the cold hard to bear. Not wanting to be ill again, he asked a member of his host's staff to fetch his overcoat. The Argentinian Ambassador, who had been rather over-generous to himself with the drinks, was passing round the tables talking to his guests. When he came to the official table, he noticed M. Sepahbodi wearing his overcoat. He took offence at this, considering it to be an insult to his arrangements for the party. Heedless, or unaware of his guest's state of health and anxious only to repay the imagined slight, he said loudly, "How dare you wear Mossadegh's[1] overcoat in my house?" There was a stunned silence. The remark was an outrageous insult. The Iranian Ambassador stood up and made a dignified departure. The following day, he made an official complaint to the Egyptian Foreign Office who transmitted the complaint to the Argentinian Foreign Office in Buenos Aires. The Argentinian Ambassador was immediately recalled.

As I was the only journalist present at the party, I had exclusive coverage of the incident. For a reporter, it was quite a scoop.

---

1 *Mossadegh. Leftwing Prime Minister of Iran 1951-53 and political opponent of the Shah, bent on discrediting the Royal Family. Dismissed in 1953.*

King Paul and Queen Frederika of Greece at a celebration of Greek Navy Day in Athens in 1953. Isis is on the left.

KING PAUL AND QUEEN FREDERIKA OF GREECE

Madeleine was a first cousin of mine who had married an Egyptian diplomat, Ibrahim Amin Ghali. In 1953 he was serving in Athens, and Madeleine invited me to spend a few days with them. At the time, I was working for a well-known Egyptian weekly magazine, *El Messawar*. My chief editor hoped I might be able to turn my visit to good account, saying, "While you are there, if you manage to interview King Paul or Queen Frederika, that would be quite something."

So in July I travelled to Athens with this aim partly in mind and enlisted my cousin's help. "We should be able to manage something," she said, entering into the spirit of the challenge. "We know some of the important people at court. We'll have a little cocktail party; that will give you the chance to make some contacts." No sooner said than done! However, during the party, Marshal Levidis, the head of the King's Cabinet, took my cousin Ibrahim aside. "I don't wish to disappoint your charming cousin," he murmured, "but unfortunately a court ban came into effect a fortnight ago, prohibiting any interviews with Her Majesty the Queen." Later on I learned the reason for this ban. The Queen had been giving interviews to the press, especially the American press, saying things that the court had to contradict afterwards. There had been some unfortunate repercussions as a result, so the court had decided there would be no more diplomatic incidents and therefore no more interviews. One person I did meet at the party was the Queen's uncle, who was one of her court chamberlains. I was to meet him again in the near future.

The next day, when Madeleine's husband returned home from the Egyptian Embassy, he had a message for me. "The Egyptian Ambassador wishes to make it clear to you that he will not risk any diplomatic incident, especially as Nasser has proclaimed Egypt a Republic and Greece is a monarchy, so forget about royal interviews."

Madeleine and I received the news in silence, but as we were both fighters, we did not abandon the idea. "I know for a fact," my cousin told me, "that in a few days time there is going to be a dinner at which the King and Queen will be present – and another one a week later." By a stroke of luck, the Egyptian Ambassador was just about to take his summer leave, and, who was to deputise for him but his Chief of Mission, none other than Ibrahim, Madeleine's husband. Madeleine persuaded him to arrange for me to have invitations to both events.

The first dinner took place but I missed it. On the day before the event, I had caught my foot in a hole in the street and ripped a toe-nail. I had to go to hospital to have the nail removed. Madeleine consoled me after the dinner by saying that I would not have had any chance of meeting the King or Queen. It had been a formal seated dinner, with no one circulating afterwards.

I was determined to be fit for the second occasion. This was an altogether different affair, being held to celebrate Greek Navy Day. The host was the Navy Minister, Admiral Tombas, the venue a Greek warship. The gaily illuminated vessel was not in harbour but anchored some distance off-shore, so all the guests, in evening dress were taken out to it in launches. I had not been aboard many minutes before the Chamberlain I had met at Madeleine's cocktail party came up to me and said, "His Majesty King Paul has no one with him at the moment. Come with me and I will introduce you." Thus I had my opportunity!

I knew that during the Second World War when the Germans invaded Greece in 1941, King George of Greece was forced to flee the country. He and the royal family, including his younger brother, Paul, who succeeded him in 1947, spent five months of their exile in Egypt. I asked the King about his recollections of his stay there. "I have fond memories of those days," he replied. "I remember my fencing lessons every morning with a German instructor. I made some progress but then other circumstances intervened." He smiled. "There is one incident I shall never forget. I used to go swimming alone in the Mediterranean Sea near Aboukir. I enjoyed the solitude and beauty of the spot. However, on one occasion a patrolling Egyptian soldier who must have thought I was a German spy or an escaped Italian prisoner of war arrested me. I was taken to the guard post and locked up. My attempts to explain were shouted down. The duty officer made phone call after phone call. At last I managed to make him take a look at my identity card. His face fell. "Your Majesty," he stammered, "Why didn't you tell me you were a Prince?" He apologised profusely, and offered me tea. "If you ever need anything in future I am here at your service." I promised I would call in when I went swimming, and I often did." He continued the conversation by saying how sorry he was not to be able to go further south to visit the marvels and beauty of Ancient Egypt.

We left the world of memories and returned to the present. I asked what was foremost in the minds of the Queen and himself. He answered by saying that two of their major aims were to raise the standard of living and reduce the high level of unemployment in Greece.

At this point, the King's reminiscences were interrupted. Queen Frederika, who was sitting only a yard or two away talking to one of the guests, looked at me, perhaps wondering who I was. "Why don't you both come and join us?" she remarked. Deep down I was highly delighted to have the opportunity to talk with this Queen who was so sought after by the world's press, drawn to her no doubt by her strong personality and physical beauty. When I had been introduced, I mentioned how much the Greek people admired her humanity and particularly the work she was doing for deprived and orphaned children. "Yes", she replied, "These children are the future generation of the Greek nation and it is our duty to look after them." The Queen had herself founded an organisation for the thousands of starving children made homeless during the 1946-

1949 civil war between Communists and anti-Communists. She had launched a worldwide appeal for funds and succeeded in raising six million dollars - a large sum at that time. Over ten thousand Greek children benefited from her work; so at this point in her reign the Queen was held in high esteem by the nation.

She and her husband spent little time in their palace. They travelled widely in Greece, in difficult and sometimes dangerous conditions, going from village to village to meet the people and to talk to factory workers in the cities. The King recalled an occasion while he was walking round a village in Macedonia. When he stopped to take a breather, he was approached by a workman who said to him, "I hope your Majesty will not think I am impolite if I ask to shake your hand." The King held out his hand, struck by the sincerity of the man's gesture.

The Queen described how one day when she was resting in her bedroom in a village inn, a simple peasant woman somehow managed to enter the room and begged her to intercede on her behalf to have her son freed from prison. The Queen had smiled, saying, "I am sorry I cannot do that, because justice is above the King himself."

My audience with the King and Queen came to an end. I was so pleased. I had succeeded in the mission, which at the beginning of my stay in Athens had seemed an impossible undertaking. During the navy ball that followed, my cousin Madeleine and I danced the night away with a light and happy tread. Yet I was still left with a problem. I had my interviews, true enough, but in view of the ban in force, was I in a position to give them to my magazine? Journalists as a body are not customarily over concerned with niceties and take it for granted that they can publish what they like, but I never followed this policy. I was always discreet - a rare attribute these days - and honest with all the celebrities I interviewed.

In this instance, I decided that my best course of action would be to approach Marshal Levidis. My request for an appointment was granted. I submitted the text of my interview to him and he approved it. When I asked him to sign it to this effect, he made no objection. Back in Cairo, after my holiday was over, I presented my chief editor with my story. He was delighted, as well as surprised, by my achievement, and gave it front-page treatment.

My principles in relation to my profession were formed in my early days - on my first visit to Paris. At the Bristol Hotel during the course of an interview with some distinguished Egyptian Pashas, one of them, Ali Chamsy Pasha, for whom I had the greatest admiration, said to me, "My child, let me give you some advice. If you want to succeed in your career, always be discreet and honest; you will gain by it." I took his words to heart and never regretted it.

Who was Queen Frederika? She was born in 1917 a Princess of Hanover, the granddaughter of Kaiser Wilhelm II. Her father was a direct descendant in the male line of George III of Great Britain, so she was born a Princess of Great Britain. She was educated in England and Germany. As an adolescent, she was forced to join the Hitler Youth. In 1938 she married her cousin Prince Paul, the brother and heir of George II of Greece.

When the German occupation of Greece became inevitable in the Second World War, she fled in 1941 with the rest of the royal family first to Crete, then to Egypt, often parted from her husband. Five years in exile followed, much of it in South Africa where the Prime Minister, Jan Smuts, became her close friend and mentor. After the war, a plebiscite restored the monarchy to Greece. George II died in 1947; Paul and Frederika ascended the throne just as the Communist war began in Greece. It was a time of widespread destruction and civil strife. Frederika founded and co-ordinated various establishments and funds for the dispossessed and disoriented villages, being especially instrumental in the creation of shelters for children and orphans. Despite her work in this field, she was the object of frequent criticism. Her welfare activities, being independent of all parliamentary regulations, were looked upon with suspicion. Essentially anti-democratic and with reactionary advisors, she was thought to have too much influence over her husband and was feared because of her German ancestry. Many insults and accusations came her way.

When her son Constantine became King in 1964, Frederika as Queen Mother still remained a centre of controversy. She was accused of being the *éminence grise* behind the throne. Her annuity became a subject of bitter debate in the press. She renounced her grant and retired to the countryside where she lived an almost reclusive life. In 1967, Greek internal politics forced the exile of the royal family. During the exile in Rome, spirituality became Frederika's main interest and she played no part in politics. She went to India in 1973 to study philosophy. Her final years were spent in London where she died at the age of sixty-three shortly after an eye operation in 1981.

KING HUSSEIN'S FIRST MARRIAGE

Of all the royal figures I have met, King Hussein ben Tallal of Jordan is undoubt-edly the most courageous. His background is an interesting one. On 12th August 1997, he celebrated forty-five years as king, an extraordinary achievement for a young king who assumed power at the age of seventeen. For the whole of his reign he was at the head of a kingdom trapped between Arab countries and Israel.

Hussein succeeded to the throne whilst his father, King Tallal, was still alive. Suffering from what the doctors called 'mental instability,' Tallal was forced to abdicate in favour of his son. It was Hussein's grandfather who, with the consent of the British, had received the Emirate of Transjordan, a kingdom created in the Middle East after the First World War.

There had been several attempts to assassinate Hussein but death did not yet have him in its sights. After one failed attempt, the king repeated words his grandfather had spoken and which he always remembered, "If my time has not come, no one can harm me. If my time has come, no one can protect me."

King Hussein has always aimed to be a 'King of Peace'. There is no doubt that 25th October 1994 was the most important date of his reign. Inside a Bedouin tent, Hussein was host to Israel's three most important men, President Ezer Weizman, Prime Minister Menachem Begin and Foreign Minister Shimon Peres. There the peace treaty between Israel and Jordan was signed. It was the occasion for Hussein to say, "One of the aims I dream about is to obtain a just and lasting peace for the people of the Middle East. Even if I do not see this dream come true in my lifetime, I shall devote all my efforts towards it to the end of my days."

Through my social contacts in Egypt, I had often met and talked with Princess Dina, the future wife of King Hussein of Jordan. The Princess was pop-ular and well liked by all her entourage and friends. She lived with her mother on the outskirts of Cairo in the fashionable suburb of Meadi.

Dina was a niece of Hussein's mother, Queen Zein; early in 1955 his moth-er introduced him to her. The King was twenty. Dina a little older. The two were engaged soon after. The news was warmly welcomed in Egypt. In April of the same year the marriage of the King and Princess Dina Abdul Hamid took place at the King's Palace in Amman. Among prominent guests from the Middle East were such personalities as King Faisal of Iraq[1] accompanied by his regent Abdul Illah. I was the only woman journalist present, having received a personal invi-tation from Princess Dina. When I arrived in the capital of the Hashemite

---

1 *King Faisal was assassinated in Baghdad in 1958. He was the last King of Iraq.*

Interview with King Hussein of Jordan on the second day of his wedding to Queen Dina. On his right is his Chief of Cabinet Bahgat El Talhouin, who was a faithful and reliable aide to the King all his life. Isis has her back to the camera.

Kingdom, I contacted the court officials. The future Queen had given them instructions to make the necessary arrangements for my stay.

After the signing of the marriage contract, a private soirée was held in the evening at the Palace. Apart from married couples, family and close friends, the guests were mainly ladies. The King's Head of Cabinet, Bahget El Talhouni and his wife drove me from my hotel to the palace.

As the royal procession walked down the line of assembled guests, the two mothers followed the ritual tradition of tossing little gold coins among them. I still possess the two that landed inside the front of my dress! Some of the ladies ended up with ten or so, not necessarily obtained in the same accidental way! After that piece of excitement, we all took our seats in the magnificent concert hall. Well-known actors, singers and dancers from various eastern countries provided the entertainment that lasted until the early hours of the morning.

I shall never forget being woken up in the morning by the beautiful, pure voice of the famous Egyptian singer, Farid El Atrach singing the Koran.

I was back at the Palace by midday to conduct the exclusive interview I had been granted by Queen Dina. The King came in just as we were about to start. My first question was, "As a new Queen, what rôle will you play in your country?" He intervened immediately. "The Queen will have no political rôle." Silence fell. Having made that point clear, the King left us to take off in his private plane and show his watching guests his skill as a newly qualified pilot. Once my interview was over – I refrained from any subjects that might be considered at all political – I went straight to the Palace of Queen Zein, now the Queen Mother. We had an animated conversation on a wide range of topics – the new Queen included. It seemed as if some strong mental power was flowing between the Queen Mother and myself. During our conversation, I became her confidante and a strong bond of friendship was suddenly forged between us. That is how she came to tell me about her apprehension for her future status with the Jordanians, her fear that she would fade away and disappear from the scene, in view of Dina's more forceful personality. Our friendship of a day did not end there. Some months later the Queen Mother sent me a wonderful letter in impeccable French.

This episode illustrates the difference in nature between Western and Eastern women. At the time it was quite usual for two Eastern women meeting for the first time to become friends there and then, exchanging details of their private lives and offering each other advice. This warmth and spontaneity of relationships exists even now, but is more restrained. In educated circles, westernising influence has altered many aspects of daily life; greater reserve is now exercised with casual acquaintances. Even so, the level of welcome and hospitality remains extremely warm and cordial.

If, in some circles of society there is now a greater reserve, ordinary people are still very welcoming and friendly. On one of his visits to Egypt my husband was sailing on the Nile. Two young brothers sitting near him quickly became acquainted and in no time at all they had invited him to take tea with them at their home. This is one example among many of the hospitality and welcome shown to strangers by the man in the street.

I left Amman with deep forebodings. There was no doubt that the King intended to exercise his authority over Dina and I knew Dina had a strong personality. The Queen Mother was already seeing the new Queen as a rival and threat to her own status. I wondered what the future held for this union, which, after all, was a marriage of convenience. They had one daughter, Alia Hussein. The marriage came to an end in 1960.

In 1961, Hussein married an Englishwoman, Antoinette Gardiner, who took the name Princess Mouna. There were four children. This marriage ended in divorce in 1971.

Hussein then married Alia Toukhan in December 1972. Tragically, Alia was killed in a helicopter crash in 1977, leaving two children.

In June 1978 Hussein married Lisa Halaby, who became Queen Noor. There are four children of this marriage.

"THE TEN COMMANDMENTS"

Generally speaking, the public is more interested in reading about famous stars from the world of entertainment than about diplomats, politicians and world statesmen. This preference was not obvious to me when starting out on my journalistic career; in any case, my own interests and preferences led me to concentrate on the latter group of personalities. However, when the opportunity arose, I did, of, course interview film actors and actresses, both in Egypt and on my travels abroad. My interview with Robert Taylor was in Guizeh in 1956 when he came to Egypt for the making of *The Ten Commandments*. He was staying at the famous Mena House Hotel, just a few hundred yards from the Pyramids. He was up at dawn to be driven to the desert location where the film was being shot.

One Saturday afternoon, my chief, Moustafa Amin rang me. "Isis, I have an important job for you. Drive out to the Mena House straightaway, spend what you have to, and stay there until you get an interview with Robert Taylor." So, young and full of enthusiasm, off I went. The first thing to do was to seek the assistance of the head doorman. Suitably bribed, he told me that Taylor had gone out early in the morning and had not yet returned. Another sweetener elicited that his rooms were on the second floor. Discreetly, I sought out the chambermaid and was lucky enough to find her in the corridor. Money changed hands. " I'll show you where his suite is, but come quickly; he is due back anytime now, and I don't want to be seen with you. We've got instructions to keep our mouths shut. The press has invaded the place. There! The room at the end."

All I could do then was to go down again and wait patiently in the lounge. Eventually the doorman came over. "You know," he said "Robert Taylor is in his room. He came in through a door at the back of the hotel." I thanked him and was soon at the film star's door. I could hear running water. He was having a shower. I knocked. What a stupid thing to do! He wouldn't hear anything over the sound of the water, and anyway, did I really expect him to interrupt his shower to answer a knock at the door? Then silence. The water stopped. I was still so excited that I didn't allow the man time to get dressed before I knocked again. "Who is it?" "Me!" The door opened. Taylor was bare-footed, wearing a white bathrobe. I had of course seen him in films, but his appearance now, without make-up, was a great disappointment. His face was lined and wrinkled. For me, in my twenties, he was an old man. In my eyes, he seemed at least sixty-five.

We had a brief conversation at the door, but I was not invited inside. Taylor said a little about the fascination of dawn in the desert with the Sphinx and the Pyramids, but avoided saying how hard it was to work all day out in the burning sun. Then, suddenly, he seemed realise what was happening. His mood became aggressive. "What are you doing here? Who gave you permission to come up to my room?" "I'm just doing my job," was my answer. "I've got nothing further to say to you. Go and see my public relations man. Answering questions about me is his job." The door slammed shut but I already had enough for my article.

Back at the newspaper offices, I wrote my story and took it to Moustafa Amin. He was pleased with it but no sooner had it appeared than Taylor's public-relations man rang up the chief editor to complain. "How dare that woman reporter say that Robert Taylor is old and wrinkled and that he is sixty-five. I want a retraction printed in your paper." He did not get one. What I had written was that I did not know exactly how old he was, but he seemed sixty-five.

This is how I learned, at Robert Taylor's expense, that age is not a subject to mention, especially in articles about members of the acting profession.

Just one more little incident, but at second hand, involving Robert Taylor and me. It took place in the early days of his stay in Egypt. It so happened that the chauffeur engaged for Taylor by the film company was a friend of my mother's chauffeur. Through this connection we learned that the film company wanted to buy a private car for Taylor's use, and had asked his chauffeur to look out for something suitable on the second-hand market. The car I had at the time was a large Buick. I had been wanting to change it for something considerably smaller. The Nasser regime was in full swing. In press circles, I was considered very bourgeoise and my ownership of a Buick was much criticised, with remarks like, "Who is this reporter in a car like that when some of us don't have a car at all?"

Robert Taylor's visit solved my problem. Via the two chauffeurs, the film company acquired my Buick. All went well on Taylor's first trip through the desert to the film set. Not so on the second one. Two of the car's tyres, which I knew were somewhat worn, developed punctures. Taylor had a long hot wait. It is perhaps just as well that he knew nothing of the car's previous owner!

When, in 1956, the filming of *The Ten Commandments* was complete, its famous American producer Cecil B. de Mille, then aged seventy-five, gave a spectacular press conference in Cairo at the Semiramis Hotel. I was present, along with hundreds of journalists and reporters from all parts of the world. What I was hoping to obtain for my Sunday column was an exclusive interview. The chances were not good. I asked no questions at the conference, but when it was over I ran after de Mille and his escort of imposing bodyguards. Of course they stopped me but I persisted, and when I began to argue, they shouted that the press conference was finished. Hearing the commotion, de Mille turned round, saying, "Let her through. Well, young lady, what would you like to know?" "I have a personal question that nobody asked you. Who has been the great love of your life?" Accustomed to American-style questions of this kind, de Mille replied seriously, "I met the woman who is my wife when I was twenty-two, fell in love and married her." Wondering how a man who had his life in the cinema world had resisted temptation, I blurted out, "All these years with the same woman!" De Mille smiled. "Yes, my dear, but that's because I never met you before!" was his charming reply.

TO CUBA VIA MADRID

One Sunday morning I was relaxing at home keeping my mother company. About the middle of the morning the phone rang. The speaker was a Cuban woman, unknown to me, who said, "The Cuban Ambassador has told me I ought to make your acquaintance. Would it be convenient for me to come and see you now?" Although on Sunday mornings I normally wanted a rest, I could hardly refuse. Mrs Maria Alfonso Rubio duly arrived, accompanied by a man who turned out to be her uncle. She was a Cuban tourist, visiting Egypt for the first time, highly delighted and enthusiastic about what she had seen and especially so about Egyptian people with their generous hospitality.

She said to me, "No one in our capital Havana knows about your country, so you are just the right person for me to invite to Cuba to represent Egypt. I would be honoured if you would accept an invitation from me to be my guest. I have a large house in Havana with a private suite for guests, so you would be staying in my home. You would also have your own private swimming pool." She added, "I shall be leaving Cairo soon, but my uncle will stay behind until you are ready and then travel with you to Havana." I replied, "I have to discuss this with my superior at the newspaper as I cannot leave without good reason." Maria said she would wait a few days until I could give her an answer. In 1958, no one could travel abroad unless they had special permission. To obtain a visa, even a journalist had to have an official form signed by the Director-General. At that time Anwar El Saadat (later to become President of Egypt) was in that position and was therefore my "boss."

When President Nasser came to power, one of the first things he did was to nationalise the newspapers; today they are still the property of the State. The group of newspapers was an important one in which I was involved with before nationalisation, and was owned by an English woman, a Mrs. Findley. The group was composed of three newspapers, one Egyptian. *El Goumhoureya* one French, *Le Progrès Egyptien* and one English, *The Egyptian Gazette*. Now, however, Saadat was in charge. His main quality, which everyone admired, was his 'willingness to listen.' Although it required courage on my part, I knocked at the door of his office. I told him about the proposal I had received from Maria Rubio. He approved of the idea immediately as there was no expense involved for the newspapers and my trip might give me the opportunity to cover some interesting and unusual stories.

On flights to Cuba from Egypt the first stop was Madrid, Spain. When the Spanish Embassy in Cairo heard about my proposed trip to Cuba, the Spanish Ambassador in Egypt told me he would call the foreign office in Madrid. The result was that I was invited for a fortnight's official visit to Spain. When I arrived at the airport to leave Egypt with Mrs. Maria Rubio's uncle I was surprised to find that there was a young man with him (a so-called photographer); he was a complete stranger to me. I arrived in Madrid on 10th July 1958. My travelling companions and I went our separate ways.

General Franco was still in power, and the absolute dictator of Spain. Almost as soon as I arrived in my hotel room, the phone rang. It was the receptionist saying. "There are some people here who want to meet you." My journalistic curiosity was aroused. Who could they be? I went to reception where I met three men; they did not say who they were or whom they represented, but they said to me, "Listen, we have heard that you have been invited as a journalist by the government. Don't believe what you are told. Be careful you will be followed and all your movements recorded. We live under a terrible régime." They went on and on criticising their government. I listened but did not comment. I never did know the truth about them. Were they sincere and honest, or were they *agents provocateurs* sent by the government to incite me to speak against the régime so that my political views could be determined? An attaché from the press department of the Ministry of Foreign Affairs was with me all the time and had to accompany me the whole day, wherever I wanted to go.

Whilst in Spain I never could acquire the habit of having lunch at three o'clock in the afternoon, even four o'clock sometimes. Dinner started at the earliest at 10pm. One day a Spanish family invited me to lunch at 2pm. I arrived on time and rang the doorbell, again and again. I heard noises, movements, and then at last the door opened. The family was not ready; other guests did not start to arrive until three o'clock. We finished lunch at half-past five! This experience taught me in future to arrive for an invitation an hour later than the time stated. As for dinner, the Spanish time for eating it became obvious, when I wanted to have mine about eight o'clock, the restaurants were just opening and my press officer escort appeared reluctant to eat a proper meal. While I was having a full dinner, he had only a snack. We finished our meal and talked until about ten o'clock. He walked with me back to my hotel, and then said with a smile, "Now it's time for me to have my dinner".

Whilst I was staying in Madrid I had to go and see Maria's uncle from time to time. Both he and the so-called photographer waited patiently and without fuss until my official visit was over. The purpose of the young man's invitation to Cuba never dawned on me at the time; neither did the real reason for mine. I carried on with my schedule and interviews. I asked to visit Carmencita Franco whose husband was the Marquis de Villaverde. Carmencita was essentially a kind of public relations officer for her father; it was she who went with him on official visits abroad. I had known her in Egypt when I had the honour of being chosen to represent my newspaper to cover her visit. She remembered me and invited me into her beautiful apartments. With enthusiasm and wit, Carmencita reminisced about her unforgettable visit to Egypt, especially recalling her excursion by boat down the Nile. On this occasion Mrs. Abd El Khalek

Hassouna, the wife of the Egyptian Foreign Minister, had accompanied her; I had also been invited; so we talked happily about our recollections. During the conversation, Carmencita invited me to the great festival being given by her father, General Franco, to celebrate National Day, on 18th July 1958. This reception was held at La Granga[1], the Palace he used most for entertaining officialdom.

The Egyptian Ambassador and his wife were kind enough to take me there with them. Dress for the occasion was formal long dresses for the ladies and black tie for the men. Upon arrival at the palace the Chief of Protocol welcomed us. In one of the rooms, the entire Diplomatic Corps was waiting in line for the arrival of General Franco. At 8 p.m. exactly, he made his appearance, accompanied by his wife. Franco was a cold, hard man. He was haughty in his manner with never a looked towards the diplomats around him. It was as much as he could do to greet them all. No courtesy; here I am... look at me!

As it was the height of summer, the soirée was held in the open air in the palace park and gardens, which resembled a miniature Versailles. It was a long party with a variety of entertainment. For three hours famous Spanish artists, singers and dancers performed popular and traditional acts. Supper was served with all the ceremony accorded to a head of state. Butlers and waiters were dressed in the eighteenth-century costume of the reign of Louis XV. It was a splendid meal consisting of Spanish soup, lobster, York ham, veal and chicken, with a variety of vegetables followed by *La Granga* iced cake and a selection of tarts and delicacies. Champagne accompanied the meal.

The lavish spectacle of the soirée made an impression on me, which proved unforgettable. Although it was an official event, the atmosphere was cheerful and easy-going. Carmencita and her friends were very high-spirited, but Franco was always the same - aloof, unsmiling, and pompous!

During my stay in Madrid I was attracted by the idea of going to a bullfight, although I am not an enthusiast of this 'sport'; indeed I am an opponent of it; for years European countries have denounced its cruelty and urged that it be banned. I even heard similar views being expressed by Spaniards in the streets of Madrid. Nevertheless, this famous, or infamous, sport attracts thousands of spectators. I did not find the spectacle exciting. What I enjoyed far more was an interview with the most famous toreador of his day, Antonio Benvienipa.

It is not easy to gain access to such personalities; how I managed to secure an appointment to share a drink with Benvienipa and his wife in the privacy of their home was due to a combination of circumstances. I was immediately impressed by the refinement, which greeted me. Antonio and his wife were impeccably elegant in their dress and manners. I was surprised because, in my ignorance, I had expected a Spanish bullfighter to look and behave like an American cowboy out of a Wild West film. Mrs. Benvienipa was very pretty with delicate features, quietly spoken, wearing the Spanish national costume. Numerous old paintings decorated the walls and there were interesting displays

---

1 *A Spanish Royal Palace, built for King Philippe V (1683-1746), a grandson of Louis XIV, in a picturesque, baroque style with gardens and fountains 'à la Française,' with important collections of paintings and sculptures.*

of objets d'art, porcelain and silver.

I asked Antonio to tell me about his childhood.

"My childhood thoughts were dominated by bulls. From the age of five, my only desire was to be with bulls, to overcome them. I went to school, of course, but once I gained my leaving certificate, I had only one future for myself in mind - to become a toreador."

"What did your parents think about it?"

"It is always the women - mothers, sisters and wives, who are afraid. For my wife, the day I give up my job can't come soon enough. When I started out in my career, I was earning thirty pounds. At present, I am paid five thousand pounds for each performance!"

"What are your feelings each time you confront the bull?"

"Inside me I feel a kind of fear – is he going to get me? But the support and excitement of the crowd create within me a feeling of extraordinary strength, which will protect my life as I overcome the bull.

"How many bull-fights do you take part in each year?"

"About fifty, the season only lasts eight months."

"How often have you been injured?"

"Eleven times so far; the last time was just three weeks ago."

"When you aren't involved with your work, how do you spend your time?"

"Oh, in various ways not at all connected with bulls. Just now, most of my thoughts are concentrated on income tax!" Then he added, "A toreador's life must be disciplined. No alcohol, no late nights, no over-work. In other words, he must lead a very healthy, active life. I swim a lot; I go horse riding and I enjoy fishing.

I turned to his wife who had been listening to our conversation.

"Do you enjoy bullfights?"

"I have never been to one!"

"What do you do when your husband is in the arena?"

"I pray to God that he will send him back to me safe and sound."

"Have you any children?"

"Yes, three boys. I hope that none of them follows in his father's footsteps." Finally, she remarked, "I keep asking my husband to give up this cruel sport. He smiles, doesn't argue, shrugs his shoulders and just says, 'Well, it's an idea.'"

On that note we ended our conversation. For me it was an unusual interview as well as a fascinating one.

Before leaving Madrid, after all these official functions and interviews, I had only time for a short visit around this lovely city with its museums, the most famous of which is the Prado.

Here are to be found many of the greatest works of famous artists including Goya, Rubens, Titian, El Greco and Velazquez.

After my stay in the Spanish capital, it really was time to leave for Havana, accompanied, of course, by the uncle and the photographer. It was a twenty-four hour flight, with three stops. The first port of call was Lisbon, the capital of Portugal; after thirty-five minutes we took off again on the six-hour flight to Santa Maria in the Canary Islands, islands that summon up a picture of the wondrous and the exotic. Just time to re-fuel, then the long journey, hour after hour, to Bermuda. The beauty of the Bermudan islands justifies their fame: a panorama of silky pink coral beaches, green seas, trees and flowers everywhere. For privileged Anglo-Saxons it is a honeymoon destination. We had an hour in this little paradise before setting off on the last leg to Cuba where we landed at ten o'clock in the morning, six hours ahead of European time.

When I arrived at Havana airport, a smartly dressed man was waiting to greet me. He was Mrs. Rubio's husband, the owner of six cinemas in Havana. I noticed however that the 'uncle' had disappeared, along with the 'photographer'. Eventually I discovered why I had been invited. I was a cover for Maria who had fallen in love with the young photographer in Cairo on the roof of the Semiramis hotel. She was in her fifties and Mohamed the photographer was only thirty. So I had become involved in a love triangle. Her lover had travelled to Cuba under the pretence of being my official photographer. I was completely unaware of the whole affair. It was only when we reached Havana that Maria told me the full story. I admit, I was somewhat amused by the clever deception!

This exotic land of Cuba had a charm all of its own, thanks to its style and civilisation that were so different from Europe. "Havana? Oh yes!" people said, that means sambas and cha-chas on every street corner. In fact to savour these folk rhythms one had to go to the popular dancehalls, not to the smart places like the "Tropicana" nightclub.

Since I was the first Egyptian journalist to visit Cuba, I was very warmly welcomed in Havana. Every day there were parties to greet me, but more than anything else I was an item of curiosity. Once a Cuban journalist asked me: "Are the clothes you are wearing just for your trip? They are like ours." I laughed and replied: "I live and dress the same way as you. These are the clothes I wear in Egypt. Each day at these social functions I had to describe the Egyptian way of life, our customs and traditions. Cubans had no idea what Egypt was like. Maria had been right. In the end, I was glad she had invited me. I lived for a whole month in another world.

One of my most fascinating encounters in Havana was with the King of Sugar, Julio Lobo. When I managed to obtain an interview with him, my friends nicknamed me 'the charmer'. After my meeting, they were even more surprised. As Julio Lobo was the 'first' man in Cuba. All in all, a visitor might more easily see the President of the Republic than succeed in disturbing the King of Sugar. He was a very busy man, with the power to send the price of sugar up or down by picking up the phone. "A country's standard of living depends on its potential as a sugar consumer," he told me and with a broad smile. He added, "Sugar is my one and only love, just think, for the whole of my youth it was my ambition to become an actor. Look at me now: a man turned into sugar!"

The 'King' was in his sixties, yet still worked an eighteen-hour day. He employed forty thousand workers. He had three mansions in the capital and a Cadillac with an automatic folding bed. He was a major art collector and possessed, so it was said, two hundred thousand historical letters including six thousand signed by Napoleon Bonaparte!

In his private life, Julio Lobo was a single man. His two marriages had ended in divorce. One of his daughters was married to a Londoner, the other aged twenty-four, lived with him. Oddly enough, he was not a native of Cuba but a Venezuelan whose father immigrated to Cuba when his son was a child. Lobo spent his weekends in one of his plantations with a small circle of friends from various countries. It was at one of these plantations that I was invited to spend a weekend. With his friends around him, Lobo seemed to forget his business kingdom. Always elegantly dressed, he was a most charming businessman. His view on life was: "Man's only value is the thickness of his wallet," hence his own long working day and appreciation of the value of time. After a hectic day's work, his only pleasure was to return home and watch television. This seemed to be his only link with the outside world, apart from sugar trading.

My hostess Maria Rubio had several journalists as close friends. Once she invited a chief editor to give me information and to explain the current political situation. Fidel Castro was preparing the revolution up in the mountains. The atmosphere was menacing even when walking in the streets. The police were everywhere. General Batista was still in power. I was fortunate enough to be granted an interview with his wife at their residence. Mrs. Batista entertained me in her drawing room. We sat together on a sofa. Behind us was a policeman with a machine gun. The first lady of Cuba was very much on edge. She told me, "The situation is very bad, we don't know what is going to happen and when!" In fact all the important people I met said the same. They all knew that the revolution was inevitable, but social life still went on.

One day two policemen came to Maria's house where I was staying. The frightened gardener brought me the message that they wanted to see me so I went out to meet them. They gave me an invitation from the Minister of Defence to spend the day at his country house on the Sunday. At that time the Minister of Defence was a cousin of the Cuban Ambassador in Egypt. His daughter Helena came to fetch me in an official car; while passing through a small village, our car was pelted with eggs and tomatoes revealing the people's feelings towards their government.

My misgivings were becoming more acute. A kind of impending fear was throwing a veil of mourning over Cuba. Families were haunted by the possibility of one of their friends or relatives disappearing. Numerous young people left home in the morning, never to be seen again. In Havana blood had been flowing in the streets for several years during internal struggles. Certain aspects of this terrorism were apparent. An individual walking alone in the street would be seen as suspicious and likely to be apprehended as a revolutionary! Imprisonment could follow, which was, one could say, a better option than being tortured.

Wanting to have a more personal and more accurate perception of the situation, I asked my friend Maria to take me on a tour of downtown Havana. I saw first-hand the police vans patrolling the streets, stopping and interrogating even the most inoffensive looking passers by. Their role was to arrest every young man walking along the road, take him, at this stage, to the police station, and declare him to be a suspected supporter of Castro who was allegedly fleeing after learning of the arrest of a friend or acquaintance.

As for remains, one found twenty to thirty dead bodies a day thrown here and there. They had been found even in the entrance of the most important Cuban weekly newspaper.

The following real-life anecdote of events I witnessed personally gives a taste of the terrorism that, at that time, menaced every Cuban. One evening, at the home of some friends, we suddenly heard the cries of a woman piercing the stillness of the night. The police had just arrested two young girls who were passing in front of the Central Office of Revolutionaries. The following day some forty corpses lay scattered across the streets. This state of affairs could not continue without some kind of mass social hysteria building up.

Another evening, dining at home with friends, we heard police whistles raising the alarm. The neighbour was feeling ill, her nerves stretched to their limit, she fell unconscious. While taking her back home, her husband explained to me that she was actually suffering from a form of depression. He also told me that on the previous day the police had forced his door and at bayonet point, asked him if he had given shelter to one of his friends. His negative response did not prevent them from firing on their home, right into the remote corners, awakening their little girl who was only eight years old. One of his friends who had answered the police back had a similar experience. "Why fire on my home when I have already stated that the person you are looking for is not living with me?" The result? The police stationed themselves by the house of this peaceful family man and shot him in public. His two children ran out in alarm and quickly suffered the same cruel fate, watched by their distraught mother. In the space of a few moments, a family had been wiped out.

Such fear and terror will be the two by-words remaining in the history of Cuba. A sort of defensive reflex was encompassed by all social groups – from the worker to the artist, from the engineers to lawyers and doctors, from the young to the housewife. Power politics was the predominating obsession pervading everyone's most intimate and social life.

Only the name of one man signified the revolution. Batista, the Cuban dictator who all the people wanted to overthrow. But if Batista relinquished power, he would become virtually the prisoner of his own following. His presidential mandate, in principle, ended on 24th February, 1959 but the dictator clung strongly to power, not giving up before that date, doubtless wanting to prolong his authority in office. His love of power was balanced by the enormous material gains he had built up. Blood continued to flow. One could estimate, that so far, there had been twenty to twenty-five thousand executions. This figure surpassed the huge number of deaths in Cuba's own fight for independence from

Spain, its mother country. Fidel Castro, the leader of the revolutionary movement had taken refuge in the mountains where there was constant fighting
between Batista's troops and the revolutionaries. From its inland base the revolution spread its tentacles to the rest of the country.

But how could this situation be reversed? The Cuban army amounted to
thirty-five thousand men and the population stood at six million, which could
quickly destroy the police force. The weak point of the regime lay, in the words
of Batista, in the army's internal divisions over which the dictator no longer had
great influence. It is useful to recall briefly the economic situation of the era. In
1958 the United States attached great importance to Cuba, owing to its geographical situation and its sugar production. On the one hand, Cuba constitutes
the line of union between America, Mexico and Venezuela. On the other hand,
the United States is the major purchaser of sugar, which forms the staple economy of Cuba, buying at a low price.

My investigations in Cuba complete, I decided that it would be interesting to
return to Egypt via the United States and Europe. I was intending to set up a
meeting with Che Guevara but unfortunately, when he arrived in Egypt, I was
in Paris attending the Summit Conference with de Gaulle, Khrushchev,
Macmillan and Eisenhower.

WASHINGTON DC

No sooner had I left Havana in August 1958, than I was touching down at Miami Beach after a thirty-five minute flight. It is nicknamed the city of millionaires. At the time, it was harbouring opponents of Batista's regime who were subsidising Castro with arms and money. Miami Beach, famous for the beauty of its beaches and its palm trees, is a particular attraction for tourists and the beautiful women of Hollywood and Broadway.

By 1958 Miami Beach had become the most famous international centre for holidaymakers, especially in the United States. Originally, some ninety years ago it was a small village of twenty-nine thousand inhabitants. My visit was a lightning one as I was not very attracted by it. I made only a brief stop there. I was impatient to reach Washington. D.C.

I will not hide my surprise from you, for the reality of 1958 corresponded so little to the fiction, and to the idea I had of it. Far from finding myself in the middle of some industrial centre, I was landing in a city surrounded by forests, brick-coloured villas with grey roofs, and no skyscrapers! A quiet city, whose inhabitants were almost afraid that it might become busy and over-populated and lose its character. It is, one can say, the political centre. It is here that the government, the army, and the representatives of foreign countries reside to the exclusion of all industrial and business life.

When I arrived in Washington my first visit was to the Egyptian Embassy because it is a matter of courtesy to initially visit one's Ambassador, who was at that time Moustafa Kamel, a bachelor, always impeccably dressed and very elegant. He had been in Washington hardly two months and was a hard worker, ten to twelve hours a day. I admired the way he had acquired a thorough knowledge of the staff and all the various departments in so short a time. He was not a career diplomat but originally a professor of law at Cairo University. His first diplomatic post was Ambassador to India. He has a very precise idea of life. It is not defined by words or literature but in a concrete way. That is how he was able to tackle all problems brilliantly, with politicians, economists and journalists. This I was able to discover when he invited me to lunch in his residence with American businessmen. As he walked over to them, he said, "We are meeting here to have a purely constructive conversation."

As is right and proper, a journalist has especially to make contact with the Press Counsellor; it is courteous and can also be very useful. It was very effective for me during my stay in Washington and New York. At that time the Press Counsellor at the Egyptian Embassy was an ex-colleague of mine, a journalist called Mohamed Habib. We had worked in Egypt on the same newspaper *Akhbar El Yom*. He said, "It is very rare for one of our journalists to come to the United States these days and so I'm going to organise a press conference for you at the Embassy." I replied that would be fine although I was not all that enthusiastic about the idea.

It turned out to be a very tough experience for me. American journalists, especially women, have a reputation for being aggressive. As I had feared, there were several awkward questions including this one, "Is your government Communist? It is very friendly with the Russians." I answered, "Egyptians are anti-Communist. Anyone who goes to the Soviet Embassy too often or has too much contact with Russian diplomats is blacklisted."

The next day, in the *Washington Post*, there was a whole page about this press conference and a big picture of me. The headline read, "Egyptians are anti-Communist says a newspaper woman from Egypt." This was enough to cause a minor political row between the two Embassies. The Soviet Embassy protested immediately to the Egyptian Embassy. The Egyptian Ambassador was obliged to summon me to his presence and deliver an official reprimand about my remarks. He treated me very courteously and I felt that in private he approved of what I had said. In fact, I was right but he could not say so.

At that time, during Nasser's military regime, the military attachés in the embassies were more important than the Ambassadors, especially when the Ambassador was a civilian diplomat and not an ex-military man. On my way out of the embassy, I was approached by one of these young military attachés who snapped at me, "You come here for a few days, you appear in the newspapers, and cause a diplomatic incident!" I did not answer, but I was very worried that on my return to Egypt I might end up in jail, as had happened to some of my colleagues.

When I did eventually return to Egypt, the first thing I did was to ring Military Headquarters and talk to Nasser's Chief of Cabinet, Amin Chaker (who later became a well-known Egyptian Ambassador), I told him what had happened during my visit to the States. He already knew about the incident, and his comment was. "You did right to say what you said." I breathed a sigh of relief.

In my career as a journalist it is obvious that I sometimes make contacts who become personal friends. Almost as soon as my interview appeared in the *Washington Post*, a couple of American diplomat friends who had served in Egypt telephoned the Egyptian Embassy to try to get in touch with me. During this brief visit, I was staying with an Embassy Counsellor, one of Nasser's men of course. He was responsible for checking on all my movements and especially for keeping my contacts under surveillance. My friend Penny Williams was talking to me on the phone trying to organise a luncheon in my honour where I would have around me all our mutual friends then serving in Washington, so that I could see them again. I accepted her invitation. It was a pleasant surprise to meet old friends, including the Lebanese Ambassador Nadim Demeshkié and his wife. As I was ending my conversation, I heard the Counsellor complaining to his wife that she had not taken down the name of my caller. He had to know who she was in order to be able to make his report on my movements and contacts in Washington.

One interesting thing I learnt in Washington was that there are courses for diplomats including counsellors, first secretaries, and attachés, when they return from their postings abroad. They attend these courses during their stay in their own country. More interesting is that there are courses for the wives of diplomats. Training wives to help their husbands during their missions abroad is a wonderful idea and a very important one.

While I was staying in Washington D.C. I heard that there was a weekly press conference for which I enrolled. Gaining admission to the White House was not easy, and one had to undergo a fairly rigorous police check. At the outside main gate the police had the list of invited journalists. After I had shown my card, a phone call to the policeman at the second door to check that I was on the second list of guests. Next I had to go to a secretariat, which finally gave me the requisite invitation card. What struck me as I went on into the White House was the simplicity of the interior decoration. Plain white, and very modern.

To speak in front of the media, one has to have the appropriate make-up. This was done for President Eisenhower. Surrounded by microphones, he was asked twenty-five questions, of which twenty-four were on subjects of domestic or foreign politics, the burning questions of the day: Little Rock, China and the Middle East among others. In the middle of all these issues of world significance, a colleague, a short, stocky man, called out, "Mr President, what do you think about the two teams in tomorrow's baseball match?" The question was greeted with general laughter, but this did not stop the President from replying seriously about the team he thought would win. I was surprised, but my neighbour explained to me that such interventions are typically American. For the whole of the session the President kept his left hand in his jacket pocket. At exactly eleven o'clock, the conference came to an end, and before the President left the room the journalists rushed out to cable their respective agencies. Always the same length of time: twenty-five questions and answers were disposed of in exactly thirty minutes.

While in Washington, my professional curiosity led me, with the Egyptian press attaché, to the State Department. The building had two thousand rooms: five thousand staff worked there, but in all some thirty-five thousand people worked for the State Department in various buildings in the city. Then the press attaché invited me to visit the National Press Club. It is situated in the centre of the city and is one of the most important buildings in Washington. In its fourteen storeys the world's press agencies had their offices, equipped with telegraph machines and typists. The whole of one floor is taken up with lounges, bars and restaurants. However, one fact scandalised me. Women journalists were not allowed in the club. Thinking this was a joke, I tried to defy the rule and walked into one of the lounges, I had hardly taken a few steps before a woman came up to me and announced that women were not allowed in this lounge, which was

guarded by two representatives of the so-called weaker sex. My American colleagues were as astonished as I was by this prohibition.

Television was then the favourite pastime of Americans. The average
American owned a set. Whether eating, entertaining friends or relaxing, they
were sure to be watching TV. It formed the backcloth to life so to speak. I did
not want to leave Washington without visiting the main television centres. Two
interesting programmes were broadcast every Sunday: *College Press Conference*
and *Face to the Nation*. The aim of the first one was to give an opportunity for
university students from different parts of the world to interview politicians. On
that day, there was a political debate on the problem of the Middle East between
five English, French and American students on the one hand, and Mr. Francis
Willcocks, the Under Secretary at the State Department on the other.

Before leaving, I took a quick ride around the City. In a large car park near
each parking space there was a microphone and a tray with a menu. To place
one's order, one had only to press the microphone button. While the order was
being prepared, music of one's choice kept one company. This only lasted a few
minutes because the service was so quick, the purpose of "hot Shoppe's" being
to save time for people who were in too much of a hurry to go to a restaurant.
All the mechanical inventions – American fast food!

Next, a visit to the famous National Art Gallery with 1,400 paintings filling
eighty-six galleries in which the paintings were examples of French, German,
Italian, Flemish and Pre-Colombian masterpieces with Italian art predominating. Egyptian art was worthily represented in a gallery containing thirty
pharaonic statuettes from different dynasties, and tomb fragments dating from
the fourth century. I also saw there a statuette of Osiris and a model of a solar
boat. Gulbenkian, a famously rich Armenian, donated this precious collection to
the museum.

I shall end this tour of the Washington scene with a highly amusing anecdote
told to me at the time of my visit to the home of our Embassy Counsellor. Two
policemen had been keeping permanent watch in their street for two days. The
reason for this was that a lady had made a complaint to the police alleging that
the dog next door was tormenting hers. The neighbour defended her dog by
maintaining the opposite. To get to the truth of the matter, two policemen were
sent to determine which one was the tormentor. What a world! Some way away
from ours!

NEW YORK

The next stage of my journey from Washington took me to New York, which most tourists arriving in the United States have already decided is the one city above all others that they must visit. The reaction of Americans to this attitude is an odd one. "New York," they say, "does not represent the USA."

When the embassy staff in Washington learnt that I was about to leave for New York, they informed the Consulate there, at the same time advising me: "Be careful. It's a violent city. You're a foreigner, young and pretty. Don't get mugged – or worse. Don't walk in the streets at night!" They should also have warned me to expect the unexpected, as I discovered during the course of various mishaps.

First of all, as I alighted from the train, I was completely flustered by the pace of life around me. Passengers grabbed their luggage and made straight for the escalator. For my own case, I had to call on the services of a porter. The only other person looking for one was a woman in military uniform. Having called over a porter, I walked along the platform looking for our Consul and Press Counsellor. Suddenly I heard a voice calling me; it was the porter saying, "Ma'am, keep close to me, otherwise you will lose all your luggage." My attempt to explain that I was looking for someone made no difference. As if deaf to what I was saying, he kept on repeating. "If you leave me for a single second, you'll lose all your luggage, and it won't be my responsibility." I walked up to the woman in uniform. "Are you an officer?" I asked. "Yes," she replied, "I am an air-force major, and I do a lot of travelling." I asked her to speak with the stubborn old porter, but this was impossible as he was leading us at the double up one escalator after another towards a taxi rank. Suddenly I became aware the air-force officer too had disappeared.

Alone and bewildered, I gave a cab driver the address of the hotel where I had a reservation booked for me by the Consulate. He gave me a strange look. "Are you certain about this address?" I answered him I was. As we drove off he again questioned the address. Subsequent events explained the drivers' attitude, the hotel was very close to the station, and perhaps it was that. Arriving at the address the driver gave me another strange look but said nothing; he just followed me carrying my luggage. We entered the hotel and passed through the lounge to the reception desk. I became aware that the residents were giving me strange looks. At the desk I asked the clerk. "Is there a room booked in my name?" No, was the short reply. "Then the cab driver said. "Ma'am, this is a hotel for men only, there must be another one for women. His manner altered and became sympathetic to the confused, young traveller, and so, with my driver, I came to discover a new American institution as I went the rounds of hotels for businesswomen. Seeing my distraught and tearful state, the cab driver finally came up with an idea. "I'll take you to the YWCA Ma'am." His idea was a welcome one. The YWCA had four premises in New York, all of which were comfortable and smart. At the desk I was told, "You're asking for a room when you haven't made a reservation? Membership card please." I explained that I did not have one and that made things worse. After several minutes of discussion and argument, I was given a room for one night only. I thanked the cab driver, paid him, and carried my luggage to my room.

I began to feel better but tired and hungry. It was about midnight when I walked around the streets in the district looking for a restaurant. Finally I discovered a grocery store not far from the YWCA. I entered and found two old men. We quickly fell into conversation; they asked me what I was doing alone on the streets at this time of night. I tearfully explained my predicament and how I was hungry and tired; they listened with interest. "Miss, can we offer you a bowl of soup and a sandwich?" I accepted their kind offer. One of them asked. "Where are you from?" "Egypt." "We are Greeks from Istanbul." They were two old brothers, both bachelors. One of them said to the other, "We ought to visit that part of the world before we grow too old." Thanking them for their hospitality, I went back to the YWCA to my room where I did not sleep for as long as I needed to. I was suddenly awakened. I looked at my watch. It was five in the morning. There was a sort of rustling and scuffing outside my door. It was only a short journey from bed to door. A note had been slipped into my room. It read, "You must vacate your room by twelve noon." Well, I certainly did not intend to stay in it any longer than necessary, and I did not really need seven hours' notice, especially at that time of day.

At seven in the morning the frenzied activity of New York put an end to sleep. New Yorkers wake up very early and sleeping beyond eight in this city is inconceivable. So I got up early. After all the adventures over my accommodation I could have done with a better night's sleep. Where could I have breakfast before contacting the Consulate? I went out again into the street and found a bar open serving coffee and toast. I took a seat at the counter and whilst I was having breakfast a man on my left was talking loudly to himself. Nobody said anything. He was drunk and smelt badly of alcohol. I gulped down my coffee and went back to the YWCA, from where it was possible to call the Consulate. That was when I learned the Press Counsellor had been waiting for me at the railway station information desk. Oh well! I explained where I was and a car was sent to fetch me. Once in the car I felt more secure following my recent experiences. On arrival at the Consulate I was met by the Counsellor who asked, "How was your accommodation? I hope you were comfortable." I smiled, and briefly explained what had happened, apparently the secretary who had been instructed to book my accommodation was under the impression that it was a man arriving from Washington; they did not expected a woman journalist. So, all was now clear and apologies accepted. For the rest of my stay in New York I was a guest at the house of an Egyptian journalist and his American wife.

One little anecdote worthy of mention. When I picked up the phone, I said good morning to the operator. His reply was. "What do you want?" That was when I realised that saying good morning in New York is a waste of time. "Time is money, Ma'am!"

Once in New York, I was impatient to visit and learn as much as possible about the headquarters of the United Nations. I had visited New York several times since 1958 and each time I visited the UN. There was always something new to learn and experience in those fabulous buildings, which are a microcosm of the world; in fact the headquarters was a world of its own.

Since its creation membership of the organisation has steadily grown, and consequently the number of staff. At its birth in 1945, there were fifty-one member states and by1980 were more than a hundred and eighty-five, represented by a permanent staff of some fourteen thousand men and women.

My first glimpse of the outside of these huge buildings made me all the keener to pass through the doors and explore all the rooms that were open to the public, and if possible some that weren't! A hundred yards or so in front of the buildings was a row of flagpoles, bearing the flags of the member states. The most important building was the Secretariat with its 39-storey tower rising to a height of 550 feet. Huge though it is, it does not now offer sufficient space for all the international staff. The exterior is exclusively of aluminium, glass and marble. What impressed me was the huge number of windows, so I asked: "How many windows are there in all those buildings?" The answer was, "A total of 5,400." The building looks rather like a matchbox, hence one of its nicknames, the other being the 'glass-house.'

Much of the headquarters is underground. Basements connect the Secretariat to the conference buildings. The Assembly Hall itself was decorated in blue, green and gold. In the Meditation Room a stained glass window caught my eye. It was a beautiful symbolic depiction of Man's struggle for peace by the famous French painter and engraver Marc Chagall. There was also the Dag Hammarskjöld Library, inaugurated on 16th November 1961 in honour of the late Secretary-General. The building, in harmony with the architecture of the other UN structures and designed to meet the growing demands for library services, consists of six storeys that accommodate some 400,000 volumes.

Throughout the buildings one can admire the dozens of gifts from member states, either incorporated into the fabric and furnishings. I was fascinated particularly by the American donation of a piece of moon rock and the UN flag carried on the Apollo Eleven mission. The Russian donation was a bronze sculpture of Sputnik, the first space satellite; and, from Egypt, an authentic gilded bronze statuette dating from about 700 BC of the god Osiris.

The whole headquarters complex received several thousand visitors per day. Entrance was free. This fact particularly attracted my attention because the UN could collect a substantial amount of funds by making a small entrance charge, which, in my view, could be put to good use in helping the very poor and starving third-world countries.

During my visit I wondered why New York was chosen for the site of the UN headquarters. The decision was taken in London. At the first session of the UN General Assembly on 14th February 1946, it was agreed that the permanent seat of the UN would be near New York City. On 14th December the same year, the General Assembly accepted by a huge majority an offer by John D. Rockefeller of 8.5 million dollars to purchase the present site on the banks of the East River, New York. On these sixteen acres converge the representatives of the five billion people who inhabit our planet.

The site of the UN Headquarters is owned by the United Nations Organisation and is international territory. Each member state contributes to the annual budget. The amounts are determined by the General Assembly and depend on each country's ability to pay. The UN has many specialized agencies including the International Atomic Energy Agency.

The celebration of the founding of the UN is on 24th October each year. Cocktail parties and receptions are given in UN offices throughout the world and I have attended several of them. I found them identical to parties given by diplomatic embassies on the countries National Day of their country.

As I walked through these unique buildings I felt as if I was living for a brief moment in a world that brought together all the peoples of the earth. My sightseeing was interrupted by a meal at lunchtime in the UN restaurant, where I met many friends and diplomats from various countries, quite an unexpected pleasure. In that dining room with its lively international atmosphere, I felt that we all knew each other despite the differences in our traditional customs, and ways of thinking, If only the friendship within these few acres could be reflected in peaceful living throughout planet earth.

New York is renowned the world over for its shops. People ask you if you have been to the department stores before they ask if you have visited the Empire State Building.

For tourists in New York, there were two "musts," the Empire State Building and Radio City. The former had the title of the eighth wonder of the world. In the lift, I went up eighty-nine floors in just one minute. Then another lift to the 102nd, and finally another to the 122nd floor. The building was illuminated at night and for good reason. A few years previously, a plane had crashed into it, which is not surprising. From street level, it is difficult to see the top. That was if one could see it at all. The descent in the lift was so fast and testing to the nervous system that it would be easy to faint.

On my second night in New York I went to a Parisian show, but it was not easy to get seats at weekends, especially for not resident in New York and just visiting the city as this was the most popular time.. My friends and I queued for an hour to get in, and what did we discover once we were inside? A giant five-thousand-seat auditorium with programmes running from half past nine in the morning to half past ten in the evening. The most remarkable was a truly spectacular live show. This included musichall routines performed by two hundred identical chorus girls – same height, same legs, and same looks. This was followed by an operetta in typical Parisian style. Everything was based on Paris, for I ought to mention that the current vogue in 1958 America was for anything closely or remotely connected with Paris, whether in fashion, in art or even existentialist philosophy.

My last day was spent at Greenwich Village, the American Latin Quarter, situated in the heart of the university district. We went by taxi. The driver's name and religion were displayed on a sign next to the meter. My friends and I were terrified by the speed. I asked the driver why he was going so fast, since we were not in any hurry. "Well, I am," he replied tartly. "Time is money, ma'am!" The first striking feature as we entered the village was the number of painters lining the pavements on both sides of the street. They were exhibiting, selling and occasionally had even set up their easels to paint the various views. Further along we came to Amsterdam Square, the site of the university. Prisoners built this square when the city was still a Dutch colony. In their life, the students were fond of imitating the young Parisian existentialists who can be seen on the left bank. One group had acquired a garage and turned it into a restaurant with the French name *Bizarre*. Everything about it was bizarre, from the broken chairs to the packing cases used as tables and the fishermen's nets draped round the walls. The waitresses were students wearing tight black slacks. Oddly enough, my friends and I thought the atmosphere was dismal, a far cry from a Parisian discothèque in St. Germain-des-Prés.

My visit to the United States was coming to an end. An American journalist interviewed me and asked for my general impression of the country. My first reaction was that it was a continent completely different from Europe and of course the Middle East – a world apart. My personal impressions were that Americans are very welcoming, hospitable and generous to foreigners with whom they come into contact. They are good-natured and openhearted, but not when it comes to business. In that they are voracious and aggressive. In scientific research, atomic and otherwise, they are very strong, thanks to the huge amount of capital at their disposal. A French professor of medicine once told me, "If we had their dollars, we could do as much research, if not more." As for American cultural life, it does not come up to French standards. The marvellous thing was that I never came across a poor American (perhaps there were many). I was struck by the wealth of America but also by the number of new rich and by the fact that if you say you do not have money people turn their back on you and you have no value. That was what struck me most of all.

When I was asked if I would like to live in America, I had no hesitation in saying that the idea had no appeal for me. On the other hand, I would enjoy being a frequent visitor. Americans are so different from Europeans and that was what was so interesting for me.

BACK TO CAIRO

Arriving back in Cairo from my trip to New York where I had been inter-viewed by the American press, I now paid for my Egyptian anti-communist statement. I was blacklisted by the Soviet Embassy in Egypt and received no more invitations to any of their official parties. This ban did not affect me par-ticularly as there were so many other social events for me to cover, and anyway I did not like vodka, which was an integral item of Russian hospitality. I was not very good at knocking back toast after toast of vodka in company with the rest of the guests. When it was announced some time later that Nikita Khrushchev and his wife were to pay an official visit to Egypt I was resigned to the fact that I would be one diplomatic journalist not invited to the social functions that would be taking place during their visit. This would be 'the' event for the whole week, so there would not be much work for me. Therefore, I spent the weekend prior to the arrival of the Khrushchevs staying with friends just outside Alexandria at Agami. This area is famous for the snow-white sand of its magnificent beach. Just desert really, with a few small shrubs dotted here and there.

With the weekend over, my friends had to go back to their desks. I returned home to Cairo early on the Monday, luckily as it turned out. At about ten o'clock, when I had been in the house for only about half-an hour, the door-bell rang. The caller was a messenger from the Soviet Embassy bearing an offi-cial invitation from Mrs. Khrushchev to a tea party she was giving at the resi-dency of the Soviet Ambassador! There were about fifty guests, including Mrs. Gamal Abdel Nasser and the wives of all the high state dignitaries. I was very surprised when I discovered that I was the only journalist present at this exclu-sive official gathering. I was able to approach Mrs. Khrushchev who told me how much she was enjoying her visit to 'this beautiful country of Egypt.' You can imagine how delighted I was at having exclusive coverage of this social event of the year.

At this point in my career I was writing a weekly column on Sundays in *Le Progrès Egyptien,* a well-known Egyptian newspaper. This column appeared under the byline "*Ainsi passent les Jours*" (How time flies) and consisted of accounts of current important events in the cultural life of Cairo, especially in the social and diplomatic world. On Monday mornings my office phone would ring continuously with some callers thanking me, but others with some reproaches as well, "You quoted Madame so and so but you didn't mention me at all." I wrote this column for about twelve years, but it was discontinued when I finally left Egypt in May 1967.

More than one Ambassador's wife would ring me up with news of various parties and events at which I had not been present. In return I was expected to quote them in my articles.

For me it was entertaining to know all the gossip, the inside stories, the 'Who's Who' of society. But it was not easy all the same. There was so much material to select from and, more important than anything else, I had to make my choice as objectively as possible. It was because of my column that the Sunday sales of the newspaper were so high. For this reason my senior editor, Georges Zezzos, read very carefully through everything I wrote.

Zezzos himself was very much the socialite. Evening invitations to embassy receptions were very much part of his daily life. If, as sometimes happened, an Ambassador invited me more often than he invited my editor to important social functions, Georges would lose his temper and cross out references to the offender in my articles. On such occasions I found that the best policy was to shrug off his editing without comment.

Interview with Ludwig Erhard, then Vice-Chancellor, later Chancellor of Germany.

GERMANY

Bonn

In June 1959, I was invited by the press office of the West German Ministry of Information to pay an official visit to Bonn. This city had been the seat of the West German government since 1949 and was to remain so until 1990. After the re-unification of West and East Germany, the German parliament voted in 1991 to move the seat of the united government to Berlin over a ten-year period, with the major phase of the move planned for 1999.

I was impressed to be invited to stay in Bad Godesberg at the Dreesen Hotel, where the British Prime Minister Neville Chamberlain and the German dictator Adolf Hitler had conferred in 1938 prior to the signing of the Munich Pact, which delayed for a year the start of the Second World War.

Bad Godesberg, a health resort in the state of North Rhine Westphalia was in 1959 an exclusive suburb of Bonn, although it was incorporated into the city of Bonn in 1969. It possesses warm mineral springs known since Roman times.

At the time of my visit, the Vice-Chancellor of the Federal Republic of West Germany was Ludwig Erhard.[1] As it had recently been announced that he might be going on an official visit to Egypt, all the press agencies were eager to interview him for information about his visit. Forty Egyptian journalists travelled especially from Egypt to Bonn, including one of the two proprietors of the newspaper for which I was working. No one succeeded in meeting the Vice-Chancellor. Requests for interviews with him were routinely made through the official press office, with only a ten per cent chance of success, at the best. I was told by one of the press officers, "There are so many journalists waiting to interview the Vice-Chancellor that the situation has become impossible. We cannot disturb him." I fared no better than anyone else, but being stubborn I refused to take no for an answer. When my official visit came to an end I explained to the West German press officer who had been looking after me that I intended to stay on in Bonn on my own account and keep on trying to obtain an interview. So I moved from my luxury hotel into a modest one. It was a big change, but it did not bother me. My philosophy had always been that as long as I had a clean room, the rest was unimportant. After all, a hotel room is just somewhere to sleep.

When journalists received official invitations to visit a country, they were given press attachés who, from early morning until evening, acted as ever present escorts. Their official purpose was to be on hand to render assistance, but

---

1 *West German Finance Minister from 1949-63. The architect of West Germany's economic recovery after the Second World War, a recovery known as the 'German Miracle,' Ludwig Erhard was Chancellor from 1963-66.*

their real function was to keep an eye on all our movements. In my case, although my official visit was over, Hermann, my press attaché, made it his business to keep in regular contact with me.

Bad Godesberg possessed a very famous restaurant called 'Maternus,' with its equally famous proprietress, Ria.[1] One evening, Hermann, seeing that my spirits were becoming rather low, took me there for dinner. During the course of our meal, he remarked. "Do you see that man who has just arrived in the restaurant? He is the man who can arrange an appointment for you with Erhard. He is his chief of cabinet." In a state of some excitement I exclaimed that I must go over and speak to him. "Calm down, calm down, Ria will arrange everything for you. Politicians frequently come to her restaurant and she has considerable influence with them." Herman called her over to our table. My knowledge of German was very limited, but with Hermann acting as interpreter I managed to explain how important it was for me to be introduced to Erhard's chief of cabinet. Ria promised to see what she could do. After a while it became clear to us that Ria was not making any attempt to approach the man, so we called her over again. "Stop worrying. He is with company, I will find the right moment." When he and his guest stood up to leave after their meal, Ria went over to him. She told us afterwards what happened. "Who is that lovely young woman who has been staring at me?" "That is precisely what I want to talk to you about," replied Ria. She explained who I was and how desperate I was to secure an interview with his political master. "That can be arranged," he replied.

The following day the press office informed me that Ludwig Erhard would see me that afternoon at four o'clock. The meeting duly took place in his office. Although he knew English, he preferred to speak in German with an interpreter present, to avoid possible misunderstandings. What I wanted to know more than anything else was whether the Vice-Chancellor really was intending to visit Egypt in the coming autumn.

Egypt was extremely anxious for economic talks with West Germany, particularly in relation to possible financial aid for the Aswan Dam project. In reply to my questions on the subject, Erhard declared that via this interview he was officially announcing his intention to go to Cairo in the autumn for political and economic discussions with particular reference to the construction of the Dam.

Once the interview was over I was able to transmit the news immediately to my Cairo newspaper *El Goumhoureya*, which published it the next morning, 21st July 1959. The Vice-Chancellor's announcement appeared on the same day in the German newspaper *Die Welt*.

Sometimes, indeed often, in the job of a journalist patience and determination are required if success is to be achieved. For me, this interview with its important news was a big scoop. My boss sent me a congratulatory cable and of course my report made the front page of the newspaper. The headline was, 'Through restaurant owner Ria, our correspondent meets the Vice-Chancellor.'

1 *Restaurant Maternus and Ria were still there in 1999.*

Although he was suffering from a bad cold at the time, Erhard did make an official visit to Egypt in the autumn of 1959, declaring that he would not post-pone it because of his health. He had several meetings with President Nasser, but the talks were interrupted when Erhard fell very ill. He had to leave Cairo to return home on a special flight declaring, "I shall be back!" Full stop!

Berlin Film Festival

I received a further invitation from the Press Office of the West German Ministry of Information in June 1963. This time it was to attend the Berlin Film Festival, an annual event in June to this day. I was happy to accept. The film world was not my speciality, but the opportunity to see Berlin was too good to miss.

The West German government allocated a budget of thousands of Deutsch marks to entertain the press, the actors and actresses, producers, directors and other invited guests from different parts of the world. Over a hundred journal-ists were accommodated in the most luxurious hotels; a fleet of cars was avail-able for our use. We ate at the best restaurants; we were even provided with pocket money – on a generous scale. Everything contributed to give the event a vibrant international atmosphere which, my colleagues assured me, made this film festival different from all others.

The Germans have an inborn capacity for organisation and this was appar-ent at the festival. The first event was a party arranged for journalists to meet the stars. There I was able to talk to Cary Grant, my favourite actor. I was not dis-appointed. He was very much like the characters he portrayed on the screen; despite his fame, he was full of good humour, always laughing and joking. I met him again the following day, accompanied by a pretty Finnish actress, at an open-air party. Suddenly, torrential rain made us all run for shelter. We ended up in the same cabin where he kept us highly entertained with amusing stories.

Party followed party. At one I met Hedy Lamarr. Her husband was furious with her for talking to me when she was very much under the influence of an excess of alcohol. I also had a brief encounter with John Wayne. He was rude and aggressive, I soon moved from his table, where he was sitting alone, moody and unsociable, unwilling to talk. Maybe he too had drunk too much!

Among the actresses present at the festival was our most famous Egyptian filmstar, Faten Hamama. One of her films, *Les Jours* (The Days) had been cho-sen for a showing and we Egyptians were hoping that it would win a prize. The book on which the film was based was the work of our famous writer Taha Hussein. It had won international recognition, and been translated into twelve languages, including Russian. No luck at the festival though.

Faten was the ex-wife of Omar Sharif and is now married to an eminent doctor. Despite his success with countless women of different nationalities, Omar Sharif himself never re-married. He still says, "If I ever get married again, it will be to an Egyptian."

One little story about Faten at the festival involved me in a rather amusing way. Naturally, autograph seekers pursued all the celebrities, and Faten was no

Willy Brandt, the mayor of Berlin and Faten Hamama, the most famous Egyptian actress and former wife of Omar Sharif at the Berlin Film Festival in 1963.

exception. Now, although I was taller than Faten, people had come to the conclusion that our general appearance and looks were similar. One day, when we
were both at the same party, I was mistaken for her and the autograph hunters
started to gather around me. I tried explaining that I was not Faten, but without success, and, in desperation, appealed to her publicity agent. All he said was,
"Oh, go on, please sign for her and make them happy; they will never know."
Faten, who did not put on airs and graces, thought it was all very funny, remark-
ing to me with a laugh, "I shan't be travelling with you again."

Esther Williams made a brief appearance at the Festival. She engaged a
German guide for the two days of her visit. She sent her husband, the actor Bob
Iller to Hamburg to arrange some of her business affairs. When he arrived at the
Festival she was in the swimming pool doing more deals – he had travelled from
Hamburg to Berlin to be with her. She stayed the first night with her husband
but the following day abandoned him to move into the Hilton. Marriage,
American filmstar style!

I enjoyed the fascination of meeting all these famous stars from the world of
entertainment. How different it all was from the world of diplomatic and society functions.

An unexpected opportunity and pleasure for me during the Festival was to
have a conversation with Willy Brandt, the Mayor of Berlin. I was impressed by
his strong personality and by his open, friendly, modest nature. Despite his countless activities, he never failed to attend a Film Festival to meet and talk with the
stars of the day. With me, he talked about the impressions he had brought back
from a visit to Egypt, where he had been the guest of the Mayor of Cairo, Salah
Dessouki. A distinguished cultured man, Dessouki was later to serve Egypt as an
Ambassador. What gave me the greatest pleasure during this visit was the exclusive interview I had with Mrs. Willy Brandt. Knowing that she had been a journalist herself, I mentioned this to her. "That is true. My first job was in the
Secretariat of the West German Ministry of Defence as journalistic correspondent for the Norwegian press. I expect you know that I am Norwegian. When
my family duties became more demanding, I gave up my job."

"Are you interested in politics and do you think you have a part to play in
that field?"

"I absolutely refuse to become involved in politics. That is my husband's rôle,
not mine; but the fact that I live in Berlin means that I have to be interested in
politics. The problem of a divided Berlin is a human problem. For example,
Berliners living in West Berlin are not allowed by the East German authorities
to cross over into East Berlin to see relatives, whereas Germans living in West
Germany proper are allowed to visit East Berlin."

Then she repeated, "But no, taking an active part in politics is not my job. I
became, and remain, a housewife. I go to the market, do the cooking and look
after our three children – all boys. When our youngest child was born, my husband was on an official visit to the United States. Chancellor Adenauer rang him
to give him the news that he now had a third son!"

"But as you are the wife of the Mayor, you must have a lot of social engagements?

"Yes, I do indeed. I also receive thousands of letters – it's a good job I have a secretary to help me. Then again, I welcome many women from different parts of the world, from Europe, Asia, Africa."

"So what is your opinion about all these women of different nationalities?"

"A woman is a woman wherever she comes from. However, before I meet them, I read and learn about their countries and their problems. The questions they ask me are always about the same problem – the Berlin wall and all that it represents."

A few years later Willy Brandt and his wife were divorced. He had fallen in love with his secretary.

While in Berlin, I took the opportunity to go on a sightseeing tour with several colleagues. I particularly enjoyed two unusual items, which gave us amusing talking points and a great deal of hilarity.

When lunchtime arrived we were taken to a very popular restaurant called the *Hummer Hugo*. From the outside, the premises looked simple enough, just like an ordinary shop, in fact. Closer inspection through the window revealed not a typical display but a large cage containing lots of fluffy yellow baby chicks. Inside the restaurant there was a queue of people waiting for tables, of which there were only a dozen or so. The menu had few options, offering nothing but chicken soup and chicken portions of various sizes. Why was the restaurant so popular? What made it different was the cutlery. There wasn't any. The soup had to be soaked up with bread, the hot chicken with its bones had to be manipulated with one's fingers. As you can imagine, this situation created a jolly, friendly atmosphere in which perfect strangers could have a good laugh together, especially those whose digital skills did not come up to the standard of the regular practitioners. We were sorry that our German was not good enough for us to join in the general conversation and share the jokes, but we could all enjoy the fun of being in the same boat together. At the end of it all we cleaned up at one of the small fountains thoughtfully provided, and, of course, there were noisy queues for those as well.

In the evening we finished our tour at an establishment called the *Resi*. It was a large hall were one could eat, drink, dance to an orchestra and enjoy several interesting features which gave the place its originality. Each table was provided with a telephone, which had a large, illuminated number. As these were visible from table to table, it was simple to pick up the receiver and dial the number of someone who caught your eye, at another table. Hence the popularity of Resi, especially with single men and women who could come in, sit at a table and establish contact over the phone. We saw one pretty young woman, who, in no time at all had her number flashing, collecting several men over to her table and dancing with each of them in turn! There was a second method of communication. On the tables was a supply of small tubes into which one could slip a roll of paper with a message on it, leaving the end of the roll sticking out, all one had to do was to print a table number on it and have it collected by a waiter. The tube was taken to a 'sorting-office' behind the scenes and eventually reached its destination via the appropriate table-waiter. We had plenty of fun watching the faces of the recipients!

The evening's entertainment was brought to a spectacular close by what I can only describe as a water ballet, created by a piece of technical wizardry unique to the Resi. The circular dancing platform around which the tables were arranged sank down into the ground; water poured into the space creating a large pool. To match the rhythms and moods of Gershwin's 'Rhapsody in Blue' played by the orchestra, ripples and waves appeared in complicated patterns on the surface of the water, fountains and water-jets rose and sank with the whole scene illuminated by lights of changing colours. At the end of the show, the unseen technician who had operated the display appeared and took his bow to warm applause.

I could not leave West Berlin without satisfying my curiosity about its counterpart East Berlin, isolated behind its notorious wall in the so-called East German Democratic Republic. It was a visit for which I needed, and was granted, special permission from the East German authorities. I shall never forget the profound difference between what were in effect two separate cities. It was like going from day into night. From the prosperity of thriving West Berlin one passed into a world of drab building, empty streets, few traffic lights few cars, dull ill-stocked shops and shabbily dressed inhabitants - a sad, lifeless, depressing atmosphere.

SIWA OASIS

"You know," my hostess was saying, "a week from now we shall be going on an expedition to Siwa Oasis.[1] It's going to be so exciting I can hardly wait for the days to go by. The Japanese Ambassador and his wife are coming with us as well."

I was at the home of Mrs. Stuart, the wife of the Australian Ambassador. "You don't know how lucky you are," I remarked. "It's not at all easy to get to Siwa!"[1]

"Well," said Mrs. Stuart, "Would you like to join us? I can have a word with my husband, if you are keen on the idea. Our expedition is being organised by the Government Desert Development Project." I jumped at the invitation.

As Egyptian journalists seldom go to Siwa, I told myself what a marvellous opportunity it would be for me to write an article that would be different, something quite out of the ordinary.

The Ambassador did indeed arrange for me to accompany the group, so on 20th October 1961, we set off on the first stage of our journey as far as Marsa-Matrouh. The next morning at eight o'clock we started our expedition into the desert. Travelling in three jeeps, we had as our guide Mr. Mahfouz Salem, a government agricultural officer.

Siwa lies 280 kilometres almost directly south of Marsa-Matrouh. For nearly half this distance, our road was just a sandy track (today, alas, there is a road). Along this desert trail, we had to follow the electricity poles to be certain not to lose our way. All was complete calm and silence in this arid desert. It was an adventure indeed. I for one felt like a real explorer venturing into the unknown. Even with modern transport, danger did exist. A couple of summers previously a group of young Germans, travelling in their Volkswagen, did go astray. Search parties eventually found their bodies. Occasionally we came across groups of nomadic Bedouins. At this time, there were throughout this vast desert region some hundred or so tribes, perhaps a hundred thousand Bedouins in all. The most famous of the tribes called itself 'The children of Ali' and was divided into the children of 'Ali the Red' and those of 'Ali the White'. What the difference between them was I was not able to discover. Sheep are the main source of wealth for the Bedouins.

One might think that an eight-hour journey through the desert would be a monotonous experience, but not so. The terrain is not one of flat, uniform sand. In places it is raised up in substantial dunes. Elsewhere stand rocky hills tinted in various colours. A wild place for all that. On our outward journey we met no other vehicles at all. One lorry was all we encountered on the way back. It came

1 *Siwa is situated in the western Egyptian desert, not far from the Libyan frontier.*

as something of a surprise when about half way along the route we arrived at a deserted police outpost. There we stopped for lunch, like picnickers on an outing. Our arrival some hours later at our destination was not one to forget. Over this oasis, rich in date palms and greenery amid the wilderness, there reigned a serene tranquillity. To my eyes it was like an extraordinary biblical vision, disturbed now by our noisy jeeps, the camels of the modern explorers we imagined ourselves to be. Yet we aroused no curiosity. Nobody gathered round.

The five and a half thousand inhabitants of Siwa seemed completely indifferent to everything, especially any visiting tourists. Our accommodation in Siwa was not of the most luxurious – it was a primitive house usually occupied by government officials. There were no hotels to offer comfort to travellers. It was essential to bring one's own supply of water, food, and even bread. I was lucky to be part of an expedition well organised for two ambassadors. We lacked nothing.

Siwa is surrounded by a number of low mountains. The largest, almost five kilometres away, is called 'The Mountain of Death.' This seems a strange name for it because it is here that Siwan families of standing had their summer residences. It was another nickname for which I could find no explanation. What was even more strange, a local practitioner, Doctor Soutouhi practised here. He treated his Siwan patients by a primitive, natural method – sand baths. Between twelve and three in the afternoon, patients were brought to this 'mountain of death' to be covered up to their necks in sand for a length of time varying between ten and twenty minutes. They were then placed in tents while their sweat dried. When this part of the procedure was over, they were moved again to the doctor's villa, which rejoiced in the name 'clinic', where they were given a meal of soup and chicken.

Dr Soutouhi insisted that his patients slept and rested during the whole length of time for which they came to him for treatment. I was quite keen to try out the treatment myself, but unfortunately (I think), I did not have the time to do more than meet him and talk about his treatments. He always dressed in a white djellabah and wore a small white hat. Very confident and self-assured, he enjoyed a reputation as a sacred figure.

In local legend it was said that during the Second World War Rommel made the journey to Siwa and to the 'Mountain of Death'. What is certain is that during the war when danger threatened, the inhabitants of Siwa took refuge up on the mountain or in the ancient city about five kilometres from modern Siwa, which was on our itinerary to visit. This city stands on top of a low hill. Guarding the entrance was a huge gateway. Once through the entrance we were faced with extensive ruins on all sides. Before us stood the remains of a Pharaonic temple dating from the sixth century BC, the famous oracular Temple of Ammon,[1] the great and most important god of Egyptian Thebes. Despite the erosion of time and the elements, there were temple stones on which it was still possible to see painted pharaonic inscriptions.

1 *'Ammon' – The Hellenised form of the Egyptian 'Amun.'*

The Spartan general Lysander came after defeating Athens in 404 BC, to be followed by some seventy years later by Alexander the Great. For some time Alexander had thought he was divine, claiming to be a descendant of Zeus. His pilgrimage to the oracle in that year reinforced his belief and from that time on he called himself the son of Zeus Ammon. In Roman times, Siwa was famous as a great agricultural centre. The oasis, also known in antiquity as the Oasis of Ammon, still enjoys the reputation of being the richest of all Egyptian oases in the abundance of its date palms and olive trees, which contribute so much to the beauty of the town. Wealth comes to Siwa not only from its dates and olives but also from its precious stones, which are renowned and sold all over Egypt. The wives of the well-to-do farmers owned and wore them in abundance.

The way of life in Siwa was governed by the very special and ancient customs and traditions of its inhabitants. Even in 1961 harem life existed in its fullest form.

As I was strolling through the town centre one afternoon with Mrs. Stuart and Mrs. Wajima, the local women, all heavily veiled in black, took exception to our approach and ran off as fast as they could go, making for the sanctuary of their homes. During the daytime, few women were allowed out, except for those who worked, or who had urgent shopping. It was nearly always the man who went off in the mornings on his donkey to buy all the necessary food. Normally the women were only allowed out, still veiled, at nightfall to visit each other's homes.

It was a very exceptional event when we three women were invited to visit the home of a young married woman. The house had two storeys – as had all the houses in Siwa. The ground floor was reserved for the husband, and that is where he co-habited with his male friend. The upstairs rooms were the exclusive domain of the wife and her children. This arrangement was the normal practice. As guests, we were received in the wife's sitting room. The floor was covered with carpets on which we all took our places. A low table held plates and dishes of oriental delicacies and these were passed round. Later we were served glasses of tea. Our smiling hostess was charming throughout. We learned that she had permission from her husband to entertain friends of her own sex but was hardly ever allowed out to visit them.

We also learned about local marriage customs. Girls were traditionally married to a cousin when they left school at the age of twelve. But if he was not a consenting partner, she could marry somebody else. When a young man wants to marry a girl, he makes his wish known to the mother. If she approves, she discusses the matter with her husband. If he agrees too, a meeting is arranged to allow the prospective husband to see the girl. The girl bathes at a spring. The man is hidden behind a tree and views from a distance. If he is satisfied, the marriage is arranged. On the morning of the wedding ceremony, the bride-to-be puts on a white dress to bathe in the 'marriage spring,' the most famous spring in Siwa. If a woman is widowed, she must live for forty days completely isolated from the world, even from her children. She remains in a dark room; her food is passed to her through a tiny window. At the end of her solitary confinement, she is taken to the 'marriage spring' to be purified. This ceremonial bathing gives her the right to re-marry.

Siwa, an oasis with an international reputation for the beauty of its natural surroundings, is especially the dream oasis of homosexuals. It is difficult from their bearing, when seeing them walking from behind, to tell a man from a woman. Despite all the efforts by the Egyptian government to change the particular habits of the Siwans, behaviour patterns have not changed. The inhabitants live their own lives and do not want anybody to interfere.

A short, but true story is a typical illustration. A husband and wife, both working for the Ministry of Social Affairs, were determined to devote themselves to going to live in Siwa in an effort to attempt to change the sexual habits of the people. The result was catastrophic – for the officials. They became the object of a major scandal when in the mosque during prayers a boy yelled out accusations that he had been raped by the husband. Not long afterwards the social workers decided to leave Siwa, as they had totally failed to make any impact on the whole problem they had come to solve. On the day of their departure, certain local dignitaries appeared with a leaving present for the husband – a boy! The oasis is not a haven for homosexuals in the manner of Mykonos or San Francisco. Its originality lies in the way it brings together under the same roof and living in perfect peace and harmony all the members of the family – wife, children, husband and the extra male.

Its way of getting rid of unwanted social workers is pretty original too!

MY QUESTION TO DE GAULLE

It was late August 1961 and I was just back in Paris. For the previous week I had been relaxing on holiday in London, going to the theatre, seeing Margot Fonteyn at the Royal Ballet, taking in the sights of London and, of course, shopping!

"So what's new in the newspaper world?" I asked my colleagues, "Anything happening at the moment?" "There certainly is. General de Gaulle is giving a press conference on 5th September. We're counting the days!" "Do you think I stand any chance of being there?" "Of course. Why not? But you'd better get a move on for an invitation."

Without going into detail, I can tell you that such invitations are not handed out just like that. In my case, it was especially difficult, as at the time relations between de Gaulle and Nasser were somewhat strained; the presence of an Egyptian journalist at de Gaulle's press conference was therefore not very desirable. However, a French colleague who often visited Egypt for his newspaper and knew me quite well put in a good word for me and agreed to vouch for my conduct.

The card I received through the post the day before the conference had taken some getting. Still, there it was, with my name on it, strictly non-transferable. General de Gaulle had been in power for three and a half years. The forthcoming press conference would be his fourth since coming to the Elysée. So on the appointed day the world's press was making its hurried and expectant way towards the rue du Faubourg St. Honoré. Here stood the President's official residence, the Elysée Palace and from here the conference was being broadcast live on television and radio.

At the outer gate I waited to show my invitation and press card, then walked through the huge courtyard and showed my cards again at the main door to the Palace. Yet another check on the way, and finally a fourth at the door where the conference was being held. The room was huge, one of the most splendid in all the palace, panelling and ornamentation ablaze with gilt and rich colours, gleaming crystal chandeliers suspended from high above.

The General's press conferences were renowned for their pomp and splendour as well as for the importance of their subject matter. Expectations and speculation were high on this occasion. For seven years France had been fighting a bitter war against the independence movement in Algeria. The conflict was at its height, a constant subject of concern and argument in France and within international political circles. There were optimists who thought this latest press conference would be a historic one for the future of Algeria.

I arrived an hour early, but my press colleagues had been just as prudent. However, I managed to find a seat on the second row facing the stage. Next to me on my right sat a French journalist, on my left an American. As always on such occasions there was a hubbub of voices as strangers made conversation with one another. "Which room of the palace are we in?" I asked my French colleague. "The ballroom." There must have been eight hundred people in the room, all comfortably seated on elegant gilt chairs. The General's armchair was in the centre of the stage. On his right, were Aubusson chairs for his ministers. Half an hour before the conference was due to start, they were in their places. I recognised the Foreign Minister, Maurice Couve de Murville, whom I knew well in Egypt when he was the French Ambassador. André Malraux, the Minister of Culture, was present. The Prime Minister, Michel Debré, was absent, a fact quickly noted by the press. What did it mean? Flanking the presidential chair on the left were high-ranking army officers and senior Foreign Ministry officials. Police and security guards were as numerous as the journalists. I had been chatting to the man on my right thinking he was a fellow reporter, not knowing until later that he was head of the Elysée diplomatic press department!

The television and radio crews were ready at their posts. At exactly three o'clock, the General made his impressive appearance, wearing a dark grey suit with a dark blue tie. His mere presence generated shivers of awe throughout the audience. To address him directly required an act of mental courage. The whole occasion was a solemn and intimidating ritual. De Gaulle sat down. Opening the proceedings with a few carefully chosen, sombre words, he continued, "And now, you will ask all your questions. When I have listened to them and thought about them, I will give you my replies."

My French colleagues had all suggested that as the representative of the Egyptian press, I ought to ask about the current situation in Algeria. Now was my chance, but I hesitated to face such an ordeal, especially as I was a woman, one of the few present. I turned to one of my colleagues, "Should I ask my question?" "Of course, go on. Why else have you just spent ten days wearing yourself out to get an invitation?" No denying the logic of that! But still I could not find the courage. I heard a question being asked about the Berlin wall, and told myself, "It's now or never," and forced myself on to my feet. "Monsieur le Président," I began, "At a reception you gave to a group of MPs in the Elysée, did you say to them, 'I would like to be rid of the Algerian problem by the end of the year?'" The General gravely acknowledged my question that opened the way for a series of questions on the same subject – the future of Bizerta, the role of the army, the conduct of the war. As the questions became more searching and hostile, so the General acknowledged them in ever more serious tones.

After listening to twenty or so questions on different topics, the President called a halt. After some consideration, he announced that he would deal with four, one on the Berlin wall, one on Algeria, one about the army and the one concerning French agriculture. "And now," he said, "I shall start with the Berlin wall. Will the reporter concerned please repeat his question?"

"Next, I shall deal with Algeria". I was so petrified I forgot to stand up. The General looked at me, saying, "Madame, will you kindly ask your question again?" I stood up and put it to him, but this time in a slightly different form, adding two important factors. "General, when and how are you going to settle the Algerian problem? Will it be before the end of the year, by giving Algeria its independence?"

For all of fifteen minutes the general explained his position again and again. He spoke confidently and as if unconcerned, ending with the words, "We do not in any way believe that the interests, honour and future of France are for ever linked to the circumstances as they at present exist, to the preservation of French domination over these people." But to the key questions of 'when' and 'how' there was no reply. Politicians and statesmen are adept at answering without answering; de Gaulle was renowned as a master of the art.

At the end of the conference, and much to my surprise, I was surrounded by journalists and reporters, especially those from the left-wing press. "Well done! You were the only woman brave enough to stand up! Congratulations! But the General didn't answer your question!" As if I needed telling! I heard subsequently that de Gaulle had asked about me, wanting to know who I was. The manner in which the President dealt with the Algerian question was a great disappointment, not least in the minds of the young French national servicemen listening and watching, glued to the radio or television, just hoping that he would make a decisive announcement about ending the war. A few days later, the son of a friend of mine, home on leave for the weekend summed it up, "We were all waiting for his answer. When? But it didn't come. Up to now, we have all been behind de Gaulle and his policy of bringing the war to an end. Now we've had enough. It's obvious, he can't, or won't make the final decision."

For some time afterwards I achieved a sort of fame in as much my questions were taken up by the satirical singers of the day, especially by Tisot, who was famous in his songs for imitating the voice of well-known personalities, especially de Gaulle. In a new song, which was made into a record, he now imitated my voice, with his repeated, "General, tell me when and tell me how". Of course, I was delighted as well to have been on television with de Gaulle on such an important subject as the issue of Algerian independence.

As they left the Elysée, those who knew de Gaulle or had seen him several times in the past seemed to be agreed. The General's self-confidence and belief in himself remained as strong as ever, but there was a sadness about him, a great sadness. At times a degree of bitterness showed through, at others he seemed to be implying, I have had enough. You refuse to understand me. And above all, you won't help me.

Three days after the press conference, an attempt was made on the General's life. It failed. This incident provoked a hostile reaction, even amongst the anti-Gaullists, who were afraid that the death of the General would lead to immediate civil war. The OAS (Secret Army Organisation)[1] which carried out the assas-

---

1 *Terrorist organisation set up in February 1961 by civilians and military deserters in France and Algeria to oppose Algerian independence; committed atrocities in both countries.*

sination attempt took note of the public mood, and especially the fear now in the minds of the European population of Algeria. Conscious of its growing unpopularity and afraid of losing its own supporters, the OAS started to deny responsibility for the attempted coup, claiming that it was a theatrical piece of bluff masterminded by the General's own supporters to show the strength and protection that de Gaulle enjoyed. As it became increasingly clear that de Gaulle would eventually take the unavoidable decision to grant independence to Algeria, the OAS intensified its savage campaign in metropolitan France, especially in Paris.

An English tourist walking in the Champs Elysées was seriously wounded when a flying splinter of glass caused by an exploding bomb, struck him in the face. The incident received a lot of publicity in the media, and brought about a big drop in the number of English visitors. Editors or proprietors of French newspapers that criticised the OAS had bombs planted outside their offices or homes. A week before I was due to leave Paris, I had personal experience of a bomb outrage at close quarters. I was having lunch in a restaurant near the Paris Opera House. Suddenly, 'Boom' and all the windows, and they were large ones, shook. I was considerably frightened. My first thought was to stand up and get out immediately. However, nobody else in the restaurant started to move. In fact, the other customers were all looking at me. I was an attraction. A lady sitting nearby said, "Haven't you encountered bombs before?" "No, madam," I replied, "and I have no desire to make their acquaintance. Goodbye!" Choking smoke filled the street outside; I wasted no time in leaving the area, but around me people seemed to be taking no notice. It was as if Parisians had become used to bombs and explosions and had accepted them as part of their daily life.

I knew that de Gaulle had been told who I was and where I came from. Encouraged by his interest in me and still under the spell of his personality, the following January I sent him a New Year's card from Egypt. Shortly afterwards I received, written in his own hand, a card of thanks and best wishes.

"Of all the famous people you have met, who fascinated you the most?" I have been asked this question countless times. My answer has always been the same. It requires no thought – General de Gaulle. I have never been apprehensive, never in my life been intimidated by anyone, except de Gaulle and the sheer force and magnetism of his personality.

Some years later, at an Embassy reception, I met de Gaulle's son, Admiral Philippe de Gaulle. In appearance he resembled his father. In conversation he was courteous and somewhat reserved. When I remarked how happy I was to meet him because he reminded me of the time I had questioned his father, he replied, "Of all the women journalists I have ever met who knew my father, you are the first to say a kind word to me. All the rest have been very aggressive."

The Count of Paris, Pretender to the French throne, at the Château de Montmirail in 1962. Isis is on his right.

THE COUNT OF PARIS
PRETENDER TO THE FRENCH THRONE

In March 1962, the resumed talks held at Evian in Switzerland between France and representatives of the Algerian provisional government, agreed the independence of Algeria. However, just as de Gaulle's position as President had been under threat in preceding months, it was by no means secure now. Apart from any legitimate political opposition, the danger of assassination attempts by the OAS remained very real. For some time there had been murmuring in Parisian diplomatic and political circles about a possible successor. Who might 'inherit' the Presidency? Opinions were divided; every politician imagined or hoped that a new President would be someone from his own party. Even so, one name in particular, and a prominent name it was, figured prominently in all the rumours. The future President could well be the Count of Paris, the Orléans Pretender to the French throne. Word had it that de Gaulle was thinking in terms of bringing back the monarchy. Approaches had been made. I was reliably informed by a source close to the Count of Paris that General and Madame de Gaulle had dined with the Count at his residence in Louveciennes.

Sometimes luck plays a large part in the working life of a journalist. In early July 1962, I was invited by the Duchess Edmée de La Rochefoucauld to spend a long weekend at her château in Montmirail. When the Duchess was in residence there she always used to invite friends and well-known public figures to lunch on Sundays. On the Saturday evening of my visit, she said to me as we were chatting, "Tomorrow there will be eighteen of us for lunch. The guest of honour is the Count of Paris." I jumped for joy. "I've tried everything to get an interview with him!" "Well, then, I'll fix it for you. It's easy. Don't worry, my girl; you'll get your interview. I know you want to go back to Paris tomorrow. I'll ask the Count to take you back with him in his car. You can have a talk with him on the way!"

And so it turned out. The Count answered my questions all the way back to Paris. Once there, he drove me to the flat of my friends, Nora and Philippe Noyer who had invited me to stay with them for a few days. With royal courtesy, the Count carried my suitcase up to the sixth floor. It so happened that the concierge of the building saw him doing it. She spread the word. For the whole of the following week, the major item of gossip between the concierges along the entire street was: "And do you know, the Count of Paris carried the case of the young lady staying with Madame Noyer!"

Before I relate my interview, let me describe its subject. The Count was nearly fifty, slim and dynamic. He was married and had eleven children. One of his sons had died the previous year in the Algerian war. Despite this, and before

Algeria gained its independence, the Count was one of those who played a large part in support of independence for that country. He was sent to the Middle East many times by General de Gaulle as an emissary to meet representatives of the FLN.[1] The Count had an office in Paris in the rue de Constantine where for most of the time he met visitors from abroad, intellectuals, politicians and ordinary people. His office published a monthly bulletin dealing with current events and problems both at home and abroad. Sometimes the articles he wrote bore his signature, but this was the exception rather than the rule. The Count was well known for his socialist principles.

At the start of the interview I commented, "It appears that you were sent on many occasions by General de Gaulle on secret missions to the Middle East to meet Algerian officials."

"Yes, that is so", was his reply, "I can say that my mission is over."

"What do you think about the Algerian problem?"

"I think that all the internal difficulties will disappear. After seven years of war, it is only natural that the Algerians will not be able to rediscover order and stability all at once. They are a courageous people, and I have confidence in them. It is no use imagining that everything will be settled right away. It would be madness to think that."

"What do you think about those French people who are furious because Algeria has obtained its independence?"

"People who come into that category have to realise that they cannot keep on clinging to what is unreal. Reality and the facts exist; we must live in the real world. The loss of Algeria is not a tragedy. After all, it was a territory that was not ours."

"But the French settlers in Algeria think that the territory does belong to them, pleading economic reasons and the length of time they have been there."

"So what? I would compare the situation to that of parents who have made sacrifices for the education of their son who, when he is twenty-one, takes leave of them. It must be realised that at a given moment in time, it is over, and we must always recognise when the time to depart has come, and know how to do it. General de Gaulle understood that it was time to accept independence for Algeria, and he has done it."

"What is your opinion about the politicians who criticise de Gaulle?"

"It is quite simply jealousy of his power. Do you know that I was the target of a bomb attack in my study at my home in Louveciennes at nine o'clock one evening, just at the time I usually go to my study? The bomb blew it up. It is just as well that I was not there."

"What are your political inclinations?"

"I am a socialist. I believe we have to progress, to march with the times and live in conformity with them. I even think that despite all the reforms already carried out, not enough is being done; more should be undertaken and co-

1 *The National Liberation Front, a revolutionary Algerian guerrilla organization, founded in 1954.*

ordinated efforts made to do better. I repeat, to accomplish something in life, we must look reality in the face and stifle all our personal feelings and passions. Besides we live in a revolutionary age. All countries are following the same destiny and moving towards democracy. We must live with the atomic age and develop economically and socially. Unfortunately, few people want to live with their times."

"Do you think General de Gaulle is popular?"

"Yes, I do. Very popular. An opposition exists in Paris, but the capital is not the whole of France. In the countryside, the population is massively for de Gaulle."

"What are your principles in life?"

"Patience is necessary, optimism is a pleasant thing to have and is useful in life. One can manage to achieve a lot with these two attributes."

"Tell me about your bulletin."

"Well, I choose my own public and send the bulletin to 70,000 people, not only in France but abroad as well. I am the one who chooses the subject I want to deal with."

"May I ask you a rather delicate question? Do royalists come to see you..."?

Before I could finish my sentence, the Count said without hesitation.

"If they do, I do not see them. The best way to waste one's time is to have contact with the people you call my supporters; apart from a few rare exceptions, the aristocracy does not come with the spirit and mentality of the times."

"What do you think of present day youth and its evolution?"

"First of all there isn't just one 'youth'. There are several. For instance, one can make a first distinction between youth which is engaged in studies and youth which is at work, earning its own living and no longer dependent upon parents. Equally, there are differences between the youth of the countryside and the youth of the towns, although these differences are tending to become less marked, country-dwellers being more firmly rooted in their family and local group, but more sensitive to the uncertainties of their economic future, which is rather bleak at present.

Military service, because it is long and involves the risks inherent in war, is another frontier between youth that is yet to don a uniform and youth which has already served in the forces. The first group feels bored and finds it difficult to find a place for itself in society; the latter is more mature, keen to settle down quickly, make a home and take on adult responsibilities.

Another feature that distinguishes today's young people from those of the past is the desire to tackle problems in a concrete, realistic way. High-minded principles have lost their emotional appeal. On the other hand, there is a capacity to become committed and devoted to positive enterprises. Political parties have all but lost their power to interest youth in their respective ideologies."

"What are your thoughts about mods and rockers?"

"The ridiculous publicity they are given can easily lead to a false diagnosis in moral terms. True, the predilection for going about in distinctive, mutually hostile gangs, the absence of facilities for healthy and agreeable leisure activities, the unfilled spare time created by the reduction in working hours, all account for the spread of these gangs, but in truth there is no immediate danger. Juvenile delinquency is low in France, a tenth of what it is in America per head of population. The courts tried 21,000 juvenile delinquents in 1949 but dealt with only 16,000 in 1957.

Other features, newer in a different way, are the consequence of the confrontation between youth and contemporary society and civilisation: it is difficult for young people to fit into a society in which it can find no clearly discernible lines of force or direction, and for good reason!

Mr. Yves Singer, sifting through a survey comprising 40,000 replies, noted that fifty per cent of young people said they liked modern music because for them it represented an escape. Eighty per cent liked it because of its rhythm, forty-seven per cent because modern songs enabled them to understand the world, as if they were a mirror of their own confused consciousness of it."

"In your view how should children be brought up?"

"In today's world, moderation is needed in everything, and an upbringing based on religious principles is essential."

As a postscript to the interview, it was said that de Gaulle conducted a discreet poll among those close to him concerning bringing back the monarchy, but in the end it came to nothing.

History tells us that de Gaulle remained in power for seven more years. Playing 'if' with history changes nothing, but it is sometimes hard to resist. On 22nd August 1962, barely six weeks after my journey to Paris, de Gaulle's car was ambushed as he was returning from the airfield at Villacoublay to his home at Colombey. In the car with de Gaulle in addition to the chauffeur were his wife and son-in-law, General de Boissieu. By extraordinary luck, they all survived. Now if ...

AN EMBASSY PANIC

My work brought me into frequent contact with Ambassadors. Sometimes a degree of friendship and trust grew up between us so that I was taken into their confidence and privy to certain secrets in their personal life. An amusing example of this 'special relationship' started for me at home one Sunday evening with a frantic telephone call from Senhor Figueiredo, the Brazilian Ambassador. He was regarded in Brazil as one of his country's most talented diplomats, but now he sounded panic-stricken. "Isis, come round quickly. It's urgent. It's a catastrophe. It's Flora. Someone's stolen Flora!" Flora? A top-secret state document perhaps? But no. If that was all Flora had been I think he would have been less concerned. "She's my life, you know. I need your help!"

The Ambassador had three fine poodles and Flora was the one he doted on.

At the Ambassador's residence I heard the sorry story. That afternoon the butler had been walking the three dogs at the Guezireh Sporting Club and he happened to meet one of his friends. Deep in below-stairs embassy gossip, he had ceased to pay attention to his precious charges. It eventually dawned on him that although he was still holding three leads, only two of them had a dog at the other end. Flora had slipped hers and vanished. A frantic search produced nothing. The butler had been obliged to return to the embassy and face his employer.

"Isis, I don't care what it costs to get her back. How about an announcement on the radio? I'm going to speak to your Secretary of State. He's a friend of mine, see if he can help." He was talking as if it were a national emergency, not a missing poodle. "Please, please, calm down! I'm sure you'll get Flora back. We'll start by putting an announcement in tomorrow's papers. There's still time." So we composed a suitable paragraph – description and name of the animal, anyone with information please report it to the Brazilian Embassy, reward for safe return. No, that was not enough. "Isis, put a large reward, in capital letters. What time do the papers come out?" I doubt if he got much sleep that night.

Figueiredo's agony was of short duration. He rang me up about eleven o'clock on the following day. He sounded a different man. "Isis, all is well, all is well. Flora's back. Come round for lunch and I'll tell you all about it. I can't say how relieved my wife and I are. We've already opened the champagne!" A jovial Ambassador and a happy smiling wife greeted me. Over lunch, they managed to tell me what seemed an unlikely story. During the morning, the doorman at the embassy had sent a message to the Ambassador that in the entrance hall he had a man, a small girl and a poodle. The Ambassador left his desk and went charging down. In a side room the little girl recounted how she had bought the dog for a few coppers from a boy.

All she could say about him was that she knew he was one of the boys who worked at the Sporting Club – they were employed for next to nothing to go round with the golfers to look for and retrieve any balls that went astray. The girl's father had seen the notice in the paper. It made him wonder and when he called the poodle by her name she came bouncing up. There wasn't any doubt about it, so he hadn't wasted any time and they all came straight to the embassy.

"I couldn't care less about the boy and the way he sold something that was not his to sell," the Ambassador told me. "I don't want anything done about it. I suppose he's poor and was only trying to make a penny or two. Anyway I gave the reward to the little girl." He had simply opened his wallet and handed over, much to the delight of father and daughter, the equivalent of £150 – a huge sum in those days in Egypt. "So, everything is all right again now, isn't it," he said, beaming happily at his wife – and at me.

That was not quite the end of the story. When lunch was over and the champagne finished, Senhor Figueiredo took me into one of the embassy drawing rooms. "I want to show you how much Flora means to me." He walked over to an exquisite eighteenth-century chest. "There's a secret drawer here," he said with a smile. He opened the drawer and lifted out what it contained. It was a solid silver tray. Set in the middle, also in solid silver, was a large medallion bearing the life-like portrait of his beloved Flora. "There," he said, "Now you can see what I mean. But this is just between you and me. Please don't mention it to anyone else. They might think that I am peculiar!"

Well, would they?

SEKOU TOURE

In June 1962, the President of Guinea, Sékou Touré accompanied by his wife made his first official visit to Egypt at the invitation of President Gamal Abdel Nasser. It was exceptionally hot at the time. A fact I have often noticed is that people coming from certain African countries find the heat of Egypt difficult to bear, in the same way that the heat of their country can be worse for us.

During his visit Sékou Touré travelled to Upper Egypt. He came back very tired, overcome by the heat. But he had to follow his schedule. For the evening of his return to Cairo his Embassy had arranged a reception at the Semiramis Hotel mainly for him to meet the Egyptian press. Many journalists were present, all shouting and asking their questions, but the questions were in English. Poor man! He stood there, put out his hands and said, "Me no speak English, do anyone speak French?"

I answered, "Yes, Mr. President, I speak French." He smiled, a look of relief came over his face, he beckoned to me saying in French,

"Eh! alors, nous allons nous entendre." (Oh! In that case, we are going to understand each other).

I approached him and said, "Mr. President, I am going to ask you the traditional question. As a President visiting Egypt for the first time what has impressed you the most up to now? Please say something unusual. "

Spontaneously he replied:" It's you!"

Our interview did not progress any further; he just wanted to escape from the pressure of the journalists. It seemed that his visit to Egypt was not going to be very positive. What was interesting for me was that I succeeded in obtaining an exclusive interview with his wife.

On 15th June 1962, at ten o'clock I had an appointment with Madame Ahmed Sékou Touré in the Koubbeh Palace (before the revolution this Palace was where Queen Farida, the first wife of Farouk lived and since the revolution it had become the residence where most official guests were invited to stay.) When I met Madame Sékou Touré she was accompanied by the wife of the Minister for Foreign Affairs, Madame Louis Sansana, both elegantly dressed in their national costumes of long colourful dresses.

My first question was, what were her views on legal rights between men and women?

"Our government," she replied, "in Guinea supports the matter of legal rights; we have women ministers and women in the political bureau and other departments.

What fascinated me most in my interview with Madame Sékou Touré was the subject of polygamy and divorce. I asked her, "What do you think about the problem of polygamy?"

She replied, "Last year a resolution was passed condemning polygamy. These measures ensure that a man cannot marry a second wife without the consent of his first wife. If the man does not respect this rule, then the first wife can complain to the social and political bureau of her area, which will try to resolve the problem. If they cannot, the case is referred to court. If the case ends in divorce and the blame is on the man's side, he has to pay a pension to his wife. If, however, it is the wife who is guilty, she must pay a penalty."

I then asked, "Are Guinean women interested in politics?"

"Oh yes, more than you think. They have equal rights and equal wages."

At the conclusion of my interview I asked Madame Sékou Touré, "Please tell me about your life." She became modestly shy and smiling, but I managed to persuade her to talk a little about herself.

"I am twenty-eight years old, have been married for nine years, and have one son called Mohamed; my hobby is photography."

My last and final question to her was, "What rôle did you play for the liberation and independence of your country?"

"Like all Guinean women, I was a militant."

Suddenly the wife of the Foreign Minister, who had been very quiet throughout the interview, interrupted, stating, "Madam President played a very big rôle working with her husband for the independence of our country."

AN UNEXPECTED VISITOR

Shortly after I returned to Egypt in September 1963 following one of my lengthy visits to Europe my sister Aïda came to see me. During the course of our conversation she put on one of her enigmatic expressions and said, "There is something I would like you to do with me tomorrow." I asked her what she had in mind. "I'll tell you afterwards. Just be ready in the morning about eleven o'clock. I'll call for you in the car."

An elder sister has to be obeyed. I was ready and waiting when Aïda arrived the following day. As I got into her car I was surprised to find we had a passenger, Mr. Shafik, the treasurer of the orphanage founded by my mother. I was more than a little intrigued. "Where are we going?" "You'll see," was Aïda's only reply. We drove into Guizeh, one of the suburbs of Cairo and stopped at a large house situated on the bank of the Nile. I followed Aïda and Mr. Shafik out of the car. "Good," said Aïda, "the butler is waiting for us at the door. You stay here." She spoke a few words to the butler, and then returned with him to where we were waiting by the car. Pointing to the treasurer, she asked the butler, "Do you recognise this man?" "No I have never seen him before. The man who came here was tall and thin, with grey hair." All this mystified me, as it did the treasurer who seemed also not to know what was going on! "We can go back now," said Aïda. "I'll drop Mr. Shafik off in town. I'll tell you the story when we are back in your flat."

Back at home I could not contain my curiosity any longer and asked Aïda to explain the mystery. She handed me a letter. "What do you think of this?" The paper was edged in black; it was a letter of condolences to a family who had recently suffered a bereavement. It had been written on behalf of The Coptic Ladies' Charitable Society – which is my mother's orphanage. The signature at the foot of the letter was mine, Isis Fahmy, excellently forged and followed by the word 'Secretary'. Aïda explained that the letter had been delivered by a man who asked, in my name, for a donation to the charity. There was an impostor at large!

As time went on, I began to receive enquiring phone calls from Coptic families who had recently been bereaved. They all had the same theme. "You are Isis Fahmy, aren't you? We've had someone claiming to be here on your behalf and asking for a donation for the orphans." I would reply, "I didn't send him. Try and keep him there," only to be informed, "It's too late; he's gone. We didn't think that Isis Fahmy would behave in such a way." As a journalist, I was well known in Coptic circles and this story could affect my career as well as the reputation of the orphanage.

The phone calls became more and more frequent, but always of course, after the collector had gone. The description of him was always the same – he was tall, thin, had grey hair, wore a navy-blue blazer and grey flannels, and was very presentable. We had to stop him. But how?

A visit to the public prosecutor's department with my elder brother, Adib, left us with the following advice. "Unless you catch him red-handed, there's nothing we can do." Over the telephone I kept on saying, "Catch him!" but it was always too late.

Sadly, on Christmas Day 1965, death struck my own family. My brother Mounir died suddenly and unexpectedly at the age of fifty. My mother was herself quite ill at the time and it was after the funeral, which was attended only by close relatives, that my brother Adib broke the news to her of her eldest son's death. Not until then was notification of Mounir's death placed in the newspapers. As is usual with bereaved families in Egypt, we began to receive a stream of relatives, uncles, aunts and cousins – coming daily to offer their condolences and sympathy.

The thought had crossed my mind that perhaps the 'charity collector' would soon be paying us a visit, but I dismissed it. The impostor was clearly obtaining his names from notices in the newspapers. He would hardly be stupid enough to call on a family where one of the family members expressing their grief was Isis Fahmy! Fate, however, had intervened. It so happened that my brother Aziz, who was very conservative and traditional in his thinking, was the one who placed our announcement in the press. In line with his conservatism, he gave for publication only the names of the men in the family.

I believe in telepathy. My subconscious seemed to be saying, "He is going to come, he is going to come." But when? A few days passed. About five in the afternoon, when I was in my bedroom getting ready for the evening family visits of sympathy, Aunt Lily, who was staying with us to help look after my mother, came to my room with a letter edged in black. I knew! Sure enough, the letter was signed by me! Great excitement. We had got him! But how to keep him? "Quick, Aunt Lily! Don't let him go. Get your husband to stay with him while I call the local police." The officer I needed to speak to was not there, because it was the time of the Iftar.[1] I went to the drawing-room to join my uncle and our visitor and started to play for time. "I'm sorry," I said, "the lady who will give you a donation is having a bath at the moment. She will be here shortly. You won't have to wait long." Asking a few questions about the man's phoney charity, I finally mentioned Isis Fahmy. "What does she do?" I enquired. He replied disdainfully, "She's just a little secretary, a nobody!" I swallowed my fury. Under the pretence of going out to see if "the lady in the bath" was nearly ready, I made a second phone call. This time I was able to speak to the officer in charge. "I'll send a policeman round immediately. When he arrives he will bring

---

1 *My brother's death had occurred during the Moslem fast of Ramadan. For a month there is strict fasting from dawn until dusk. The firing of a cannon announces the daily end of fasting. The 'Iftar' is the meal that follows.*

your suspect here. You come as well to file your report." Back in the drawing-room, Mr. Charity Collector was becoming impatient. "I won't disturb you any longer," he said, "I'll leave you now and come back later." "Oh, no you won't," I replied firmly. "You will stay here until the police arrive. I've been on the look-out for you for a long time. Let me introduce myself. My name is Isis Fahmy, your nobody of a little secretary. It's high time I caught you." Meantime, my sister Aïda had arrived and the reinforcement was soon knocking at the door.

After heated arguments and denials, we set off to the station – in my car. I drove with my uncle beside me. In my mirror I saw the thief slip a bank note to the policeman. I said nothing until we reached the police station. Without getting out of the car, I yelled at the two policemen on duty outside. "Quick. Come over here. Your colleague has just been bribed by this impostor to let him escape!" Eventually the man was taken in. I made my statement and was told I could return home. As we were getting out of the car, my uncle remarked, "That envelope on the back seat, is it yours Isis?" It was a fat envelope and it was not mine. Inside was a sheaf of begging letters. The signature on some was Isis Fahmy. On others it was Zeinab Labeeb. What better proof could there be? I drove straight back to the police station with the evidence.

Who was the bogus collector? He was a teacher in a small primary school where his salary was only twenty-five Egyptian pounds a month. To supplement these meagre earnings, he had been visiting up to six houses a day, making about ten pounds. And who was Zeinab Labeeb? Not satisfied with collecting from Coptic families for a Coptic charity in my name, he was also using a Moslem 'secretary' to collect from Moslems for a Moslem charity as well!

He was sentenced to six months in prison.

THE ASWAN DAM ADVENTURE

In May 1964, some four hundred miles down the Nile from Cairo, the first stage of the Aswan High Dam project was completed. I was sent by my newspaper to cover the opening ceremony. My brief was to write a feature not so much describing the official proceedings as conveying the general atmosphere of the occasion, the feelings and thoughts of the ordinary people about this massive undertaking.

The building of the dam, with its promise of controlled and permanent irrigation in the Nile valley, represented Nasser's single most important achievement for Egypt. Apart from the material benefits, the dam was the symbol of Egypt's emergence from backwardness and poverty, the visible sign of modern, scientific progress.

The opening ceremony was the occasion for national rejoicing. Nasser had invited Middle-East heads of state; all the Egyptian top military and civilian officials were there; but most important was the presence of Khrushchev, the Soviet Prime Minister, who six years previously had committed Russia to providing all the huge capital investment needed for the scheme.

In recognition of this contribution, Khrushchev was the guest of honour, and was invited to perform the opening ceremony. The event naturally attracted the world's press. Some two-hundred-and-fifty journalists and photographers descended on Aswan. Accommodation was provided in the recently completed blocks of flats built by the government to house the future workmen who would be needed for the continuing construction of the dam. The flats were now being used for the first time, so the journalists took a real part in somewhat less spectacular inauguration proceedings.

I was sharing a room hardly big enough for two with a pretty young Swedish journalist who was on the look-out not only for news but also for someone to spend the evening with, or to be more precise the night. By chance I had earlier interviewed a young relation of one of the visiting Arab heads of state. Well, I had tried to interview him; but it soon became obvious that he wasn't interested in the questions of a woman journalist, just in the woman journalist herself; so I tactfully thanked him for answering my questions and made my getaway. Keen to help my Swedish roommate – and to have a room to myself – I suggested that she could probably get a good interview from a certain young Mr. X if she went to the Cataract Hotel, which was where all the important guests were staying. She seemed to think my idea was a good one and off she went. The next time I saw her was the following day, amongst the crowd of journalists at the dam. Problem solved, for both of us!

At the ceremony, speeches by Nasser and Khrushchev. Khrushchev pressed a button. A symbolic mountain of sand cascaded down. The rocks excavated to make a new channel for the Nile had been used to block its original course and to form the foundations of the High Dam proper. It was to take a further six years to complete the project.

I was walking amongst the crowd of onlookers, doing my job listening to what ordinary people were saying and asking them questions. I asked a local person, dressed in the customary djellabah,[1] what he thought about the dam? "It's a marvellous thing, he replied; it will bring benefits to everyone. We're taming nature to bring prosperity to Egyptian agriculture. No more unpredictable Nile floods." I was impressed by his words and said to myself, "The locals are well educated in these parts." I spoke to a second man and then a third. They too surprised me by their intelligent and enthusiastic comments.

As I carried on through the crowd, I noticed a little boy was following me; he was about ten years old. In the end I got a bit irritated. I turned round and asked him, "Why do you keep following me?" He replied, "I just want to tell you that the people you were questioning were policemen in disguise. You didn't notice what they were wearing on their feet, did you? Policemen's shoes!" He was right; we both had a good laugh about it. So much for the man in the street. Just how many policemen had I been interviewing?

Later on, back in the lounges of the Cataract Hotel, I managed to get the views of some of the public figures. Naturally enough, they were all full of praise for Nasser's achievements.

Now that the show was over, I wanted to get away from Aswan as quickly as possible and avoid, if I could, the crowd on the train back to Cairo. In the hotel I came across Marshal Sedky Mahmoud, the Chief of the Egyptian Air Force. I knew him quite well. All the journalists including myself had come down to Aswan on a special train. The only aircraft to make the trip were military ones. I asked Sedky Mahmoud if he could do me a favour and get me on a plane to Cairo. He was eager to oblige, called over his aide-de-camp and told him to give me a ticket. This he did. It was not an ordinary airline ticket of course, just an official pass with 'Admit one' stamped on it. I dashed to the airport where I was eventually given the last place on a waiting plane. There were six passengers in all. One was Nasser's Security Minister, three were other government ministers, including Nasser's brother-in-law who was the Minister of Education. The plane had only four seats. Behind them was enough space for two other passengers, me and, believe it or not, the head cook of the President of Egypt. He was already sitting on the floor with his piles of pots and pans all tied together with string and rattling noisily, the very utensils which had contained the meals served to the visiting Heads of State! The Aswan High Dam might have arrived, but the technological revolution still had some way to go! I found myself a space facing him.

---

1 Djellabah - *the usual daily dress for men, a long loose-fitting white gown.*

Completely ignoring the presence of the VIP passengers, who never gave us a second look, the cook proceeded to give a loud, never ending commentary on what had been in each of his pans, how many meals he had served, what problems he had had to sort out. On and on, I listened. So much for custom and tradition which decreed that men should not speak to women they did not know. The pilot eventually broke the monotony.

"I'm sorry; we haven't enough fuel to take us to Cairo. We'll have to land at Luxor to refuel."

At the airport we all got out, and there we were stuck for the best part of an hour. There was a slight problem. Whatever kind of fuel our plane had left in its tank, it was not the same as the fuel at Luxor. Anything landing at Luxor could only get Russian aviation fuel. Was it safe to mix it with what we had? "Probably not", the chef confided to me, but in a whisper this time, "I thought the Russians used vodka, the speed their fighters go." Whatever the Russians used, the decision was eventually taken. Mix it; we'll take the chance.

So, by yet another miracle of modern technology, we completed the journey, arriving at one of the military airports outside Cairo at seven in the evening.

Chauffeured limousines were already waiting to whisk their ministers to Cairo. None of them had the courtesy to ask me how I was going to make the journey into the city. It was no thanks to them that a minibus shortly arrived with Ministry of Information stickers on it. The bus had come to collect mail sent by the journalists from Aswan. With a bit of persuasion, my journalist's identity card and a piece of paper saying 'Admit one', I managed to get a lift into Cairo. One more journey, this time by taxi, and I was back in the newspaper offices. I had achieved my mission at Aswan and returned with plenty of material for my feature.

And the cook? When I left the airfield he was still waiting, with his pots and pans, for his transport to arrive.

SILVER SERVICE

It was Italy's National Day, 2nd June 1965. To celebrate this event the Italian Embassy in Cairo, as usual, gave a reception. Social events at the Embassy had a reputation for magnificence, gaiety, and the length of the guest list. On the National Day it was customary for the press attachés to invite their own friends and contacts from press circles and for the military attachés to do the same from their own service. Many of the guests would consequently be strangers to the hosts.

The event was, as expected a great success being enjoyed by hosts and guests. As the reception was drawing to close, I went over to the Ambassador to take my leave and in the course of the conversation he said, "Oh, by the way Isis, there is something I wanted to ask you. You know everybody. Who are those two couples?" He nodded towards four persons who were standing just two or three yards away, near the table in the centre of the entrance hall. Whether our glances in their direction made them nervous is impossible to say. As they moved towards the main door, one of the men bumped into the table. To our astonishment a couple of little silver dishes fell from his pocket. The Ambassador reacted quickly. Dashing forward, he grabbed hold of the culprit shouting to the staff on the door to stop the other three. "Quick Isis, go and fetch the Chief of Protocol." This I did. He rang for the police and the four were taken away, but not before a search of pockets and handbags produced about a dozen pieces of the embassy silverware.

Who were these light-fingered guests? Two bank clerks and their wives. They said they had read in the morning paper about Italy's National Day and the large reception the Ambassador was giving. So they had just put on their best clothes and managed to slip in and join the reception!

Invitation cards at the Italian Embassy – and others – were checked much more carefully after that. Perhaps appropriately, the name of the Italian Ambassador was Count Magistrati!

Count Magistrati remained as Italian Ambassador to Egypt for four and a half years until October 1965. When I interviewed him before his departure, he expressed his hope that the close understanding and co-operation between Egypt and Italy that had characterised his service in Cairo, would be maintained.

SWEDEN

My love of travelling took me to Sweden several times but only twice as a journalist, in July 1960 and July 1966. I did not submit my articles to my Egyptian newspaper straightaway, as I knew that there would not be another Egyptian journalist visiting Sweden for some time. Therefore, when I returned home, at the end of September on both occasions, little by little I fed my articles and reports through to my editor for publication. A mini series was therefore created and I maintained the interest of my readers.

I was always, as far back as I can remember, in those early days in Cairo, attracted by the names and impressions of countries far away from Egypt's shores. My imagination painted wonderful images and my desire was always to travel and test out my imagination in reality. Places I had heard about from family, friends and visitors were places I wanted to see when I grew up.

In my early working days in Egypt as a Diplomatic Correspondent, I was fortunate in being able to meet a wide variety of people from different countries around the world. During the following years considerable travel became part of my work, and I became particularly attracted to the Scandinavian countries.

In Cairo I was very friendly with a lady we nicknamed 'Lolly', the wife of the Swedish Ambassador, Mr. Croneborg. Lolly was always full of life and fun. One day, she said to me "Isis, have you ever been to Sweden?" I had not but I really did want to go and soon the opportunity arose. "Then it's very simple. You shall. We'll invite you to our house in Sweden where our daughter, Christina, is living." I had, in fact, met Christina some time earlier when she had visited her parents in Cairo. "Christina will take good care of you and will occupy your time! As regards your air ticket, I will arrange for Scandinavian Airlines, SAS, to invite you as a journalist."

The air-ticket arrived as promised and away I went. I remember it to this day, arriving in Stockholm on the evening of 21st July 1960.

The 23rd July was Egypt's National Day and the cause of much celebration at home and abroad. I was invited to attend the reception given at the Egyptian Embassy in Stockholm. On arriving in the reception rooms I was not alone for more than a few seconds before I was approached by a lovely young Swedish woman who enquired whether I was on my own and asked if she could introduce me to her friends. I was introduced to several, among them a Swedish journalist, who asked if I was free that evening. I was, and an evening out was then arranged for me.

Stockholm is a large capital city, like a paradise island to me from a range of viewpoints. The landscapes were beautifully surrounded by water. It was built on several islands within a wide lake. The huge concrete and glass skyscrapers stand side-by-side with old traditional houses, which date back several centuries. Many of these ancient dwellings stand in equally ancient twisting streets and lanes within the old city. I was fascinated by Stockholm, a city exuding feelings of strength and glory. The statues, the old churches, the royal castle with its royal family, the museums, all created a sense of history and a sense of a proud heritage.

Sweden really did enchant me. It was not a country like any other that I had visited or reported on. I found it to be quite exceptional. To my mind, Sweden had everything I could have wanted. Life progressed calmly and easily in a spirit of happiness. Visiting Europeans whom I spoke with found Sweden in general quite different from Europe. The Swedes, however, had no problem at all with the rest of Europe and, indeed, felt a strong sense of commitment to their neighbours. Yet within this regulated, ordered, calm and peaceful Swedish life-style, free from warfare for the last hundred and fifty years, there is room for a little boredom. I found that good order and a strong domestic focus could border on becoming something of a 'complex.' In political life, Sweden refused to belong to any military bloc or alliance. However, the high standard of civility, charm and politeness were as appealing to me as the love of education and a developing culture, which beat within the very heart of the country.

The youth of the country had a somewhat undeserved reputation with tourists for being far too liberal. Personally, I think that the world press did much to create and exaggerate this view of youth culture. I did not find the Swedish young people to be any more 'liberal' than those I had encountered in other European countries. Quite the reverse, in fact. In the case of some families I had met they were very strict with their children.

The people worked very hard. Holidays were very often alternative working periods. I saw a girl ten years of age working in the local Post Office on one occasion. The granddaughter of the Foreign Minister worked as a tourist guide. Many women were to be seen working on the transport system. Throughout, I found two main qualities always present, firstly there was careful attention paid to punctuality and, secondly, all the workers were very diligent. No matter how late an evening had been enjoyed, everyone was at work the next day by eight o'clock sharp. The Swedish character is phlegmatic, marked by a coolness of character certainly not to be found in most Egyptians! In all matters, a calm and almost impassive approach predominated.

One evening, an Egyptian diplomat and his wife invited me to their private flat. Whilst we were having dinner, the doorbell rang. It was the caretaker of the building who warned us that there was smoke coming from the upper floor of the flats, caused, he thought, by an electrical short-circuit. He was concerned that the smoke and fire might spread. We asked him whether he had called the fire brigade. "No, not yet," said the caretaker, "I'll get round to doing that when I've seen whether it is going to be a serious fire or not. Not before..." The Egyptian family and I were feeling very frightened at this. We quickly grabbed the children and hurried out of the building, passing through the smoke as we went. Other Swedish tenants gazed on us with a most perplexed look as we sped past. Meanwhile, the caretaker continued to insist that he would not be calling any fire brigade until he had gauged the size of the fire. Such coolness in the midst of heat! The diplomat and his family accompanied me back to my hotel where he waited around for a time, assuming, I suppose, that his flat had been burnt to ashes.

Swedish women whom I met were very beautiful and very shy but not very elegant. The interiors of the apartments that I visited were impeccable. So neat and tidy! Married or not, the women had jobs and worked hard. Remember that this is the early 1960s. Jealousy seemed rare. There seemed to be a very relaxed approach to the behaviour of some of the men in partnerships or even to the predatory women one occasionally finds.

"So what? It's not of consequence..." I was advised.

This phrase "It's not important" was one that I met with time and time again; a positive Swedish motto for others. Life was to be approached calmly and without agitation.

What did surprise me on one occasion, being thousands of miles away from my home in Egypt, was when I was walking along a small, narrow street in one of the old quarters and found an Egyptian Museum. It was full of Egyptian antiquities. There were even five mummies on display.

I learnt that the King of Sweden was very interested in this particular Egyptian Museum. He had tried to improve it, donating several sculptures from the pharaonic period of the third to the sixth dynasty. There was a statue of Queen Hatshepshut and many other wonderful art treasures.

The 'Sophia Albertina'

As a guest of the Ministry of Foreign Affairs, I was invited the following day to a club called the *Sophia Albertina*. The club's president, Mrs. Cecilia von Ryding hosted my visit and subsequent excursion. The Sophia Albertina was, in fact, the local name given to the building that housed the Ministry of Foreign Affairs. Constructed during the reign of King Gustavus III, the King had so loved the finished work that he named the building after his wife, Sophia. A club had then been established within the building for the wives of foreign Diplomats posted to Stockholm. This women's club had a mainly cultural function; visits were arranged to places of interest in and around Stockholm, as well as various artistic presentations being held within the club itself. From time to time, foreign language classes were arranged for those interested amongst the membership of three hundred.

My excursion with some thirty members of the club began at 7 pm prompt; the assembly point was the port area of the famous Lake Malar. A boat was waiting. Its owner, Baron von Eissen, was our host, accompanied by a Mr. Blom, an architect and director of the public parks and gardens in Stockholm, who was to be our tour guide. As we sailed through the Lake Malar valley, we were given a potted history of Sweden. Alongside the lake were the castles and manors built by wealthy Swedish lords and nobles of yesteryear. The enormous number of private boats on the lake was apparently due to the fact that anybody who was anybody had to be able to run their own boat. A gauge of respectability was the number of boats owned! As we continued we saw the huge buildings belonging to important newspaper companies as well as the tiny holiday-homes much loved by the Swedes for relaxation and summer holidays. We passed the famous Palace of Drottningholm, the usual summer residence of the Swedish royal family and where they also enjoy Christmas and the New Year. Next to the palace stood the Royal Theatre of Drottningholm, a building with a two-hundred-year history, going back to the time of Gustavus III.

As I wandered around the boat, I was surprised to find that the Captain of our vessel was a young woman. This was quite unusual in the rest of Europe during the 1960s, but not in Sweden. She was timid, reserved and spoke little. She did, however, recall "I was already a sailor by the age of eleven. Then I entered the officer training school of the merchant marines at Göteborg. I passed my training, received a marine certificate and became a second-officer. Last winter, I received a scholarship from a navigation company to study in Paris. As for now, I command the private boat belonging to Baron von Eissen."

I really enjoyed this lovely introduction to Sweden by means of an evening cruise. Back ashore, I was invited by Baron von Eissen to one of the best dancing restaurants in Stockholm, namely *The Strand*. The Swedish people I met loved to dance, whether young or old. Thus there are many such dancing restaurants. This then was my first day in Stockholm, and what a day!

The mornings seemed to pass very rapidly as lunchtime began as early as 11.30 am. One·day I was lucky enough to be invited to the *Maertha Skolan*. This was, at one and the same time, a club, a restaurant, a school and a 'maison de couture' or sewing salon! The aim of the club was to provide a sound fine arts education for young ladies of high society. The Countess Von Schwerin had founded it in 1927. The club is named after the first Swedish princess who attended it when it was first set up in order to learn sewing. Subsequently, all the Swedish princesses have been there, achieving a finishing diploma after about two years of study. The club, as you might well imagine is very select. The choice of students is solely the responsibility of the Club President. "From around 140 students who apply each year, I have to select just sixteen. I choose young girls who have a good basic education so that later they will be able to easily find suitably promising positions of employment," said the President. Lunch was served in one of the salons within the club and at the same time a fashion show was presented to the diners. The garments modelled were designed in the style of Parisian couture The President added "All these garments and indeed the models themselves came from Paris. It would be dishonest of me to say that it is all our own creation." Sometimes the ladies who attended the shows used to bring their husbands or boyfriends along in the hope that they would be tempted or persuaded to buy a dress for them. Some succeeded!

Co-operative life

I was so interested by the elegant civilisation and culture of Sweden. The word 'poverty" seemed to have no meaning here. The fundamentals of the economic and social systems in Sweden seemed to hinge on the people's involvement in their own style of co-operatives. In spite of rather high taxes, there was a real commitment to collective societies and companies. Hence it was possible to purchase anything one wanted.

In the centre of Stockholm, there were four massive buildings that were the central headquarters of the co-operatives. Within them worked some 1,200 civil servants who led the management of the co-operative companies, which employed a further 50,000 people. Some one million Swedish families were members of this co-operative movement. At that time, the population of Sweden was seven million.

As part of my interest, I asked my hosts if it were possible for me to spend some time with a typical Swedish family. It was agreed that I spend a day with two families of modest means.

My first family visit was to the home of two schoolteachers. Mr. and Mrs. Yngve Lundell and their three children. Their home was a very nice one, modern in Swedish style. On the first floor there was a large living-room; a modern useful kitchen which had, close by, a washroom possessing all the domestic equipment necessary for washing; then a type of 'hobby room' containing many DIY items for maintenance and repair. The second floor comprised three bedrooms and a bathroom. Close to their home, Mr. Lundell escorted me to one of his neighbour's houses. The family, friends of the Lundells were Mr. Karlsson, a bus driver, his wife, a postwoman and their twelve-year old daughter who enjoyed stamp collecting. The family was most welcoming but did not speak any foreign language so the teacher translated for us. The Karlsson's home was almost identical to that of the Lundells except that the living room was somewhat smaller. Again, every modern convenience was to hand. The teacher and his wife were kind enough to invite me to lunch and we had an interesting talk about the Swedish education system, which struck me as remarkably democratic.

Sporting activity was of great importance with football and ice hockey being predominant. English and German were taught in school. Less academic students are directed to secondary schools with a technical bias that is more employment-related. I found my day fascinating as it helped me to gain a view of normal Swedish life.

Swedish hospitals are noted for their high standards and innovative approach. The one I was able to visit was the Carolinska hospital in Stockholm, which had a worldwide reputation. The hospital used a 'television system' to examine patients' problems, quite revolutionary in its day.

An evening with the Prime Minister

Although the Scandinavian countries, apart from Finland have a monarchy, Sweden is governed by a Prime Minister who is the Chief of State and the most powerful and important man in the country. In 1966, Mr. Tage Erlander was Prime Minister. In February of that year, he was officially invited with his wife on a visit to Egypt, hosted by President Nasser. On that occasion, the wife of the Swedish Ambassador in Egypt, Rudolph Croneborg, invited me to an exclusive lunch at which the guests were the wives of the Vice-Presidents and Ministers of the Egyptian government. I was the only journalist invited, as I was a good friend of the hostess who had given me this chance to gain an exclusive interview with Mrs. Erlander. During the cocktails, I had the chance to speak with Mrs. Erlander. "I have been invited to Sweden by your Ministry of Foreign Affairs next spring. I wonder whether it would be possible for me to interview your husband." "That is very simple to arrange. Please call me as soon as you arrive in Sweden." That is exactly what I did.

I was visiting Christina, the daughter of Ambassador Kroneborg, and asked her how I could contact Mrs. Erlander. The answer was both simple and astonishing. She took the telephone directory and looked up the phone number of the Prime Minister then dialled the number and Mrs. Erlander answered directly. She asked me whether I wanted to interview her or her husband. I was a little taken aback by this and replied that I would like to speak to them both, although, in truth, it was her husband that I really wanted to interview. Mrs. Erlander asked me to phone her again in two days time at 9 am. In the meantime, she would arrange an appointment for me with her husband. On Thursday morning at nine o'clock on the dot, I called again. Mrs Erlander answered straightaway, inviting me for coffee at their private residence at 6 pm. How times have changed. In those days there was no security, no bodyguards.

The Prime Minister lived on the seventh floor of an apartment building. Christina, my photographer and I duly arrived and pressed the relevant intercom button. It was Mrs. Erlander herself who answered: no housekeeper, no doorman, no cleaner. Mrs. Erlander managed everything herself with the occasional help of her sister-in-law. She opened the door and invited us in. The Prime Minister came over to welcome us. They had also invited – in my honour I was told – the top columnist and journalist Marianne Hook. I was taken over to the window and shown the beautiful panoramic view over Lake Malar and Stockholm.

"We thought that with such a view, we do not need paintings on the wall," said the Prime Minister. "We have a living painting to look at." He showed me the panorama with great excitement and enthusiasm.

Their flat was modern but sober. The windows were full of plants and flowers. We sat down and Mrs. Erlander served coffee together with a range of traditional Swedish snacks and cakes.

My first question to the Prime Minister was about Egypt, remembering that he had been there some three months earlier.

"How did you find Egypt?   Did it live up to your expectations?"

"We had many images in our heads before we set off for Egypt. My wife and I had spent some time reading about your country before our trip. However, when we arrived we were surprised and somewhat unprepared. We did not expect Cairo to be so large, so modern and so full of life. The traffic was so heavy!" He added that he thought Aswan was a beautiful place and that he preferred it to Luxor. After these opening remarks about Egypt, we went on to discuss political problems and matters on the international scene.

I enquired, "How is it justified, Prime Minister, that Sweden was among the first to develop and install observation and defence posts, built underground, for the detection of nuclear activity?"

He replied, "Up to now we have tried, with much difficulty, to construct underground observation posts capable of detecting the difference between earth movements caused by an earthquakes and those caused by nuclear explosions. The Americans rightly say that one cannot accuse any State of breaching a nuclear test ban without being absolutely sure of the evidence. I attach a great deal of importance to disarmament and nuclear control. Other countries, such as Italy, Japan, India and Romania, are also very interested and recently we held a conference here in Stockholm to discuss this subject. Of course, everyone agrees that we want harmony and peace. However, it is a different and difficult matter to agree how as the largest countries are not prepared to accept any control over their actions on their own territory. I hope that at our next conference, in Geneva I believe, we can all move towards some solutions. Let's hope that our desire for peace overcomes our differing views!"

I then asked Mr. Erlander what he thought about the two great problem areas of the moment, namely Rhodesia and Vietnam.

"We had hoped that the decisions of the Security Council would bring about some concrete results. However, this has, sadly, not been the case. We must not give up hope. As far as Vietnam is concerned, our Swedish government has not changed its position. We always preferred negotiation to bombing and think that the Americans have to come to accept that the Vietcong do exist, have views, and all three parties in this dispute should meet and reach an agreement. To this end, we have tried to do all that we could. However, nothing has changed. I just wish that I was able to tell you of some news, or new initiative, on the subject but unfortunately things remain the same."

After a brief overview of international policy, we turned to Swedish domestic affairs. Although Sweden is one of the richest and best-developed countries in the world, with a high standard of living, in Parliament there are frequent lively debates on policy between the conservatives and the social democrats. At that time there was much discussion about the treatment of elderly citizens.

"Yes, that's right," said the Prime Minister. "Our policy is, at present, to offer a retirement pension to all elderly Swedish citizens who are sixty-seven years old and over. They all receive a minimum basic amount, irrespective of what their own economic situation happens to be. This basic pension can then be increased by any complementary provision they have made. From time to time, Parliament reviews this situation with regard to our relatively high cost of living. Since 1960 a new law has been applied to the provision of complementary pensions for the elderly. It will, however, take up to twenty years before the law fully takes effect and its benefits are realised. In the meantime it is the taxpayers, especially those of the wealthy classes, who have to fully fund the pensions for our old people!"

We then discussed one or two items from current Swedish newspapers, one such topic being a strike by SAS pilots. The Prime Minister said that strikes had been unknown in Sweden since 1945.

"True, there had been talk of strikes by civil servants and other employees but there had always been discussion and compromise that ended in agreement, averting any need for strike action."

Suddenly, Mrs. Erlander, a teacher, came and sat down by her husband saying, "I may be taking part in a strike myself if you do not raise teachers' pay. We are actually discussing this at the moment!"

"Oh!" said Mr. Erlander with a look of surprise on his face.

Mrs. Erlander was involved in the Youth Labour Movement. We discussed the emancipation of youth both in Sweden and in the rest of Europe. I then enquired as to her thoughts on sex education in the school.

She commented, "In my view, it is absolutely necessary to educate our young people about such subjects, subjects which they must not be ignorant about."

This led to a question about women priests who were, I found, very popular with the laity in Scandinavian countries but not so popular with the clergy.

"I am all for women priests. Why not? Surely, we have the same rights as men. We do the same studies."

Mr. Erlander remained in power from 1946 until 1969.

After Prime Minister Olaf Palme was assassinated in 1986, discreet security measures were put in place to protect those in high office. The tradition remains, however, that the Prime Minister has the same democratic lifestyle that every other Swedish citizen enjoys.

The Largest Mining Complex in the World

North of the Arctic Circle in Sweden, I visited the largest metallurgical mine in the world at that time. The mine produced 15.1 million tonnes a year, mainly iron and steel. Here I met up with Mr. Lundberg, who was head of this massive government enterprise as well as being Secretary of State for Transport. He looked very severe. He spoke little. He was not in the custom of receiving members of the press. I had not been able to find out from my diplomatic friends what sort of man I was going to interview. Any opinions, which they might have, they were going to keep to themselves this time.

As I approached the interview, having walked long corridors, passing through many different offices, I was struck by the looks of astonishment I was receiving from the employees. Mr. Lundberg receiving a foreign journalist at the mine? I even began to ask myself what I was doing here!

As soon as I met Mr. Lundberg he began to tell me about the mine. One of his largest extractions to date had been of some 21 million tonnes, half of which consisted of iron ore. His best customers were in England, Belgium and West

Germany. There were about seven thousand people working at the mine, which was so large and so important within the country that the miners were very well paid and had a high standard of living.

Mr. Lundberg explained that through export and trade, especially in metal ore, Sweden was continuing an age-old tradition. Sweden also imported rough quality ore, refined it and exported the finished product. The mine covered a vast area underground, with 800 km of roadways, like a city under the earth.

I enquired whether any women were employed. "Of course," came the reply, "Their numbers increase year on year. They are very efficient, careful workers."

Ulla!

The Swedish people were very proud of their well-known actress and Ambassadress, Ulla. Whilst visiting Stockholm during the summer of 1966, I often heard mention in Swedish society circles of this famous actress and Ambassador's wife. Her name was Ulla Zetterberg. At that time, her husband, Mr. Lons von Celsing, was one of the principal officers within the Ministry of Foreign Affairs. In any other country, it would have been unheard of for the wife of an Ambassador to be a popular actress. However, I found that generally in the Scandinavian countries the social mentality was very different from that otherwise found in Europe.

In Sweden, they were all very proud of their actress Ulla. One Sunday afternoon, a Swedish colleague accompanied me to her lovely house in the suburbs of the capital. The decor was nineteenth century, simply furnished with taste and style. Ulla and her husband received us in their beautiful garden.

Ulla shone. She was full of life, cheerful and dynamic, with a terrific sense of humour. Her husband, however, was reserved, more formal, and yet most courteous. Within her acting world, Ulla was enthusiastically preparing for the central role of Dolly in the forthcoming musical *Hello Dolly!* She told me, "It's the first time I have been asked to play such a part because my career previously has not been as a musical artist but rather as a comedienne. Yet I've accepted this role because it's a challenge to a person with a strong will! Some time later, I heard from my Swedish friends that her interpretation had been very successful.

During our interview Ulla also told me how she had started her working life at the age of seventeen. Her mother, a businesswoman, had wanted her to train as a lawyer. Ulla, however, had different views. She had heard the call of the stage. "It was my obsession to act in the theatre; to be in contact with an audience."

I then enquired, "How did you cope with being the wife of a diplomat likely to be transferred abroad?"

"I always followed my husband when he was moved abroad. For example, we stayed for three years in Iran. Whilst there, I collected various textiles, as a hobby, and I became very involved. Whatever I do, I do with great passion! I intend to make a gift of my textile collection to a museum. Of course, I was a long way from home and from the theatre for a long time. However, here I am, back again, with *Hello Dolly!*"

Lars Magnus Ericsson

During my journey to Stockholm in 1966, I was taught all about the history of the telephone whilst visiting one of the largest manufacturers of telephones and telephonic equipment in the world at that time. This was the Ericsson Telephone Company. For the tour and interview, I was fortunate in being led by Mr. Bjorn Sundwall, President of the Ericsson Society. I made it clear that I wanted to know as much as possible about the telephone, an absolutely essential tool of efficient modern communication and living.

Mr. Sundwall commented: "First of all, I must tell you that today there are no less than nine million Ericsson automatic telephones throughout the world. Half this number is in the United States of America. We have sixty offices in ninety different countries. We employ more than 62,000 people worldwide, 22,000 in Sweden alone. Working conditions are very good here. We have many workers who have been with us for up to fifty years. The pay is good. The average working week is currently forty-five hours."

The huge office headquarters, which I was visiting, had some six thousand employees. At lunchtime, I was shown to the staff restaurant, which, being the largest in Sweden can accommodate up to 2,500 people at a time. As to be expected, the Swedish democratic system was in play. Company directors, office staff, technicians, young and old all mixed and sat together. I noticed that young people with long 'pop' hair were sitting beside older, more conservative groups and they all appeared to be getting on well.

"The largest Ericsson factories are located in the United States, France, Norway, Italy, Australia, Brazil and Argentina. There is even an operation in Egypt, run by Egyptians. In 1960, a hundred thousand new telephones were installed in Cairo."

Down in the basement of the factory was the telephone museum. Here I learned the Ericsson story and was able to trace the development of the telephone through the years. It was in 1876 that an American, Graham Bell invented the first telephone. That same year, Lars Magnus Ericsson, then aged thirty, was working in the centre of Stockholm with a young apprentice twelve years of age, repairing telegraphic equipment. They soon moved on to repairing early telephonic equipment imported from America. It was a labour of love, their hobby, and their joy. In 1878, Ericsson decided that the time had come for him to create his own telephone. This became the first telephone in the world to have both receiver and transmitter in one instrument and was called the 'French Model.' Numerous other manufacturers copied the design. Ericsson's reputation nowadays is that of a pioneer in telecommunications, producing ever more modern, smaller and more efficient devices for worldwide communication.

My guide was an older man whose father had contributed to the development of the early telephone in 1885. How far we had come since then. In 1884, the telephone consisted of two separate parts connected with a piece of wood. By 1966, office workers could have all their messages automatically recorded. At that time, technicians were still working towards a push-button phone.

I was fascinated by what I was seeing and hearing. I had always had a love affair with the phone and was glad to be living in the telecommunications era. The human side of the people working at Ericsson's especially impressed me. People who were in so many ways, so different, and yet who worked in harmony in understanding was indeed something to phone home about...

Skokloster Castle

One of the most interesting castles in Sweden is Skokloster Castle, which is owned by Baron and Baroness Rutger von Eissen. I met the Baron during a boat trip on Lake Malar organised for the ladies of the diplomatic corps. He had kindly invited me to his castle that particular weekend in order to meet his wife and a group of their friends. The castle is about forty kilometres from Stockholm and thirty from the ancient university town of Uppsala.

During my visit I saw a great number of treasures, amongst them being one of the most important collections of arms in Europe as well as an impressive library of twenty thousand books and manuscripts. The Baron and his wife lived permanently in a private apartment in the castle. A further seventy rooms are open to the public. They do not live an aristocratic life but, as is the lifestyle in Sweden, what might be termed a 'democratic' one.

For lunch, there was a typically Scandinavian buffet, which, of course, was self-service, in the traditional manner. The secretary of the King of Sweden was the guest of honour. The Baron told me something of the history of the castle.

"It was constructed during the middle ages and given by the Viking owners to a religious group who turned the building into a convent. Only later, in 1654, was it redeveloped into the castle you see today by a famous General at the time called General Carl Gustav Wrangel. Skokloster Castle is quite different from the other castles in Scandinavia because of its style and the generous proportions of its construction. It is of such a size that, during one visit by King Charles XI, an estimated three hundred guests were easily accommodated.

"Regarding my collection of arms" said the Baron, "It was during the Thirty Years' War that Gustav Wrangel collected some two thousand different weapons. This private collection is the most important in the world for items of that period. There are, furthermore, 350 valuable paintings, some by Wrangel, in addition to some fabulous tapestries from the sixteenth and seventeenth centuries, together with Persian tapestries from the latter part of the seventeenth century."

The Baron acquired the castle in 1930.

I was fascinated by my visit, seeing all the treasures as well as gaining a better appreciation of Swedish history through the story of the castle. It was a lovely day; so pleasing too that I could mix with a wide range of Swedish people during my visit to that country. I found that from whatever circle or society people came, they were invariably well educated, attractive, with good manners and a sense of culture. My own view, looking back, is that Sweden through its education, manners and culture seems more civilised than other European countries. It was a world of its own in this regard.

What attracted my attention finally at the castle was the Baron's collection of old cars including an old Citroën that had belonged to the Baron's cousin, Dag Hammarskjöld, a famous Secretary-General of the United Nations. This car was a particular favourite of the Baron's.

In 1967 Baron Rutger von Eissen donated Skokloster Castle to the Swedish nation. I had been lucky to visit it in 1966.

An Unusual Evening

One evening, at a reception at the Egyptian Embassy, I bumped into one of my greatest childhood friends, Tahani Sedky. This was quite a shock!

"What are you doing in Stockholm?" I asked.

"I work in the Military Attaché's office," came my friend's reply.

The year was 1960 and Tahani was the first Egyptian woman appointed to work in a military attaché's office, especially notable as Nasser was 'reigning' at the time. Tahani had an important confidential appointment, full of responsibility. She invited me to a typical Swedish restaurant, having first enquired as to whether I liked to dance. I replied that I loved dancing and so the plan was set.

One evening later that week we visited the chosen restaurant. True Swedish restaurants in Stockholm at that time were large! Inside, sitting at round tables were only ladies having their dinner. Alongside mirrored walls, on both sides of the room, were long bars where men only were standing having their drinks.

I said to Tahani, "We have had no success at all so far, not a single man has come over to ask us to dance."

"Of course not! They are very polite in this country. Whilst we are having our dinner nobody will venture to disturb us. However, you just wait and see..."

She was right. As soon as we had finished eating our meal, various gentlemen did approach and asked us for a dance. Social rules of engagement were strict indeed. It was forbidden for men to sit down at a ladies' table unless they had been invited to do so by the lady concerned. This rule was so rigorously enforced that as soon as a gentleman sat down at a lady's table, the manager of the dance floor would immediately go over to enquire whether or not the lady had given her consent.

We enjoyed a most pleasant and typically Swedish evening.

A Portrait of Marianne Hook

My brief portrait of Marianne Hook, the best-known Swedish journalist and columnist of her time, begins when I first met her in 1966, over a cup of coffee at the home of the Swedish Prime Minister. She had been invited in my honour so that I was able to converse with a fellow columnist.

The next time we met was over a cup of coffee at a lunchtime meeting. Her husband was a most brilliant Ambassador, posted in Moscow at that time.

Marianne had a powerful pen, perhaps the sharpest in all of Sweden. People had good reason to respect, even fear, her column. She had the ability to 'make the ground shake' under those she chose to target.

At our rendezvous, we discussed the serious topic of the rights and concerns of Swedish women. She was forthright. She never let political personalities off lightly. She said, "We have equal pay in Sweden. However, when we look at the facts, women's responsibilities are far greater than those of men, and require a much greater investment of energy. On an individual level, there are many young women who have to work but have to live in the suburbs. Those who have children are obliged to leave their children with carers during the day or in a crèche. It is said that this is better for the children and creates a calmer family. However, the underlying truth is that this arrangement does not always create calmness and the women feel guilty and worry at work. These worries are due to the expectations of society and to the pressure to work outside the home.

Nowadays, our young people are educated and liberated in many ways. They cannot accept that women should come second in the economic and social queue, behind men. They are also not prepared to automatically accept that a woman's career comes to a halt when she becomes a mother. Our government supports this view but it is a topic about which there is continuous debate."

It was interesting for me to meet my Swedish colleague again. She had a column in the newspaper every Sunday, as I did in Cairo. Three days later I was featured in her column, with my picture alongside the Prime Minister.

I was devastated to learn, four years later, that Marianne Hook, such a brilliant journalist and beautiful woman, had committed suicide in February 1970.

Conclusion

Something that surprised me during my first visit to Sweden was the fact that even the richest people, for example the Prime Minister and the grandest in the land, never retained paid servants or cleaners. The prevailing social system is of such a high order that it is seen as one-upmanship to do one's own cooking and cleaning. That is the real snobbery.

I found Swedish people to be very hard working and energetic. They seemed to lead straightforward lives and peaceful ones. International politics and faraway conflicts did not interest those I met. The focus was on what was happening within Scandinavia and any problems there, which needed attention.

When I eventually left Sweden, I felt that I had visited a country apart from the normal run of places; in fact, a 'world apart'. Sweden resembled neither Europe nor America. It was truly its own place!

NORWAY

What a gorgeous country Norway is. Arriving in Oslo, in May 1966, I was amazed by the wild and rugged beauty of the landscape around me. I saw the deep fjords that cut far into the coastal land, penetrating, finger-like, into the heart of the country. Bold colours and bold forms of cliff, mountain and inlet delighted the eye. These are picture-memories I shall never forget.

Norway was surprising because of the sheer length of the country and its coastline. It constitutes the most western part of the Scandinavian group of countries, occupying some forty per cent of the landmass. It is the fifth largest country in Europe with respect to area but has the lowest population density. In 1966, there were some 3.5 million people living within its borders. This had risen by 1998 to some 4.5 million.

Along the Norwegian coast, there are 150,000 islands of which two thousand are inhabited. Each year, Norway welcomes four million tourists, which is hardly surprising given the beauty of the country, the charm of the people and the quality of the fishing and the fish! As I found in Sweden, people are relaxed, calm and good-natured, always seeming to smile. They are well educated and value their traditions and culture. Most visitors come from Sweden, Denmark and Great Britain. The English especially enjoy salmon and trout fishing, choosing camping-type holidays that are very healthy for the body, mind and wallet.

Wandering around Oslo itself, what initially caught my attention was the number of students wearing bright red caps with tiny bows and red outfits to accompany them. In their hands, they held long sticks. What was the cause of this strange display? It was 16th May, the day the results of the Baccalaureate were published. Those in the red caps and costumes had passed their exams. The celebrations would continue well into the night, or even the next morning, creating a carnival atmosphere.

Continuing my tour of Oslo, I came to the famous Holmenkollen Olympic stadium. In 1966 it was regarded as a world-leader of its kind. It could accommodate a hundred thousand spectators who came from far and wide to witness some of the finest ski jumping in the world. Norway, of course, has an outstanding tradition of expertise in all types of skiing. Each year Holmenkollen stadium hosts a huge ski competition. King Olav V, and his son Prince Harald were always present at this event, which is a highlight in the Norwegian calendar.

The Norwegian Royal Family is well known and well respected because of its democratic and straightforward approach. King Olav V, for example, regularly goes shopping in the centre of Oslo, gazing in shop windows and making his own purchases as he wanders around.

On one occasion I saw him really close to but, like the citizens of Norway, I respected his privacy and did not disturb his progress. The King's powers are those defined within the national constitution, which is one of the oldest in Europe, dating back to its formal beginnings in 1814. The King is thereby directed to follow the majority decisions taken by government Ministers within the Cabinet. He retains a power of veto when it comes to legislative action. He is also the Supreme Chief of the Armed Forces and head of the Church of Norway.

The position of the King is akin to a sacred office, in that his role is enshrined within the Constitution and he cannot be blamed, attacked or pursued.

My time in Norway, especially in Oslo, was full of variety and interest; meeting people from different circles and backgrounds, a passion of mine. I loved mixing with those from other countries and cultures. On one occasion, the Public Relations Director of Scandinavian Airlines, who was, at the time, Mr. Odd Medboe, took me to a well known local restaurant called *Blom that attracted* many artisans and authors. The origin of the name dates from the 1820s. In those days, it was a type of coaching inn, which provided victuals for horse and man. Horses were fed and watered in the stables and their riders on the floor above. As time went on, artists and intellectuals adopted *Blom* as a special meeting place and increasingly frequented the inn. It was also popular with actors, musicians, painters and architects.

Odd Medboe was a quite fascinating personality and could turn his conversation from business matters to writing, to science and new inventions. I enquired about his life and career and he told me that, at heart, he was a writer but he was one of the original founders of Scandinavian Airlines in Norway. SAS was one of the first airlines – the other was Air France – to use Caravelles. The first Caravelle to land in Cairo was from Scandinavia.

Most fascinating was that Mr. Medboe was also the private writer of King Olav V, a position that earned him the title *Saga*, a name given to the principal royal reporter that dated back to the time of the Vikings. Each time the King travelled, Mr. Medboe accompanied him and wrote a report of the trip. He thus took part in numerous royal visits. I asked what King Olav V was like. Mr. Medboe told me that the King had a great love of history and mathematics. These were his two consuming interests. He had few close friends but those he did have had scientific, mathematical or archaeological leanings

Whilst in Oslo, I also had the opportunity to meet Mr. John Daniel Lyng, Minister for Foreign Affairs. We met just prior to his first official visit to Cairo. I was impressed by the Minister's close interest in the Middle East. He said he was delighted to be planning his trip to Egypt and was especially looking forward to discovering something of Egypt's ancient civilisation and rich historic heritage. He told me he was expecting a great deal from his visit. There was already a close link between our countries in that Norwegian shipping was the third most frequent user of the Suez Canal.

I asked the Minister if he was willing to give me his personal opinion on the continuing Vietnam War. Was there a solution?

He replied: "The tragic war in Vietnam is of great concern to us all, especially in this age of the nuclear threat. This war could lead to other countries being drawn into the conflict. At worst, it could degenerate into a global cataclysm. It has serious repercussions on international relations and policy. There is no easy solution, no miracle cure. Only detailed political negotiation can lead to a durable peace in Vietnam. We must all try to get the parties involved to talk to each other round the table. There must be initiatives to start negotiations."

As Norway was a member state, I then asked Mr. Lyng what he thought about the United Nations.

"I am convinced that the United Nations, given time, will become perfectly adept at facing up to and dealing with conflicts and international situations. It will prove, I am sure, an effective instrument for keeping peace and security. It will have a valuable role in assisting with the economic and social development of nations. It is in the interest of all the countries in the world that peace is maintained so that prosperity can grow. The United Nations needs to command authority throughout the globe and, to that end, requires its own strong financial base and the firm commitment of its member states; without this, it will not be able to achieve its aims."

A Focus on Fishing

One of Norway's richest industries, as well as being its principal resource, is fishing. Norwegians are the fishermen of Europe. Fishing, together with its associated industries, is a major employer and a major export earner. Fish products rate amongst the top three of the country's export earners, playing a vital role in Norway's economic health.

It is hardly surprising, therefore, that a great deal of interest is generated when, in January each year, the herring fishing season begins. The whole nation looks on as thousands of fisher folk take part in the herring campaign. Will it be a good catch this year? Many years there are over one million tons of herring caught.

Science too has its part to play. Science and fishing now go hand in hand. The migrations of herring and cod are as closely observed, studied and followed as one would survey a hostile army's manoeuvres.

In 1966, when I was visiting, there were twenty thousand boats with large engines plus some eleven thousand other boats – sailing or motorised – that put to sea for fishing. In general, fishermen are not salaried; they earn what they catch. They own their own boats and are their own boss.

Oslo's port area contained a tremendous number of boats. There were more boats than I had ever seen in my life including a newly-built boat, named *Julian*, of 88,000 tonnes, which was up for sale. The people of Norway are, first and foremost, sailors and sea-merchants. They are a noble nation.

The North Cape

The most exciting time for me was spent travelling at the Northern Cape. From Oslo, I flew 400km on an SAS Caravelle jet to a point 4° north of the Arctic

Circle, at approximately 8,000 m (26,000 ft), passing over many mountainous regions on the way, which, after Alvdal, were all snow covered. Our destination was Trondheim, the third largest city in Norway.

At Trondheim, what really attracted me were the lively colours of the painted chalets and houses. These bright colours contrast with the gloomy climate yielding a splash of gaiety.

After a short stop at Trondheim, we arrived at a place called Rod, situated 150km inside the Arctic circle. At the airport my guide, Mr. Lokke was waiting and handed me a special passport. On the cover of the passport was written the following:

'Polar Passport – As issued to all good men and true,
upon crossing the Arctic Circle, Norway'

On the inside it read:

'This is to certify that our trusty and well-beloved subject
Isis Nefertiti Fahmy is given the Freedom of
the Arctic Circle, with all the rights and privileges
thereto pertaining."

Inside the Arctic Circle one can imagine finding polar bears and seeing icebergs floating in icy seas. Not at all. To my surprise, I found a small, modern city, inhabited by 14,000 people. There were three stylish hotels; a modern youth and recreation centre; a lovely church containing wonderful tapestries depicting various aspects of local life; also an architecture school, which was one of the most up to date in Europe. It is also worth mentioning that the city of Rod was the second most important military base of NATO in Norway.

I was there at the beginning of June 1966. It was the time of the year when the sun never set. The time of the 'midnight sun' and twenty-four hours of daylight a day lasts until late July. It is the time of year when many locals stay awake much longer, making the most of the light; making hay while the sun shines!

Rod was, of course, well known for its fishing industry and port. Life was calm and regular. However, later in the year, from 19th December until 10th January, the local people experience a time of total darkness. No sunlight, no daylight, just darkness day and night.

One evening, my guide took me to see the current of the Salstraumen, a famous narrow channel, 150m wide and 3km. long, situated between the Island of Straumen and the mainland. Around 370 million cubic metres of seawater pass through the channel at each high tide, creating terrifying whirlpools and undertows. Not the place to attempt a swim! The journey there was most impressive. The landscape was filled with high mountain scenery. Local legend has it that a frightening giant died, was petrified and transformed into stone. The stone remains were called Hestmannen (the horrible man). The horrible man wanted to go to the place of the seven sisters, the name given to seven mountains nearby.

The following day, again with the help of the SAS, I journeyed to Tromso. On the way, I was invited to sit alongside the pilot on the flight deck. What a view! Huge mountains contrasted with the depths and clarity of the icy seas. Knowing that I was a journalist and a guest of SAS, the pilot took the plane down to a height of some 900m so that I had an even better view of the unbelievable panorama below. Although I saw these things many years ago, they are still fresh in my mind. Their beauty will never fade. Norway is unique.

As we flew along, we passed over an island called Red Lion Island. The pilot explained that ancient drawings, from thousands of years ago, had been discovered there. The drawings clearly represented skiers. That went to prove that even Stone Age people knew how to ski.

Very few cities in the world are surrounded by as many islands as the city of Tromso which is also important because it has the largest concentration of population in northern Norway: some 23,000 people in 1966. It is the largest city in the northern world, being at a latitude 69° 40' N. Today, it is a fine university city, centre of cultural excellence and, of course, sailing and fishing.

When I arrived at Tromso airport, I was a little worried as I could not find my guide, nor she find me. For the first time, the guide was to be a young woman of my own age. However, she had imagined that she was waiting for a very old Egyptian journalist, in the style of an ancient Cleopatra. As it was, I was dressed in normal clothing for northern Norway. It was snowing, I was wearing boots, thick trousers and two pullovers, nothing that would have found favour with Cleopatra! My guide was wearing an official outfit and by some instinct or other, we found each other. "Ah, it is you Cleopatra!" said my guide. "I have never met an Egyptian before. I was wondering what you would be like. As you are dressed in a sporty manner, please will you excuse me for a moment while I change into something more in keeping?"

As I travelled around Tromso, it seemed to me that everyone I met had blond hair and striking blue eyes. It was I who was the unusual one and quite an attraction to the local folk who would stop my guide to ask her where I came from.

The main working life in the city centred upon the fishing industry. Between May and September, large numbers of shark are brought into the port. Here men with special knives cut up the shark for its meat and its oil. The spectacle is fascinating.

We took a cable car 430m up above the city and wondered at the sights below: harbours, inlets, tiny islands and multicoloured wooden houses and shops, all encircled by the cool blue sea. Even at this time of year, there was still snow lying on the ground and, like some energetic child, I amused myself making snowballs and kicking the snow. In the evening, we watched the sun dip slightly and re-ascend, forming the midnight sun, so admired by locals and tourists alike.

When I knew that I was going to travel to northern Norway, I was intrigued as much by the idea of perhaps meeting some Laplanders as by the likelihood of seeing the midnight sun. However, I was to be as disappointed by the Laps as I was thrilled by the sun. My imagination had misled me.

The Laplanders resembled typical Asiatic types, a true Lap being very petite, well used to frequent walking in the mountains wearing flat footwear. They had dark hair and dark eyes. Most were nomadic. Their lives depended upon the lives of their reindeer. Wealth was gauged by the number of reindeer that they possessed. They lived all along the northern territory of Scandinavia, with the exception of Denmark. During the mid-1960s, the Laps began to adopt more European ways, visiting the towns and cities of the northern lands. They started to wear European dress, send their children to school for certain periods and increasingly use the Norwegian language. What a shame, I thought!

In Tromso, I visited a little museum that explained different aspects of the Laplander's life, culture and environment. The man's outfit differed from the woman's outfit only by the belt, which he wore around his fur-coat. Those who followed the reindeer lived in tents. Something, which was striking, was the fact that Laplanders love very bright colours. All of their clothing accessories, gloves, belts, hats are bright red in colour, their jewels set in copper, South-American style. I noticed that their homemade carpets and blankets seemed identical in style to those of the Bedouins in the East.

This was the end of my travels in Norway. All the people I met, all that I had seen, especially the beautiful landscapes and the fjords, fascinated me. The memories remain clear in my mind – unforgettable to me.

Midnight Sun visible (whole disc) at Bodö from June 5th–July 10th - Tromsö May 21st–July 23rd - Hammerfest, the Worlds Nothernmost Town, from May 17th–July 28th, and NORTH CAPE May 14th–July 30th

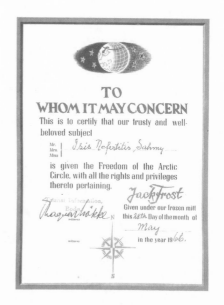

Polar Passport presented to Isis when she visited the Arctic Circle in 1966.

FINLAND

Following my stay in Oslo, I continued my travels through the Scandinavian countries arriving at my next stop – Finland, where I was invited as a guest by the Ministry for Foreign Affairs.

As a diplomatic journalist, I arrived at a critical moment because all the officials I wanted to meet were busily engaged in the visit of the then Soviet Prime Minister, Mr. Kosygin, who just before this visit had been guest-of-honour of Nasser in Egypt, enjoying a wonderful trip to Cairo and being welcomed with full honours. But it was not the same when he arrived in Finland.

Let me offer a little background. For the major part of the past thousand years, Finland was a territory belonging to the Swedish realm. In 1809, Sweden surrendered Finland to Russia. The Tsar of Russia declared Finland a semi-autonomous Grand Duchy with himself as constitutional monarch represented by a Governor-General. In 1917, Finland achieved and declared its independence from Russia and in 1919 adopted its own constitution as a republic with a President as Head of State. However, during 1939-40, the Soviet Union attacked Finland and the Winter War was fought. Fighting continued between the Finnish and Russian forces through 1941-44. Some territory was ceded to the Soviet Union but Finland was never occupied, preserving both its independence and sovereignty. In 1955, Finland joined the United Nations and the Nordic Council. Later, in 1995, it became a member of the European Union.

Through the years, little Finland (at that time the population was five million), which has a border to the east with Russia, has always lived in some trepidation of its huge neighbour. Good diplomatic relations were maintained between the Finnish and Russian governments; but ordinary Finnish citizens were frightened of and did not like the Russians.

Thus when I arrived in Helsinki during this delicate diplomatic visit by the Soviet Prime Minister, my aim was to interview the new Prime Minister, Mr. Rafael Paasio, who had been in his post for only three weeks. Achieving an interview under such circumstances was a personal challenge.

My guide had an idea. She suggested that I join the large party of journalists who were in the country covering the visit of Mr. Kosygin. This I did.

During his visit to the Finnish cable works factory, situated outside Helsinki, I joined my journalistic colleagues on the bus to the factory. As we followed the Prime Minister and government officials we passed through one small village after another beyond the city suburbs. One thing was very noticeable, by its absence. Nobody at all appeared; nobody lined the route, nor greeted the visiting Soviet leader in any way. He must have been rather disappointed.

When we eventually arrived at the factory, instead of concentrating on the technical aspects of production, I decided to search for the Prime Minister. I found him, greeted him and quickly introduced myself. He welcomed me to Finland and briefly explained that I should call his secretary to arrange a proper appointment. That was it…. "Good-bye!"

At the end of the factory tour, by chance, I found myself close to Prime Minister Kosygin. I introduced myself and found him quite responsive. He remarked upon the warmth of his reception when he visited Egypt and the coolness of the Finnish people he had encountered. What a difference!

The following day, the Finnish Prime Minister did not accompany Mr Kosygin on his next visit.

Shortly after my visit to the cable works, I was surprised to receive a phone call from the Finnish Prime Minister's Office granting me a 3.30pm appointment later that week.

So the day came and I was having an early lunch with the wife of a Finnish ambassador. She remarked, "I hear you are meeting Rafael Paasio. I pity you. He is brusque and can be quite unpleasant… especially with journalists!"

I thanked her for the advice but was even more excited. Here was a challenge.

At 3.15pm precisely, I arrived at the office of the Prime Minister, accompanied, as usual, by my Finnish guide who never let me out of her sight for even one second, wherever I went. In Denmark, Sweden and Oslo I did not have the 'assistance' of a guide from 8am until midnight; only in Finland.

Invited in, I began my interview,, "Prime Minister, I have heard that you are extremely difficult to interview because you do not speak a lot, having a reputation for being calm and quiet. It has been said of you that you can be unpleasant with journalists. Are you going to be difficult with me too?"

My guide, who was also my translator, was trembling at this point and refused to translate saying, "I cannot put all that to him!"

I replied, "If you don't translate what I say, I will not interview him."

She answered "No, no…!"

I said, "Yes, yes. You are just translating!"

Meanwhile, the Prime Minister, who was witnessing this interchange, was becoming rather anxious and asked my guide what was happening.

Finally, in a rounded, polite fashion, she translated what I had wanted to say.

He smiled. This was rare, so it was rumoured.

He answered, "I am not a difficult man!"

The ice had been broken! I then found out that he had been a journalist himself.

My next question was, "How can it be that you are both the Prime Minister of Finland and Chief Editor of a newspaper?"

"Since I was elected Prime Minister, I cannot go on being Chief Editor. I do not have the time. However, for the present, my name is still on the newspaper although I am not doing the job."

"What about the political articles?"

"Until now, I have always written my own speeches for publication in the newspaper. But from now on, I shall need some help."

"For the first time, you are in a position of power. What are the great problems that you are facing?"

"Firstly, for the past seventeen years I have been a Member of Parliament and served several times as a government Minister. So the problems are not new."

"What are the problems that you face? I have heard that your government faces three main problem areas: salaries; strike action; and the cost of living. One also hears about inflation."

The Prime Minister answered, "Concerning wages and salaries, this has recently been resolved in a peaceful way with the agreement of workers and civil servants. Regarding what some see as the high and rising cost of living, it is increasing, but slowly and gradually. There will not be inflation. In comparison with many other countries, we are proceeding gradually, slowly and carefully."

"What would you say is your major problem?"

"It is the economic situation which is our main task."

We then moved on to discuss political problems. I said, "The Social Democratic Party has not exercised power for many years, since 1958, and yet at the last general election (1966) only a few weeks ago, your party won with a great majority. Could you explain to me the essential reasons for this victory?"

"I think the reason is the general unhappiness of the Finnish people with our economic situation. Moreover, the Social Democrats have shown a united front and stood together on party, economic and political issues."

We then discussed a somewhat delicate internal government issue. In the formation of his new cabinet, three party groups were represented, and it included three communist Ministers.

"What is your personal opinion Prime Minister concerning the coalition in a cabinet where there are these three different tendencies? There are two different opinions. One is satisfactory and suggests that you are going to work as a unified team; the other is almost pessimistic."

"The three parties to which you refer have already made a programme containing a detailed plan of political lines to follow and appear to be in common accord. As to the future, that's always a secret. Who knows? All I can say, is that for the present, everything is working well."

"With these new left-of-centre elements in power, do you think that there will be changes to the government's strategic line?"

Rafael Paasio smiled as he replied, "We do not have revolutionary ideas. The economic strategy we adopt will remain on the same lines, based on the same fundamentals as before. To support a somewhat higher standard of living for the middle classes, the richest people in Finland must pay more taxes."

He added, "Our principal task is to present to Parliament a draft law for 'the social security of the family.' Such social support has up to now only been available to the civil service. Every Finnish citizen should benefit. We think that all Finnish families should be entitled to the same standard of social conditions."

My final question to Prime Minister Paasio was one dear to my own career, "Which do you prefer: journalism or politics?"

"I found that as a result of my journalism I acquired numerous political experiences. I think that every politician, before becoming involved in political life, should have a career in journalism as it is the best school for a career in politics!"

I responded quickly by commenting that in journalism one can say what one really thinks, whereas that is not so in politics.

Laughing, he answered, "That, my dear, is perfectly true!"

My next meeting was with the Foreign Minister, Dr. Ahti Karjalainen.

At the start of the interview, he commented to me, without prompting, "It is my belief that Egypt and Finland have a number of similar points of view politically, in spite of our being so far apart geographically. Our political strategy is very close. Our foreign policy is essentially based upon 'neutrality'; yours is based on non-alignment. These strategic positions are, in essence, the same, although the terms, the language, which we use, are different.

Here in Finland, we follow Egyptian foreign policy with great interest and concern, especially with respect to your strategy of independent non-alignment, which we are in agreement with ourselves."

I turned the topic of conversation towards broader foreign policy issues for Finland and its political relations with other countries of the world. Before answering a specific question, the Foreign Minister remarked, "When we had our last election campaign in this country, which happened only recently, all the political parties represented agreed that we would not change the strategy and objectives of our foreign policy. There is a common and stable point of view in this respect. That is why all government ministries have had a change in their leading Minister since the election except for the Minister of Foreign Affairs who retained his portfolio. There are, accordingly, four essential and continuing foreign policy perspectives underpinning our approach to other countries. We enjoy and appreciate very good relations with all our neighbours, including the Soviet Union and the Scandinavian countries, among others.

Regarding Finland and peacemaking; we play an active part in the workings of the United Nations. For example, we sent our troops to Palestine immediately after the Suez crisis and have forces serving in Cyprus. Finland is always there to support world peacemaking initiatives.

In the world economic sector, Finland has trading relations with capitalist countries as well as with socialist countries. Without prejudice, 90 per cent of our economy is tied up with European countries, including the socialist ones. One third of this trade is with the member countries of the Association of Free Trade and Exchange and one third is with member countries of the European Economic Community (EEC). I would say that we have 20 per cent of our trade with socialist countries, and a further 15 per cent with the USSR."

We started to talk about NATO (the North Atlantic Treaty Organisation) and the recent withdrawal of French troops from NATO operations in 1966. What did the Minister think about this action? Would it have any repercussions?

"It is certainly most interesting to follow the French policy and from our point of view, this policy may have some effects on the European situation. With respect to the repercussions that it might have on certain Scandinavian countries, Finland remains neutral and will not declare any official position on this subject. Personally, I think that there may be repercussions and that these will occur later rather than sooner; but there will be nothing straightaway."

I continued, "What do you think about Mr. Rapacki's idea, following his recent visit to Stockholm, of organising a conference for all the countries of Europe, east and west? Are you interested in such a collaboration?"

"Yes, of course we are interested. Finland is always concerned with promoting international peace and achieving inter-European harmony. However, speaking personally, it is difficult to give you a definite view as it is not easy to predict whether all countries would agree to take part in such a summit. First there must be agreement on who takes part and then they must be willing to do so!"

I concluded my meeting with the Foreign Minister by asking him what had been his most memorable moment since taking over the foreign affairs portfolio. He smiled and replied, "There have been so many special occasions since I took over this office. Of them all, two months during autumn 1961 particularly stand out in my mind. First of all, there was the official visit of the President of the Soviet Union. Secondly, I was chosen to accompany our President to the United Nations where we took part in the relevant sessions. From there, we took part in official visits to both Canada and the United States of America where we were able to spend a fortnight. During that time we had several meetings with President Kennedy. After that we travelled westwards, returning via Hawaii. It was while we were in Hawaii that we received a message from the government of the Soviet Union alerting us to an international crisis, which was developing concerning aggressive manoeuvres by West Germany. We responded immediately and flew home, twenty-five hours non-stop travelling. Arriving home in Finland, it was not long before I was travelling again, this time to the USSR to meet Mr. Gromyko to discuss this alert. A little later, I made another trip to the Soviet Union and accompanied President Kekkonen of Finland to Moscow in order to sign a trading agreement. What a couple of months those were! Two quite unforgettable months! It was a good job that I could survive the constant travelling."

"So there we are. I shall see you again in Cairo."

I was delighted to have been able to arrange these two interesting interviews during my visit to Helsinki. Looking back, although I was very impressed by the number of lakes I saw – they have been called 'the eyes of the Finnish landscape' – it was not the landscape that touched me most but the warmth, generosity and kind hospitality of the Finnish people. I had not experienced such a friendly reception anywhere else in Western Europe. I could have been at home in Egypt; the welcome and entertainment reminded me of oriental countries and the traditions of my early life.

DENMARK

I concluded my tour of Scandinavia by flying from Helsinki to Copenhagen. Denmark's unique geographical position makes it the link between mainland Europe and the lands of Scandinavia. This location appeared to give rise to a character in the Danish people more like that of southern Europe, a type of Mediterranean outlook you might say. They are full of life, outgoing and cheerful, with a ready sense of humour. Their capital city is full of vitality and joy.

The first place in the capital that visitors normally make for is the famous Tivoli area, of international reputation. Copenhagen is Tivoli! In my travels as a journalist, I was fortunate to visit the Tivoli twice, in 1960 and again in 1966.

Tivoli is situated in the centre of the city. It is a huge, seemingly endless, garden in which one can stroll for hours. This I did. It was fascinating, as there seemed to be something new and unexpected around every corner. There was an international selection of restaurants catering for every palate: Chinese, Japanese, Arabian, French and so on. I counted twenty-three eating-places in one short walk. Other attractions appeared as I proceeded: theatres, dance halls and a Luna Park. There was entertainment to appeal to every taste and fancy. It was impossible to be bored.

Here stands the Pantomime Theatre, one of the oldest in Denmark. Theatre-goers and music-lovers also have the choice of ten different orchestras and a similar number of artistic and dramatic programmes. Other attractions included a circus, a selection of nightclubs and cafe-concert bars.

With the approach of night, thousands of tiny coloured lights are lit throughout the gardens, dancing in the breeze like so many exotic fireflies performing a bizarre dance. Visitors and locals meet and talk. Conversation and good-natured enquiry stimulate even the most reluctant. Single people do not remain single for long. It is said that one never leaves Tivoli alone!

As usual during my travels, I paid a courtesy visit to the Egyptian Ambassador and his wife. His Excellency Moustapha Sadek had been our representative in Denmark since October 1958. I knew them from Cairo. Mrs. Sadek was a most elegant, attractive lady and an accomplished hostess. When they were entertaining, it was as though you had chanced upon an oriental feast, typically Egyptian. A touch of home to be relished in the centre of a Danish city!

The Egyptian government in 1960 had bought the residence of the Ambassador, situated in Hellerup in the suburbs of Copenhagen. It was in the modern Danish style. However, when Mrs. Sadek moved in with her passion for redecorating, an immediate start was made in creating an oriental ambience. It really did feel like an Egyptian setting.

With the exception of the Spanish chambermaid, Carmen and the Danish chauffeur all Embassy staff were Egyptian. The chief cook was Osman, the butler Mohammed and the housekeeper, Naïma. Thus, warm Egyptian hospitality was the order of the day with oriental food and traditional Turkish coffee.

I asked the Ambassador for his impressions of the Danish people. After all, he was a long way from home in a land that could not have been more different from Egypt. He replied, "In truth, the Danes know very little about Egypt. What they do know centres on historic Egypt, rather than the modern state and its current reforms. They are interested in our archaeology, especially in the preservation of the archaeological monuments of Nubia. As for the modern social reforms and the attempts to develop enterprise and modern industries, they know little, if anything. Therefore, it will be necessary for us to organise exhibitions and conferences, which cover the political and economic advances we have made, in addition to those in the fields of art, literature and medicine. I need to remember that Copenhagen is essentially a maritime port and that it would be very different, and very interesting, for the Danish people to meet some of our great men of letters and captains of industry like the Chief Executive of the Suez Canal, for example. My wife and I have quite a task ahead of us in developing a better understanding here of our Egyptian homeland. We work hard and frequently arrange receptions and dinners. These promote our mission and the local press seem to make the most of them! I am fortunate in having a wife who has the personality and taste that combine to make our receptions both glittering and valued."

Then Mrs. Sadek told me a little about Danish women. She said, "There have been many positive social reforms here in Denmark and, indeed, throughout the Scandinavian countries. Danish women have come to expect equality of rights and opportunity. Unlike in many other European countries, here there is equal pay for equal work. This is very advanced, I believe. Women expect to have the same rights as Danish men. Men and women both help in the home and, whether rich or poor, they do their own housework and do not employ servants or cleaners, as we would at home. Yet for a population of around four million, Denmark has 179 parliamentary representatives from seven political parties. From what I have said, you may well guess that it is the social-democratic party which is in power at the moment."

Something that particularly impressed me in Copenhagen was the organisation of the Tourist Office. Tourists are welcomed with open arms. There are facilities in place to provide visitors to Denmark with a most interesting and worthwhile stay. The main offices are situated in the centre of Copenhagen, and were then run by Mrs. Jeanne Steinmetz, the general Director of Tourism. She was young, jolly, and full of energy. With her information, I learned that Denmark spends well over two million Krone (1966) each year in promotion and publicity. In return, the annual revenue from tourism supports Denmark to the tune of over seventeen million pounds sterling each season. In terms of foreign income for the benefit of the country, tourism occupies fourth place, coming after eggs, bacon and butter, the famous Danish dairy produce. Each year, about four million brochures are printed and translated into nine languages.

This charming young Tourism Director strongly advised me to visit Zeeland of the North during my stay. I arranged this trip by joining a coach-party of tourists. An experienced and lively guide explained the interesting history of the area, a job he had been doing for the past ten years. On leaving the centre of the capital, we were taken to a popular, open-air museum, which contained old buildings and historic windmills dating back some 350 years.

As we travelled further on, we came across more and more heavily forested areas. Our guide explained that forestation accounts for 25 per cent of land-use in Norway; 55 per cent in Sweden; 60 per cent in Finland but only 11 per cent in Denmark, which is principally farming land; 70 per cent of the land is cultivated. Denmark has an important agricultural economy.

This is as true today as it has been for centuries past. However, although farming remains the main economic industry in Denmark, the number of people involved in it has declined greatly and consistently over recent years. Less than one million people are now involved in farming-related industries. The main crop is grain, covering some 60 per cent of the available land. Denmark is among the top seed producing economies in the world.

Included in the tour, was a visit to the famous Frederiksborg Slot. The Danes always translate *Slot* as 'castle,' but in most cases we would describe such a building as a manor house. Frederiksborg Slot is situated in North Zeeland. It was built between 1560 and 1620 for King Frederick II and King Christian IV. In 1859 much of the interior was destroyed by fire. Rebuilding and restoration work to original specifications began in 1877, led by the vision of J.C. Jacobsen, of Carlsberg brewing fame, who wanted the castle to be a museum of Danish history. Today it is one of the most beautiful castles in northern Europe, housing the Museum of National History and doubling as the summer residence of the Danish Royal Family. Visitors are permitted only when the royals are elsewhere!

The castle's chapel fortunately escaped the fire of 1859 and still houses intact one of the oldest German organs in the world. However, perhaps the most impressive and memorable room in the entire castle is the Ballroom. It is gorgeous. A flight of imagination allowed me to imagine myself dancing around this beautiful grand room, full of costumes, colour, vitality and conversation; Flemish tapestries and paintings grace every wall. What heady days those must have been!

From Frederiksborg, we travelled to Castle Croneborg, which enjoys a worldwide reputation for being haunted by Hamlet's ghost. More of this in a moment. The castle is very imposing, rebuilt in the Dutch renaissance style about 1574 from the remains of an earlier building belonging to Erik de Pomeranie, King of Denmark, Sweden and Norway (1397-1439). It is a royal residence of great character created by Frederick II, Christian IV and their successors.

The ground floor has been converted into a Maritime and Trading museum. Here one can see a very interesting collection of ancient objects telling the story of Danish navigation and sea trading from the time of the Vikings to today.

Our guide told us a most interesting story. This was the tragic story of Hamlet. A French author whose work was later taken over and developed by William Shakespeare originally scribed the tragedy of Hamlet, Prince of Denmark. The Danish texts, which date back to the twelfth century, tell us about a certain Hamlet, living sometime during the seventh century, whose father was a Prince of Jutland. In spite of this evidence, some historians doubt the existence of a real Hamlet and point to local folklore and legend for an explanation. Perhaps his ghost will clarify the matter some day? Whatever the answer to Hamlet is, it remains to say that Croneborg castle is one of the principal tourist attractions of Denmark. Furthermore, it is one of the richest and most opulent palaces in the whole of Scandinavia. It impressed me so much that I left it with great regret. It is truly one of the brightest jewels of construction in the world.

During my stay in Copenhagen, I was invited one Sunday to spend the day, outside the capital, in a private castle, noted for its pure and typical eighteenth-century style. The castle, called Ledreborg, is situated near Lejre which in 1966 was a small village. Now it is a very overgrown village, popular with people who work in Copenhagen because it has low taxes, is on the main railway line and lies in pretty countryside.

I took the train from Copenhagen, arriving in Lejre in less than an hour. On leaving the train, I was met by the eldest daughter of the owner of the castle. She was a well-known photographer and reporter in Copenhagen: her name, the Countess Marie Holstein. She had a marvellous personality and was full of life. Off we went in her little car to the estate.

The castle of Ledreborg was built in 1603. In 1740, it became the property of Count Holstein, ancestor of the present owner who had married the daughter of the Grand Duchess Charlotte of Luxembourg. They were the happy parents of seven daughters.

The day of my visit, I had the honour to meet both the wife and the sister of Count Holstein. The Count's sister was the Princess Brigitte de Bourbon, widow of Count Jacques de Bourbon who had sadly been killed two years earlier (1964) in a terrible car accident. Count Jacques de Bourbon's sister Anne was married to Michael, the former King of Romania.

The family atmosphere was welcoming, simple and democratic. The entire family loved sporting activities, almost as much as they loved to travel. I was first introduced to and welcomed by the mother of this happy family. Lunch followed, it was served without any butler or servants, I was presented with a range of Danish specialities to eat and enjoy. Really a buffet-style marvel.

After lunch, one of the family took me for a walk in the grounds. Typically for Denmark and indeed for the other democratic countries of Scandinavia, the parkland was open for public walks and recreation, an entry charge of merely ten pence being requested. During our walk, I saw the deer and stags. The latter were wild and fierce and would have attacked us had we dared approach them.

The little village of Lejre is sited at the head of a fjord where, according to local legend, stands the throne of the ancient Kings of Denmark, dating back to the time of the Vikings. However, that was not all, a last surprise was in store! I found out during my trip that the paternal grandfather of Count Holstein had been Prime Minister of Denmark at the beginning of the 1900s. He was a forward-thinking and politically astute man, well qualified to advance his country.

Man should live to eat and not eat only to live

I was giving some thought to the fact that the majority of people who travel by plane attach a great deal of importance to the cuisine offered during the flight. In fact, I have known people who choose an airline solely on the basis of flight menus, choices offered and the quality of drinks provided. On this basis, the company 'SAS Catering is widely regarded as providing the best cuisine for its sister airline SAS Moreover, a visit to the SAS Catering factory has become one of the most interesting places for a tourist to experience.

The company, based in Copenhagen, started in October 1961 with an opening capital of 570,000 dollars. It supplies food daily to the SAS operations in Oslo, Athens, Düsseldorf, Frankfurt, Hamburg, Rome and Tokyo. Twenty-six other airlines use its products, in addition to various food chains and restaurants. In 1966, each day some 5,000 sandwiches, 3,000 hot prepared meals and 7,000 cold meals were produced.

As I toured a huge kitchen at SAS, there were 950 employees working away. Thirty-five cooks and thirty-eight assistants were employed just to butter the bread for the sandwiches! It was a vast operation with, among others, twenty-two bakers making 4,000 small round bread buns an hour, twenty-three speciality cake chefs and 220 general packers, wrapping up the prepared food for shipment. Each day, some 2,500 eggs and a ton of meat were used as well as 450 pounds of caviar each month and a ton of salmon.

The Director of SAS Catering was Mr. Geert Horst who told me that the annual income in the mid-1960s was of the order of 40 million Danish Krone.

During my tour, I remarked on the fact that there were far fewer women employed throughout the factory than men. Mr. Horst agreed saying that it was a shame that they could not attract more women to be involved in the packing and transportation part of the operation, which involved a large number of staff.

What was interesting was the international atmosphere of the place. There were cooks from every part of the world. Each country had its own transport containers. Into these were packed the cold plated food, the cakes, sandwich varieties, meat and prawns and, finally, the hot meals in sealed aluminium cartons. All this was done a couple of hours before the food was eaten on board.

Regarding Danish food in general, one of the most striking features for the tourist strolling through the streets and shops of Copenhagen is the elaborate and attractive way in which Danish sandwiches (Simorrebrod) are presented. Can you imagine that there are two hundred varieties of Simorrebrod!

Danish open sandwiches are normally on either rye or wheat bread with lots of butter and all sorts of crazy fillings and toppings. Not crazy for the Danes though; they seem to have a very clear idea about what goes with what. Some looked rather odd to me! They are still very popular, especially for lunch. Many people take them to work in lunch-boxes specially designed for the purpose.

The origin of these sandwiches dates back to the middle of the eighteenth century. John Montagu, the Earl of Sandwich, enjoyed playing card games. He enjoyed cards so much that he played day after day and sometimes throughout the twenty-four hours of the day. He did not want to have his card playing interrupted by having to eat proper meals; so little bread and meat snacks were invented which took his name. Since then, numerous variations of the filled bread layers have occurred. However, there remains one rule for use in polite society when eating a sandwich, and that is that a sandwich should always be eaten with a knife and fork! The playing cards are not essential!

L'Art de Vivre in Denmark

To experience the Danish style of living, one must eat and drink as the Danes themselves do. This is what I did. For breakfast: a glass of cold milk mixed with cream, eggs part-cooked with grilled Danish bacon (Danish chickens produce some five million eggs each day!) accompanied by various sorts of bread; white bread, round bread buns 'rundstykker' and black bread, butter bread, together with a whole host of different pastries. Danish butter is always on the table and is an important export product for Denmark. The Danes export two hundred tonnes of butter a day all around the world.

At lunchtime, sandwiches and speciality sandwiches such as the 'Amorrebrod' are enjoyed washed down with lager, apple juice or aquavit with a glass of sherry and a cup of coffee to end with.

In the afternoon, one would enjoy a cup of tea or coffee served with a selection of Danish pastries.

At dinner, local specialities are the order of the day, for example; conger-eel in butter or a trout dish. There are five hundred lakes in Denmark filled with fish. If not fish, then a pork speciality might be served, such as pork 'frikadelle.' To finish the meal, you will be recommended to partake a sort of thickened stewed red fruit puree.

Danish Arts and Crafts

It was certainly true that whilst I was enjoying my stay in Denmark I did not want to miss any opportunity of seeing Danish artists and craft workers at work. Danish designers have a worldwide reputation for creativity and style. They are especially noted for the design and manufacture of modern furniture, which is frequently highly original and trend-setting.

In the heart of Copenhagen, there was an exhibition taking place entitled *Den Permanente de Copenhagen*, which provided a forum for Danish artists and craft experts with a wide variety of interests and skills. Here they could display their work to attract sponsors and customers. The only real difficulty was to obtain admission to the exhibition!

Towards the close of the last century, there arose a feeling, all over Europe, that there ought to be a way of preserving and protecting traditional local arts and crafts, which were in danger of being lost forever by the rapid forward march of industrialisation. It was feared that the factory would kill the artist's craft. Therefore, in many countries, associations were formed with the object of keeping local crafts and traditional skills alive.

Here in Denmark it was an artist called Kay Bojesen who promoted the idea of grouping all the little workplaces of local artists and craftspeople into a Craft Village where they might enjoy some protection and be able to practise their art and sell their creations. Thus *Den Permanente* was born, back in 1931, for the protection and encouragement of Danish art and to display, sell and promote Danish craftwork. A committee was formed from the group of artists to decide upon standards and traditional quality of workmanship. As the years have passed by so has the reputation of this craft centre grown for its variety and its excellence. Only the best is shown. Only the best is sold. Whilst I was visiting I saw specialists and buyers from all over the world. The works on sale were presented with style and refinement. They had simplicity and beauty.

There were 250 members of the craft centre, including potters, carpenters, cabinet-makers, weavers, glassblowers, jewellers, workers in ceramics and many others. Among the cabinet-makers, one in particular caught my attention. He was Niels Vadder. In 1940, he had formed a partnership with another creative thinker, the architect Fuin Juhl. These two men worked together to bring a new creativity and perspective to Danish furniture design and production. They broke away from the idea of traditional furniture manufacturing and developed furniture that resembled modern art in its new free shapes and styles.

A young woman, Hanne Backhaus, was rapidly gaining status and popularity within the craft centre for her talent in printing fabrics. She would create her designs using carved woodblock or cut linoleum-printing methods. The Danish designs and methods employed were largely traditional.

As for Kay Bojesen, the creator of Den Permanente, he also became well known worldwide for his Danish design work in silver, which belonged to the classic modern school. Equally, the famous *Bojesen Monkey* continues to be one of the most famous and popular exhibits. Copies of the monkey are suspended in children's playrooms and bedrooms the world over. Kay Bojesen is reported to have said, "What it consists of is not necessarily the precise representation of a real monkey but rather what one thinks a monkey may look like!"

A lucky accident! During my stay in Copenhagen, the annual festival of Danish ballet, opera and music was being held at the Royal Opera House for a fortnight. It attracted visitors from far and wide. The Danish ballet is very famous It has been in existence for over a hundred years and has played to audiences all over the world. It is continually setting new challenges for the years to come. It excels in classical ballet, as well as being able to adapt to and perform modern dance composition. Both dancers and technicians are wonderful.

Sex - Too Soon or Not?

I cannot leave Scandinavia without offering you some of my thoughts on Sex in Scandinavia. The topic of sex was widely and frequently discussed in all the Scandinavian countries I visited. It was one of the major 'problems' that preoccupied people and the State. The large social institutions and state schools hold that it is vital and necessary to educate the young concerning sexual matters.

Young people, it is said, should be fully aware of their sexual capacities and also be aware of the problems that can occur. Thus, there are widely presented films in the cinema on the subject; programmes on television; and explicit explanations and pictures in certain, readily available, magazines and books.

However, some people believe that by educating children in sexual matters at a young age it is possibly encouraging them to experiment with sex too early in their lives. However, what is certain is that the young of Scandinavia are exposed to sexual matters and that there is an environment of sexual openness surrounding them. I found, however, that there was a very high percentage of illegitimate children.

Although Scandinavia is an integral part of Europe, each time I visited I felt that I was in another part of the world and not within a European zone. Whether rich or poor, nobleman or working man, the people of Scandinavia all received and enjoyed a full education. All had excellent manners. As I wandered in the streets, everyone I met was clean, well dressed and polite. For me, Scandinavia was a most civilised place, on a higher plane than most countries in the world.

*Above: The Château de Montmirail, the country home of the Duke and Duchess de La Rochefoucauld.
Below: The Duchess de La Rochefoucauld (right) with Alain Poher, President of the French Senate, and
Isis.*

THE DUCHESS DE LA ROCHEFOUCAULD

In 1946 I left Egypt to study the history of art at the Ecole du Louvre in Paris. Shortly after my arrival I was invited to a reception in the Egyptian Embassy at 2, place des Etats-Unis[1] given by the Egyptian Ambassador, Ahmed Sarwat who was an old family friend. At that gathering I had the honour of meeting Madame la Duchesse Edmée de La Rochefoucauld. I was so happy to meet this *grande dame* who was so widely respected in Parisian society.[2] As we talked, a strong affinity seemed to spring up between us, leading to a friendship which was to last for more than forty years and was brought to an end only by the death of the Duchess. I left the reception with an invitation to dinner at 8, place des Etats-Unis, the Paris residence of the Duke and Duchess de La Rochefoucauld.

For the next three years the friendship between the Duchess and myself grew steadily closer; I was often invited to *le grand 8* as their mansion was familiarly known. In 1949 I returned to Egypt where I started my career as a journalist, an occupation which later gave me the opportunity to spend two or three months in Paris nearly every year. During my absence, Edmée and I kept up a regular correspondence.

Edmée's father was Count Edmond de Fels; her mother was Jeanne Lebaudy, the heiress to the family sugar refinery interests. In 1917, Edmée married Duc Jean de La Rochefoucauld, thus becoming the Duchess de La Rochefoucauld. They had four children: Isabelle, the present Countess; François, the present Duke who is married to Jeanne-Marie de Villiers Terrage, the present Duchess de La Rochefoucauld; Philippe, now deceased; and Solange, who has taken the family name of her husband – Fasquelle, the well-known publisher.

Solange herself is a writer. Her latest book on the La Rochefoucauld dynasty, enjoyed great success when it appeared in 1992. She brought vividly to life the many family ancestors, recounting accurately and in great detail the story of a family famous for hundreds of years in the history of France. I have known her since she was fourteen. She has a striking personality, showing in her character some of the features so prominent in her mother. Solange's only daughter Ariane, pretty and charming, was the Duchess's favourite granddaughter. In keeping with family tradition, Ariane now follows a career in publishing.

1 *The mansion at no. 2 had been bought from the La Rochefoucauld family by the Egyptian government to house its residents. The combination of proximity to 'le grand 8' and former ownership had led to the establishment of warm and friendly relations between the occupants of the two properties*
2 *There were several duchesses in Paris, but it was always Edmée who was known and referred to simply as 'the Duchess.'*

I had the greatest admiration for the Duke de La Rochefoucauld (the Duchess's husband). In his style, elegance and manner he was a worthy representative of the French aristocracy. I see him now, as he was every evening, always in a dinner jacket, whether there were guests or not at the place des Etats-Unis or at his château in Montmirail. Handsome, tall, slender and blue-eyed, for me he had many similarities with Sir Anthony Eden, who was often considered to be the world's most elegant man.

The Duke did not much care for social life. He never accompanied the Duchess to her various social functions, although he was always present at the lunches and dinners given at their residence in Paris where he showed the utmost courtesy to guests. One of his main interests was the town of Montmirail, of which he was Mayor for many years. In 1970 the Town Council of Montmirail re-named an avenue after him for his services to the community.

The Duke died peacefully in his sleep in January 1970 after fifty-three years of marriage to the Duchess, who telephoned me with the bad news, saying, "You are a dear friend, the Duke you were so fond of is no more." Like all the close friends of the family I went with the customary flowers to pay my respects at their Paris home. It was a truly sad occasion for everybody; to me, the passing of the Duke seemed to signify the end of an era, for in him I saw the last representative of the old aristocracy. Shortly after his death, the Duchess said, "For the fifty-three years we were together I always used to tell my husband everything about the receptions and dinners I had attended. Now it is all over. I am alone."

The Duchess's earliest hobby was painting. As a girl she was a pupil of Lévy Dhurmer. The first time I went into her study she showed me several portraits of some of her friends such as Paul Valéry and André Maurois and especially some fine lifelike portraits of her children and her husband. The Duchess was an ardent feminist. "Do you know," she said to me, "that in 1927 I joined the fight to secure votes for women. The studio on the same floor as the flat where you are living was our headquarters. From there we worked to obtain women's right to vote, which General de Gaulle granted in 1945." Once the right to vote had been obtained, she continued to work ceaselessly for women's civil rights, directing the publication of the magazine *L'Union Nationale des Femmes* and wrote a book entitled *La Femme et ses Droits* (Women and their Rights).

I was greatly interested in the books that the Duchess de La Rochefoucauld published, for she took an interest in literature at an early age. In 1925, her first books were poems, which she published under the name Gilbert Mauge. What particularly struck me in her writings was the method she used. For the most part they were short stories and observations about the various people she had met and remarks about her philosophy of life. Had she subconsciously drawn inspiration from the *Maximes de La Rochefoucauld*? Her greatest work was a three-volume set of critical essays entitled *Upon Reading the Notebooks of Paul Valéry*. In acknowledgement, the French Academy awarded her the Prix Bordin' in 1968. This work, which attracted great interest and acclaim in French intellectual and literary circles, was a commentary on the notes made by the Duchess during her conversations with Valéry, a close personal friend who stayed many times at Montmirail. So the Duchess had a dual source of knowledge of Valéry and of the 28,000 pages of his personal reflections. "It is possible," the Duchess told me, "to discover in Valéry's most private labours the very germ of his thoughts on problems of language, criticism, even his own personal metaphysics and his strange mathematics of the mind." During one of my stays at Montmirail, Edmée talked to me at length about the works of Valéry, especially about *De l'Académie Française au Collège de France*, adding that this particular work represented thirteen years of the Academician's life. Amongst other works, he published *L'Ame et la Danse*, *Méditations sur Descartes* and *Essai sur Stendhal*. "When I was writing my book," added Edmée, "I tried to extract from some nine thousand pages the main thoughts of Valéry. He himself wrote of his note-books, *'Ces cahiers sont mon vice'* (These notebooks are my vice)."

Apart from her work on Valéry, Edmée has published several books on a variety of subjects, *Femme d'Hier et d'Aujourd'hui*, *Spectateurs*, *L'Angoisse et les Ecrivains*, *L'Acquiescement*. *De l'Ennui*, on the subject of death, was one of her favourites. Edmée's work and interests in the field of literature were again recognised when she was made a member of the Belgian Royal Academy. She also received several literary prizes and decorations from foreign countries and the *médaille de Vermeil* from the City of Paris. She was President of various literary committees and was made a *Commandeur de la Légion d'Honneur*, a rare achievement for a woman. For many years the Duchess was the president of the ladies' section of the Cercle Interallié and was deeply involved in its social and cultural activities. She also enjoyed travelling all over the world and was often asked to lecture on French literature and culture.

The Duchess was fair-haired and blue-eyed, an elegant figure with her high waist, straight back and handsome legs. There was an element of stiffness in her bearing and manner, developed I think to conceal an inner shyness which showed itself to close friends in private surroundings. Fashion interested her, as did most things. I used to accompany her to the autumn collections at the Paris fashion houses. Not that she spent a great deal on dresses. There was no nonsense about her. She thought that extravagance on clothes was ridiculous, telling me, "I always go to a little shop in the rue de Passy. I can find dresses at reasonable prices there." For each of the four major receptions she gave each year, she felt she had to have a new dress, her femininity went as far as that, but did not extend to spending a small fortune in order to impress or look glamorous.

A good judge of character, Edmée knew who her true friends were and always remained faithful to them. I admired the interest and kindness she took in her staff. She did not like to tire them. It was rare for there to be any changes, except for retirement. All her staff repaid her with loyalty to the end of her days.

I often heard members of Edmée's family say, for example, "On Tuesday we're having lunch at *le grand 8* with mother, 12.45 on the dot." They knew not to be late. For their mother, punctuality was all important. At lunch or dinner, if a guest was late arriving it did not matter how important he was, an Ambassador, politician or writer, the meal started at the appointed time. Edmée did not like her guests to linger over their meals either. I would not say that she rushed them through it, but she was apt to bring the meal to an abrupt close when a quick glance told her that everyone had finished. However, her quick glance sometimes failed to spot the slow eater who had to forego what was still on the plate.

On Sundays I used to go for lunch with the Duchess and three or four of her friends at one of the little restaurants on the Champs-Elysées before we all went off to the cinema. Edmée had no chauffeur on Sundays so I used to pick her up from No. 8 in my little Renault. My flat is on the rue de Grenelle, close to the rue Cler (the well known market). One Sunday I lost track of time looking at the shops and market stalls and listening to politicians who at election times used to mingle with the shoppers and stall-holders, shaking hands and generally trying to make themselves popular. I stayed too long at the busy scene. I rushed back to my flat for the car, but too late. I arrived for Edmée at ten minutes past the appointed time. She was waiting for me outside the door, looking anxiously up and down the street, "I was worried," she told me, "I thought you had had an accident. I've been here for at least five minutes!" In her mind, an accident was the only possible explanation. She herself had the uncanny knack of never being late for her appointments. I do not know how she did it, especially as her days were always full. I suppose she thought that if she could be on time, everyone else could as well! Today's volume of traffic in Paris would be a stern test for her all the same.

Edmée owned several radios but her favourite was a tiny portable; she always had it with her when she went from room to room or was out walking in the grounds. She could not conceive of the idea of not being up to date with the latest events. She always wanted to know the news as soon as it was broadcast. In her last years when she was confined to her bedroom and sat in her armchair to receive visits from Ambassadors, politicians and friends (never more than four at a time), everyone was amazed at how well informed she was about current affairs. One day she treated me to a radio identical to hers. I still have it. When she offered it to me, she said, " It's practical to carry around, especially when you are travelling." I take it with me whenever I go away. It keeps me company, a precious and ever-present reminder of a wonderful person for whom I retain so much affection.

The Duchess played a major part of my life in Paris. For she became a second mother, affectionate and protective, as well as an incomparable guiding friend, always faithful and true, as she was towards all those to whom she extended the hand of friendship.

I remember the occasion when a jealous lady began to criticise me to the Duchess. Before she had spoken more than a few disagreeable words Edmée cut her short. "Isis is my friend, I will hear nothing against her." She had no time for malicious gossip. From her I learnt much, especially how to react and behave towards people who were determined to be offensive and insulting. Edmée would refuse to listen, turn her back with the words, "I don't want to know."

She taught me to take no notice of jealousies and pettiness, to answer them with indifference and not to descend to the same level. Even now, if I find myself in similar situations I hear Edmée's advice and follow it.

Life was never boring in Edmée's company. For all her intellectual interests and pursuits, she needed distraction and gaiety. She had a ready wit and liked nothing more than to laugh. Her daily routine resembled perpetual motion. She was always on the go. She liked to be everywhere. "Well," she would say to me, "these people have invited me; they will be disappointed if I don't go." This was perfectly true. At cocktail parties guests would look forward to her presence. As soon as she arrived everyone would say, "The Duchess is here!" Calmly, without fuss, she would go every evening to receptions, sometimes four, six or even more, but she never stayed at any of them for long. Ten minutes maximum. On the occasions she asked me to accompany her 'on her rounds' I must admit it was sometimes irritating. I would begin to have an interesting conversation with someone only to have the Duchess come up and whisper, "Come on, we must go!" There was no way out of it. We went.

Edmée came into my life on an almost daily basis. Two days never went by without a phone call from her at 08.30 in the morning. It would go like this: – "Is that you Isis? What are you doing on such and such a day? Lunch? Dinner? Would you be interested in coming with me to such and such a lecture, reception or film?" Edmée was a cinephile. Although the cinema was part of Sunday's routine, she had to see the big, much advertised, new films as soon as possible, on a weekday if necessary. Her life was like a well-regulated clock: eight o'clock, breakfast; eight-thirty onwards, telephone calls; ten o'clock, a walk in the Bois de Boulogne; eleven o'clock, back to her study to deal with her correspondence. Letters were answered the day they arrived. Afternoons and evenings were also highly organised.

In early December 1972 I received news that my mother was seriously ill. I immediately flew back from Paris to Cairo. Two days later, on 6th December I was present at my mother's bedside when she died. I returned to Paris on 20th December. I had loved my mother dearly. Losing her was the saddest and most painful event in my life. As soon as I was back in Paris, Edmée came to see me and continued to call every day to enquire how I was, trying to persuade me to go out with her when I really wanted to be by myself. "No, no," she would say, "you must not remain alone and stay in all the time." I shall always remember that Christmas Eve. Edmée had invited me to go to No. 8 for a quiet dinner, just the two of us. When I arrived about seven o'clock she was just looking at the many presents that had been sent to her. She told Arturo, her butler, to put all the presents in my car. Although I resisted, she would not accept no for an answer. I was very touched. I still have a velvet covered jewellery box, a black feather boa and a woollen cape knitted by one of her friends. Edmée then decided it would be more fun if we had dinner out. Perhaps it was what she had intended all the time. She took me to one of her favourite restaurants, an English Victorian style pub on the Champs Elysées. I can still remember what we ate.

Slowly, Edmée helped me to overcome my grief. Nothing illustrates better her affection and concern on my behalf.

Every year the Duke and Duchess spent the month of July in their château at Montmirail. Edmée loved the country air and whenever I was staying with them she would say to me, "Breathe in, breathe in deeply, my child!" My visits to the château date from 1946 when I was a student in Paris. I remember the very first time I was invited to stay and how greatly impressed I was by its majestic grandeur. The Duchess welcomed me with great courtesy. The staff immediately took my luggage out of the car and off to my allotted room. Edmée said, "Follow me, I will take you to your room. If there is anything you want tell me and I will make sure the chambermaid sees to it. What do you like for breakfast? Tea or coffee? What time?" She gave the instructions to her butler, Arturo, who each morning knocked on my door at the exact time and passed the tray to the chambermaid, who brought it to me in bed, the solid silver eighteenth century service carefully arranged on the silver tray.

For more than thirty years I stayed in the same room on the first floor of the right wing of the château, above the Duchess's rooms. The furnishings were seventeenth century style – classic four-poster bed, a desk, dressing table and a large armchair. Over the years, all the bedrooms were modernised with bathrooms added. In the mornings I liked to stay in my room to write but this caused a little problem. I was supposed to be out of the room by 10.30 at the latest so that it could be cleaned.   When the chambermaid came to do the room I would say, "Everything is clean and tidy. Just make the bed and clean the bathroom," and I would continue writing in my chair. It was a little secret between us. But if by chance I remarked that I was feeling tired or had not slept well, this news was reported immediately to the Duchess who was supposed to be kept informed about everything. Then when I saw her she would say, "It seems you slept badly last night." The chambermaid was a local girl from the village taken on for the month of July. The cook, Victoria, was Spanish. She was Edmée's cook and chambermaid in Paris and always came to Montmirail with her. One day she came to my room to tell me, "You are lucky, Miss, because the Duchess loves you."

At 11.30am I would go and meet the Duchess in the grounds. She would be sitting in a chaise-longue reading. She could easily read a book a day. Being a member of several literary panels awarding annual prizes, of which the most well known was the Prix Femina, she would read some fifty books during her stay at Montmirail. When we were alone together she would talk at length about various subjects, but especially about her philosophy of life. "Who knows what awaits us after our life on earth!" she would say. She was fond of quoting a sentence from Marcel Proust. '*Mort à jamais qui peut le dire?*' (Dead forever, who can say so?) Her great strength lay in her ability to meditate and ponder, to analyse and to synthesise. In fact she suffered unconsciously from an excess of talent. I think that is why she gave me to understand that of all the books she had written, she considered *De l' Ennui* (On Boredom) one of the best. On a different subject, one day she confided how much she still suffered from the theft from her safe in Paris of the original manuscript of the *Maximes de La Rochefoucauld*[1] one of her favourite books. Returning from the theatre one evening, she found the safe open and all her jewellery and the priceless manuscript gone. Despite lengthy investigations and the involvement of Interpol, no arrest was ever made, and nothing was ever recovered.

After a good hour spent in the grounds with their massive age-old trees, it would be time for lunch, always served at 12.45. Then to the library for coffee and above all, chocolates. All the Duchess's friends who came to Montmirail knew that chocolates were her great weakness. I liked them too, and so did they. Therefore, they always brought boxes of the highest quality. If twenty friends were invited, there would be at least that many boxes. Edmée would insist that one box had to be finished before another could be opened. Occasionally this took time, as some boxes weighed two kilos! Then a guest would whisper in my ear that the Leonidas[2] had to be eaten quickly because they would not keep for long. I told the Duchess who said, "What do you think? Perhaps we had better make a start on them." I agreed and everybody was happy!

After a short siesta in one's room, it would be time for the afternoon walk. Four o'clock sharp. The Duchess would have it all organised. Sometimes she phoned neighbouring gentry saying, "Would it be convenient for me to call on you this afternoon? I have two or three friends staying with me." We would be back by about half-past five, to be advised, "Aperitifs in the drawing-room at 7.15, dinner at 7.30." The drawing-room was magnificent in all respects but I particularly remember the marvellous Chinese vases. After dinner, Edmée led the way into the library for everyone to watch television. Even on holiday she maintained a strictly disciplined daily life. The routine was traditional!

When we were alone, she would say, "If you don't want to change for dinner it's not important." But she always did. In the days when entertaining at the château was at its grandest I had to take a whole wardrobe to change three times a day: the right clothes for lunch; a suit for the afternoon; a dress for dinner.

Every week-end in July it was a tradition for Edmée to entertain some of her close friends – for example, the Duke de Castries[3] and his wife, Prince and Princess Dedeyan, Princess Marie-Louise de Robech. Madame Cino del Duca was a frequent visitor at Edmée's Sunday lunches. The Duchess had a natural talent for organisation. Weekends apart, she always had a friend staying at Montmirail to keep her company. Sometimes it was me and other days it would be the artist-sculptress Elizabeth de Selva. Naturally there was always a happy relationship between the Duchess and myself at Montmirail, but one day Edmée asked me if I would be giving my traditional cocktail party at the end of October. "Yes, and I have had a good idea. I shall be sending the invitations for

---

1 The famous work of François, Duc de La Rochefoucauld, 1613–80. Some 500 concise, well-constructed aphorisms, which identified egoism as being the general motive of human conduct.
2 A brand of white chocolates filled with cream.
3 An eminent member of the Académie Française.

6.00pm to 10.00pm. That way, people who have other cocktail parties or dinners to go to, can come early. Younger people who have their work can come late." Edmée made no comment, but put on a grave face. I could see she was not happy. An hour or so later, after lunch, she said, "About your party, will you be putting me with the older people?" "No, no, my dear lady! My home is your home. You come when you wish. I would be delighted if you stayed all the time." Having said this, I could see that Edmée was hurt. I was embarrassed and did not know what to say. I repeated, "For you there is no timetable. Come when you like. Your presence will be an honour."

October came, the day of the cocktail party arrived. So did Edmée – at 9.15pm. Not only could she not bear to be considered old, she just had to know what the younger elements were thinking and doing.

Every Sunday the Duchess and her guests attended Mass, sitting in the family pews. The village church at Montmirail had originally been the private church belonging to the château. When I went with the Duchess we had access to the church by a door in the château. If I wanted to attend Mass without going into the church, there was a corridor on the first floor leading to a room where I could see the service in the church from inside the château.

My visits to Montmirail were a source of endless fascination and remain a wonderful memory. From books and films one may learn about country-house life, but at Montmirail I experienced it at its best. I have stayed in other such châteaux, where not only the building had been modernised, but the way of life as well. For me, there is no comparison. The Duchess always maintained a form of discipline appropriate to her traditional way of life; her guests were expected to respect her code, and did so.

I found the history of the château of Montmirail and its links with events in French history very interesting. A hundred kilometres to the east of Paris, Montmirail-en-Brie, a small town of some four thousand inhabitants is situated where three regions come together – Picardie, Ile de France and Champagne-Ardenne. Even before the twelfth century there was a fortress at Montmirail. The twelfth-century castle itself stood on the same site as the present building that was slowly rebuilt and enlarged in the sixteenth and seventeenth centuries, with later owners making significant additions and alterations.

Its historic associations are numerous. Joan of Arc passed through on her march to Paris after attending the coronation of Charles VII in Rheims. Paul de Gondi, the future Cardinal de Retz,[1] was born there. Saint Vincent de Paul[2] lived for sixteen years in a room there and acted as tutor to the young Gondi.

---

1 *Cardinal de Retz 1614-79. A lover of political intrigue and conspiracies, he played a colourful and chequered rôle in the often turbulent minority years of Louis XIV. Finally disgraced and imprisoned, he was pardoned by Louis in 1662 on condition that he gave up the position of Archbishop of Paris. His famous* Mémoires, *published some thirty years after his death, gave a lively account of the events and leading personalities of his age.*
2 *Saint Vincent de Paul 1576-1660. A simple shepherd-boy who became a priest. Renowned for his tireless efforts and benevolent works on behalf of the poor, the aged and the downtrodden. He founded the Sisters of Charity and was canonised in 1737.*

The room that Vincent occupied has been preserved as it was in his day. When I saw it for the first time I was impressed by its simplicity – a narrow bed, a table and a plain black cross. That is all. It reflected perfectly the spirit and life of this humble man. His portrait hangs on the wall. It was placed there after his death.

In 1678, Louvois, Louis XIV's well-known Minister of Defence, purchased the château. He carried out major improvements and embarked on large-scale landscaping of the grounds. The King found it very attractive and visited it on several occasions. Louvois bequeathed Montmirail to one of his daughters when she married the eighth Duke de La Rochefoucauld and the long association of Montmirail with the La Rochefoucauld family began.

The château and its owners emerged unscathed from the excesses of the French Revolution, but not from later events. Napoleon stayed there in February 1814 drawing up his plans for the battle of Marchais, later known as the Victory of Montmirail. Despite this success, Napoleon could not stop the progress of the invading Prussian, Russian and Austrian armies advancing from the East. Two months later Paris capitulated. Napoleon abdicated. Montmirail experienced the horrors of foreign occupation that brought looting and damage on an enormous scale. During the Franco-Prussian war of 1870-71 and the subsequent occupation of France until 1873, Montmirail suffered once more at the hands of the victorious Prussians, who set up a military hospital in the château and billeted soldiers in the outbuildings and nearby farms. Once again there was considerable loss and damage.

The 1914-18 war saw Montmirail at the heart of the Battle of the Marne in September 1914. The Germans occupied the château for a few days before it was recaptured. During the four years of the German occupation of France in the Second World War from 1940 to 1944, Montmirail escaped without major damage or interference. The Duke de La Rochefoucauld, who was also the Mayor of Montmirail, remained in residence throughout. A more or less happy ending to invasions and occupations now thankfully and firmly a thing of the past.

Most of the weekends I spent at Montmirail were interesting, but some were exceptional. I remember particularly Saturday, 13th July 1985. The Duchess had invited Alain Poher, the President of the Senate who fascinated me with his strong personality, his charm and simplicity. He was a good talker, relaxed in company and always said what he thought both in private and in public. He was neither snobbish nor pretentious and enjoyed explaining the latest political events to his listeners.

For this weekend the Duchess had asked Gilbert Gantier to call and pick me up from my flat on the Saturday morning to take me with him to Montmirail. Gantier was (and still is) the MP for the important Paris sixteenth district. He arrived on time in his luxurious silver-grey car. Once clear of Paris we were soon travelling at high speed. Gantier remarked, "I hope the speed doesn't upset you. We are doing 200 km an hour." (125 mph). "Not at all, I replied, I hadn't noticed. It doesn't feel like it." We chatted from time to time. He was reserved, but said what he thought all the same. He was one of the leading members of the UDF

(Giscard d'Estaing's party). I asked him if he knew we were having lunch with Alain Poher. "No, I didn't. If I had known, I would have put on a dark suit." "No need, you look fine. It's a lunch in the country." I noticed he was wearing a Christian Dior tie, the same as one I had just bought for a friend's birthday. Everyone arrived at Montmirail on time, the cars driving up in procession.

There were twelve people at lunch. As I was looking for my place, Poher gave a smile, saying, "You're here, next to me." True enough, I was placed on his right. As I had dual nationality – Egyptian and French – on this occasion for the Duchess I was Egyptian and took precedence over other guests. The Duchess had placed Poher between us. I could see the high society guests looking in my direction, keeping a watchful eye on me. President Poher had brought with him his chief of cabinet, Gisèle Lourdeaux, a very intelligent and forceful woman. When lunch was over, she came up to me and said, "You were lucky to be able to talk to the President." "Yes, I replied, it was very interesting, as usual. It isn't the first time I have conversed with him." (He had even attended one of my cocktail parties, but I did not invite him again. What! The President of the Senate at Isis Fahmy's! His presence had set tongues wagging and caused some jealousy – especially among the men. My local MP had left the party in a huff, without a word of thanks, because that evening he was not the cock of the roost).

During the lunch, I had a political conversation with Poher. I started by asking him. "Why have you stopped giving your wonderful parties at the Senate?" "What! For those people![1] The idea of entertaining them does not interest me. It's out of the question!"

"I admire you for sticking to your guns, keep it up!" "That President Mitterrand," continued Poher, "is a real cunning one. He's terrible you know. We have to be even more cunning. I remember when I had a long conversation with him about private schools. He began by saying, 'You will be spilling blood in the streets, and what's more you want to.' He spent all his time trying to attack me and make me feel guilty, but I didn't rise to the bait. Then he said, 'Those three amendments that you discussed with me, I approve of them. Enforce them.' 'That is for you, the President of France, to do, not me.' I replied. Whereupon Mitterrand got to his feet and I thought the audience was over. But Mitterrand continued towards the door, pursuing the conversation.

I asked Poher, "What do you think about the forthcoming elections?" "I am very apprehensive. I keep on preaching union, union and I shall continue to do so. Giscard is all very well, but he isn't a man of the people. He does not get to grips with them. Chirac is decent, honest and loyal."

"Well then, Mr. President, who will you be voting for?" I asked. "That will depend on the circumstances at the time. One or the other!" Poher replied. I changed the subject and mentioned that I would soon be going to Brittany for my holidays. The President is a Breton. He was going to the Finistère region; I

---

1 *The Socialist government then in power.*

would be on the North coast. I brought up the subject of the painting exhibitions I organised at my Paris flat. "I remember last year you sent me a telegram saying you were unable to come." I said. "You must come this year; it is an exhibition of the work of two Breton artists, Aude de Kerros and Lohou." "Definitely two Breton names," replied Poher.

After lunch came the ceremony of the souvenir photographs. President Poher was the last of the luncheon party to leave. On his way out he came up to me and said he would come to my painting exhibition on 18th November.

All the guests thoroughly enjoyed the opportunity to meet and speak to Poher, who impressed everyone with his simple, relaxed manner.

The next really memorable date was 11th July 1986. The Duchess always used to find one of her guests to take me to Montmirail at the weekend. This time it was her best friend, Ambassador Pierre Siraud. He was one of the most popular Ambassadors in the Parisian salons, very refined, elegant and ironically witty. He had been Chief of Protocol for several years during the reign of General de Gaulle. At five o'clock, exactly the agreed time, he was knocking on my door. As he carried my case to his car he told me he already had a passenger, Professor John Rogister who had come over from England especially to spend a long weekend with the Duchess. Rogister was one of her closest friends. He was a professor at Durham University and spoke perfect French, with no trace of an accent. He was recently elected Membre correspondant de l'Institut des Sciences morales et politiques à l'Académie française, a rare honour for a foreigner. So there we were, the three of us on our way to Montmirail. I was in the company of two very interesting men. An hour and a half later we were all sitting in the drawing room with the Duchess. Usually after dinner everyone moved to the library, to watch television but on this occasion, the Duchess said there was nothing interesting to see and it would be better if we were to sit and talk, discussing events in France. After a while, I needed to go to the loo. Near the library was a bedroom with a bathroom en suite. In I went. Smoke everywhere, coming up from the ground floor. I ran back to give the alarm. Pierre Siraud went downstairs with me. The thermostat on the central heating system had burnt out because someone had left in on too high. It was ten o'clock at night. The staff had retired to their rooms. Pierre Siraud called the fire brigade, which arrived in time to prevent the flames spreading. It was fortunate that I needed the bathroom. During all the commotion the Duchess remained calm and impassive.

In May 1989 the Duchess told me she was having doubts about going to Montmirail that summer. She was beginning to find it difficult to go up and down all the stairs. She asked me what I thought about it. I replied, "Well, it will be healthier to breathe country air than to stay here in the polluted atmosphere of Paris, even if you can't manage the steps to the grounds." "That's what I think," Edmée remarked, "but would you be willing to come with me?" "Of course I will come and stay with you. You know that I enjoy keeping you company, and besides, I am very fond of Montmirail." "Thank you my dear, its very kind of you. This time there will not be any social gatherings." "Good," I replied, "in that case we shall be able to take life easy. It will be a rest cure." Edmée asked what dates would suit me. I said I would be glad not to be in Paris when the celebrations were on for the bicentenary of the start of the French Revolution. I would be stuck in my flat all the time. So it was agreed that I would travel to Montmirail on Sunday 9th July, the day after Edmée arrived. I would be driven there by Count Régis de Causans, an old friend of the Duchess. "This time," said Edmée, "I have only invited friends who are used to coming to Montmirail, because I don't know how well I might be!" On the Sunday, the lunch went well, in a pleasant, relaxed atmosphere. This was the first of the 'no social gatherings,' the first of many. What was it the Duchess had said about them? The habit had been too hard for her to break!

On 14th July, the bicentenary of the Revolution was celebrated in Montmirail as it was in towns and villages throughout France. On that day Edmée was determined to pay a visit to a Count who lived about twenty miles away; his castle was situated in a cul-de-sac in the centre of a village. When we arrived we found a crowd of villagers dressed in eighteenth-century costume. They were blocking the whole road through the village square. The car came almost to a stop. Arturo, the chauffeur, had to wait for people to move out of the way to let us through. It wasn't easy. The crowd did not co-operate. It took us a quarter of an hour to travel the few yards to where the Count was waiting behind the railings of his castle gates with a look of concern on his face. It required patience, calmness and especially a show of indifference towards the crowd milling, looking and shouting all around us. Finally we arrived safely. I must admit I was quite scared. Edmée of course remained unperturbed throughout the proceedings.

It was during this holiday at Montmirail that Edmée's son Philippe returned home finally discharged from hospital where he had spent many weeks recovering from very serious injuries sustained in a car accident. He adored his mother, both of them were so happy to be reunited. "You know," Philippe told me, "I have come back from a faraway place. Everybody thought I was going to kick the bucket." His recovery was a miracle.

Never before had I looked so closely at my room in the château, observing all the small details and asking myself if I would ever see it again, if I would ever return. For the last four years the Duchess had said to me, "Say your farewells to Montmirail, this is the last time." Each time I had asked, "Why do you say that?" and each time I heard the same reply. "I shall no longer be of this world." During her last years Edmée had thought more and more about death. It troubled her greatly and she often used to say to me. "Alas, time passes too quickly for me." Now the last time had indeed come. After that summer we never went back to Montmirail. For the happiness I experienced during all those lovely days at the château I owe the Duchess my heartfelt gratitude, as I do for so much in my life, which she influenced for the better.

ANDRE MAUROIS

It was an encounter in 1966 that opened the way for me to interview one of France's most celebrated writers of the century, André Maurois. At a lunch given by the Duchess de La Rochefoucauld I met her eldest daughter, Countess Isabelle de La Rochefoucauld. She was Maurois' secretary. I asked her if it might be possible to obtain an interview with him. The Countess promised to see what could be done and suggested that I should call her in a couple of days. The day after our conversation, I read the front-page headline "André Maurois seriously ill." I must admit that my first reaction was a selfish one that luck was not on my side. Then I felt regret that the famous author was ill. In the circumstances I obviously could not pursue the matter of an interview; it was only some weeks later, when Maurois' health was improving, that I contacted the Countess. Maurois was out of Paris, convalescing in his country house. However, I was invited to submit my questions in writing; in due course I received a charming and courteous letter from the author, together with the answers to my questions.

Before recounting this written interview, let me say a little about his background and his career. André Maurois was born in 1885 in the small town of Elbeuf in northern France, not far from Rouen. He came from a family of industrialists who had moved to Elbeuf from Alsace after the Franco-Prussian war. In 1918 he wrote the successful *Les Silences du Colonel Bramble*. an amusing and perceptive study of an English officers' mess during the First World War. For this and a similar work, *Les Discours du Docteur O'Grady*, which followed four years later, Maurois drew on his experiences as a liaison officer with the British forces. The English versions were widely read.

Maurois' reputation on both sides of the Channel grew with essays on English writers and *The History of Edward VII and his Times*. His romantic biographies of Shelley, Disraeli and Byron became very popular in England. Other major works include studies of Voltaire and Proust, biographies of George Sand, Hugo and Balzac, and popular histories of England and the United States.

Maurois also published collections of essays and lectures dating from the time he spent in the United States during the Second World War as a professor at Princeton University. He was elected to the French Academy in 1938.

And so to the interview.

"For you, is being a writer a vocation?"

"Yes, it has been since childhood. I always thought there was no finer profession; as soon as I was in a position to give all my time to it, I gave up any other occupation."

"How difficult was it for you to find your literary direction?"

"I didn't give it a thought. I wrote my first book because it was something I very much wanted to do. After that, everything became easy."

"What are your views on twentieth-century writers and especially on the *nouveau roman?*"[1]

"I think there have been three generations of French writers in the twentieth century. One is older than I am; its leading members in my opinion are Valéry, Gide and Claudel. Then comes my own generation. Here, I particularly admire Mauriac, Romains, Montherlant and perhaps Sartre. Finally, the generation of the *nouveau roman,* my favourites being Butor, Robbe-Grillet, Sarraute and Claude Mauriac. To be truthful, I don't think the 'new novel' is very new. Flaubert and even Balzac have already put all its ideas into practice. Still, it is a good thing for each generation to think it is new.

"Would you like to write a novel in the new style?"

"Yes, I have often thought it would be amusing to do a pastiche of the genre – under a pseudonym."

"Your most recent venture into the theatre was your much acclaimed adaptation of Shaw's *Don Juan*[2]. Are you thinking of doing anything else?"

"Not at present, but circumstances may lead me in that direction."

"Do you subscribe to the view that the modern theatre is in decline?"

"There have been some talented playwrights recently – Anouilh, Ionesco, Beckett, but the 'new theatre' does not meet the needs of the public. To draw audiences, drama festivals have to put on Shakespeare, Molière and Corneille."

"As President of the Cannes Film Festival, would you give me your opinion of the *Nouvelle Vague*[3] in the cinema? Are you sorry to see the disappearance of classical ideals? What direction do you think the cinema will take in the future?"

"The *nouvelle vague* has produced some fine works – for example *Last Year in Marienbad.* As for the future, only time will tell. However, I think the cinema might well come to concentrate more on the poetic and the fantastic."

"Now that television is part of everyday life, do you think it has any influence on young people?"

"It certainly has; a good one in so far as it improves people's vocabulary and introduces them to great works of literature; it is harmful when it portrays scenes of violence which are then imitated in real life. Incidentally, I also think that television should make greater use of authors to educate the young in cultural matters. I believe such a policy would be very successful."

"Of all the books you have written, is there one for which you have a particular fondness?"

1 *The 'New Novel' based on the view that events have no collective significance or order.*
2 *Shaw's "Man and Superman."*
3 *'New Wave.' Name given to a movement in the late 1950s led by a group of young French directors aiming to bring greater realism to the cinema.*

"It is difficult for an author to choose his favourite work. He always has an affection for the 'last-born'. That is why I like my *Balzac*. Others that come to mind are *The Life of Disraeli* and my short stories *Pour Piano Seul*."[1]

"Once you have finished a book, do its characters live on in your memory?"

"They remain with me. For example, I am currently writing a collection of short stories in which all the characters from my novels re-appear. It will be called *Les Retours*."[2]

"You recently stated your views on ethics and medicine. Do your beliefs apply to all branches of science? I am thinking particularly of nuclear science."

"Yes. The moral code of medicine is respect for the individual. The same should apply in all sciences. A physicist must also be a humanist and concern himself not only with his discoveries but also with their impact on humanity."

"Do you have any strongly felt political doctrine?"

"I think that a well constructed democracy is what offers people the most happiness, but everything depends on the character of the nation; what suits one may not be good for another.

Your final question was about my memoirs. Yes, I hope to publish them and I am working on them at present. I hope your readers will enjoy my replies to your questions and regret that I was unable to speak with you personally."

André Maurois died some months later at the age of eighty-two.

1 *"For Unaccompanied Piano."*
2 *"Going Back."*

COUNTESS DE LA BAUME

In 1990, two years before her death and when she was already quite ill, it became clear to the Duchesse de La Rochefoucauld that she could no longer continue as President of the Cercle Interallié. There was only one person whom she thought suitable to replace her and that was her niece Hélène, Countess de la Baume, the daughter of her brother the Count de Fels, who was one of the founders of the Cercle Interallié in Paris.

I came to know Hélène in 1970. A pretty blonde, what impressed me about her was her class. She has a strong, well-balanced personality and the ability to make the objective decisions on the spur of the moment, if need be. A faithful friend, she always shows unfailing devotion to all, albeit very discreetly. Her life has been a happy one, lived in easy circumstances, but she has devoted much of it to helping the poor and doing social work. She appears to me the very model of French aristocracy at its best.

Hélène was the only daughter of the Count de Fels, a man of cold appearance, yet cheerful at heart, if somewhat ironic. At the Paris mansion at 31 rue Octave-Feuillet where Hélène was born – one of the finest mansions in the sixteenth arrondissement – her mother, Marthe de Fels[1] presided over a renowned salon at which she entertained a select group of interesting prominent figures. It was not easy to obtain an invitation from Marthe. I was lucky enough to be introduced by one of her friends, and as Marthe's salon was international in its outlook, an Egyptian like me was made welcome. Marthe entertained in the style of bygone days. All the items at her lavish buffets were prepared on the premises by her chef – no sending out for canapés, petit fours and the like. Hélène enjoyed a very happy childhood. She was brought up by an English nurse, which in those days meant there was an emphasis on discipline and sport! When Hélène came out in society at the age of eighteen, there was in her set a certain gentleman whose position was Treasury Inspector at the Ministry of Finance by the name of Giscard d'Estaing. The story is still told of how she turned down his offer of marriage. Later he was to become the President of France. Hélène denies the truth of the story, yet an addition to it still circulates to the effect that Hélène's mother became quite cross with her when later Giscard d'Estaing was elected President. Marthe is supposed to have remarked to her daughter, "Never mind that you could have been the wife of the President of the Republic; I could have been the mother of the wife of the President of the Republic."

---

1 *Born Marthe de Cumont, from an old French bourgeois family.*

At the age of twenty, Hélène married Count Olivier de la Baume, a member of an aristocratic family that could trace its ancestry back to Louise de la Vallière.[1] The wedding took place in Paris on 3rd July, 1946. The reception was held at the mansion in the rue Octave Feuillet. Hélène told me, "It was the first grand wedding after the war and was a spectacular occasion, with over three thousand guests. A day I shall never forget."

The marriage was a very happy one. Over the years, six children were born. Olivier worked in the import-export department of the Schneider company, and frequently had to travel throughout Europe, as well as further afield in Asia and the United States. Hélène's mother-in-law was so fond of her grandchildren that Hélène still says, "I was lucky because I had a mother-in-law who used to encourage me to go with my husband on his travels whilst she looked after my children. So for about fifteen years that is what I did. In those days few young women had the opportunity to travel so widely, especially to New York, which was always a great event." One day I asked Hélène. 'Were you ever pregnant on your travels?' "All the time."

The first social work in which Hélène became involved was in interesting circumstances. "It was in 1951," Hélène recounted to me, "A friend called on me to ask if I had a space heater, because one was needed by a certain Polish priest called Wresinsky. He was living in a tent in the Paris suburb of Joinville le Pont, with other igloo-shaped tents all around him. In this encampment Wresinsky was caring for a small colony of wretched homeless down-and-outs. So I started to go there every week, taking with me friends I recruited including a young American woman who supplied milk and other provisions."[2] At the same time, Hélène was involved in social work in the Benedictine parish at La Haye des Roses on the outskirts of Paris. The priest there, Father Jean de Féligonde was the first Benedictine monk in the world to found a parish, for it was a rule of the order that monks remain within their monastery.

When her last child was three years old, Hélène decided she could take a job. She obtained the position of Public Relations Officer at the Librairie Plon, a leading French publishing company. Here she met famous authors including de Gaulle, Kessler and Druon. "It was an exciting place to be," Hélène told me, "I used to accompany such authors when they were on television. However, after eight years I was ready for a change. An opportunity came one day, when in my husband's office I met Gilberte Baux, the most famous Parisian woman banker. I became her assistant in the European Federation of Financial Analysts. At the time I did not know what a financial analyst was, but I was interested in money matters because my father had often talked to me about the world of high finance. Gradually, I became Gilberte's right hand, so to speak, and for twenty-five years worked with her in the Federation, which met every two months in

1 *Louise, Duchess de la Baume le Blanc. Mistress of Louis XIV. She bore him two children who were legitimised.*
2 *From these small beginnings, the organisation spread throughout Europe, it took the name, 'le tiers-monde' (the third world). Its current President is Geneviève de Gaulle, daughter of General de Gaulle.*

a different European city. Eventually the Federation became international in its activities, and meetings took place in the United States, Canada and the Far East.

In an earlier chapter (Paris Days) I mentioned the Lyceum Club. For many years Hélène played the leading role in both organisations. Hélène's strong personal qualities were quickly recognised when she joined the Lyceum in 1970. She had not been a member for long before Madame Le Beck, the President, told her that she was the ideal person to succeed her. And indeed Hélène achieved the rare feat of becoming President in her first year as a member. This was also the year that I became a member of the Lyceum Club, proposed by the Duchess de La Rochefoucauld. I was keen to support the cultural activities of the club and play an active part in them and eventually Hélène nominated me for membership of the committee.

For thirty years she remained President until, in 1998, she decided to retire and make way for a younger person. Her choice was Solange de Saint Rapt, a member of the Rothschild family.

As president of the Cercle Interallié (ladies section) Hélène recently introduced lunchtime meetings with a guest speaker. She also created within the Cercle Interallié an annual prize named after the Duchess de La Rochefoucauld for the best first book of a writer of any nationality. In 2000 a young Chinese author, Dai Siedtge, was awarded the prize.

I asked Hélène how often she used to go to *Voisins*, the famous château near Rambouillet that belonged to her father. "The La Rochefoucauld and Fels families used to spend every September there. We cousins had a wonderful time. Golf and tennis were available including private tuition. *Voisins* has always been well known for its hunting parties. Famous public figures such as King Alphonse XIII of Spain, King Fuad I of Egypt, the Duke of Windsor and other famous statesmen were often among the number."

The original château had a long history, developing over the ages as a manor house. Much enlarged in the eighteenth century, it was bought in 1892 by Count Edmond de Fels (1858-1951), demolished and replaced by a new château built from 1903 to 1906. Only the best building materials were used, and the most advanced amenities of the day – electricity, central heating, and hot and cold running water were incorporated. The gardens were a major undertaking and represented on a grand scale the philosophy of the Society of Garden Lovers of which the Count was a founder member. Created over a twenty-year period from 1903 they were based on an architectural and decorative conception in which all the elements were scientifically calculated – tree-lined avenues, lawns, canal, lake with an island, waterfall, terraced flower beds linked by great stairways and a fine open air collection of sculpture to complement the architecture of the flower beds and foliage. The new *Voisins,* conceived inside and out in eighteenth-century style, was widely regarded as the most important and successful creation of classic French art since the Revolution. The park was listed an historic monument in 1983. Count Christian de Fels, the present owner of *Voisins* has continued his father's policy of maintaining the property to the highest standards.

A GLIMPSE OF SOPHIA LOREN

At the home of the ex-King of Egypt, Ahmed Fuad II, whose residence in Paris was a spacious apartment on the Avenue Foch, his wife, Fadila, enjoyed entertaining friends and acquaintances not only at grand dinners and lunches, but especially at ladies' tea-parties.

On one occasion, which I remember most vividly, there were about sixty guests, including Madame Pompidou – the wife of France's ex-President – and an exclusive gathering of ladies from different circles and countries, with royal princesses, ambassadors' wives – and Sophia Loren. For my part I had been invited that afternoon in the company of Baroness Jean de Courcel, the mother of Bernadette Chirac and thus the mother-in-law of the then Mayor of Paris.

As I strolled through the beautiful reception rooms I caught sight of Sophia Loren sitting alone on a sofa. I sat down next to her and after we had exchanged a few words, Sophia remarked, "What a wonderful party! A buffet fit for a king! But all these women! It's the first time in my life I have ever been invited to a tea party for ladies. I can't believe it. Here I am, Sophia Loren surrounded by women. A hen party! Not a man to be seen."

So we had a good laugh about it. After chatting for a while, I moved on, with the thought that her manner and personality came over exactly as they do in her films – natural and spontaneous, which in my experience is not often the case with filmstars. And, of course, she was as beautiful in person as she is on the cinema screen.

By coincidence, when Madame de Courcel and I were leaving the party we noticed Sophia Loren standing by herself outside in the street, obviously waiting for her chauffeur who for some reason was not there on time. The Baroness said to me, "Waiting about just as it's getting dark on the Avenue Foch is not to be recommended. It's dangerous for a young woman. You know what it's like here with kerb crawlers. We had better invite her to come with us."

Safely in the car on the way to her flat, Sophia Loren kept repeating, "Sophia Loren at a ladies' tea party!"

Whilst flattered to have been invited by the Queen of Egypt, she still had not got over the fact that there was not a single man at the party! I still smile to this day when I remember her disbelief.

Above: Queen Nefertiti
Below: A meeting with Jean Leclant, the famous French Egyptologist.

FACE TO FACE WITH NEFERTITI

When I first met in Paris the famous Egyptologist, Professor Jean Leclant, my thoughts turned to the 'face to face' encounter I had with Nefertiti during my visit to Germany in the 1960s. I was particularly attracted to Berlin, a warm welcoming city full of vivacity. Berliners enjoy making strangers feel at home. The main purpose of that visit was to rediscover my ancestor, Nefertiti.

Alas, the famous sculpted portrait of this beautiful queen is in Germany and not in Egypt. So my first visit in the city of Berlin was to the Dahlem Museum where she was to be found at that time. On the way to the museum it seemed that every street corner had a large poster bearing the photograph of Nefertiti and the words, "Queen Nefertiti, a rare treasure at the Dahlem Museum." The bust of Nefertiti was the most rare and precious object in the museum. For me, as for all lovers of art and antiquities, it was the main attraction.

As soon as I arrived I made my way straight to the place where our queen was displayed. She had a special area all to herself. She really impressed me. I stood looking at her full in the face and then in profile, from close to and from a distance. I had the strong impression that her gaze was pursuing me. Was there in her expression the faintest trace of a smile?

I was so moved that I became carried away to the extent that the attendant in the room started to give me suspicious looks. The queen had on the back of her neck an alarm in case anyone dared to touch her. (It made me think that the Germans imagined that some fanatical Egyptian might one day consider risking the dangers involved in coming to steal her back.) The attendant approached me. He had been keeping an eye on me from the beginning. I told him that I was an Egyptian. He smiled. "My name is Nefertiti," I added. He probably thought I was some crazy eccentric, so I showed him my passport. He became more understanding and left me to enjoy the expressive looks of my ancestor.

A review at the time stated, "One of the most popular and admired masterpieces is the exquisite bust of Nefertiti. If, with regal look, the Egyptian Queen, whose strangely modern expression remains an enigma, could cross Germany from north to south and from east to west, she would discover places where the spirit breathes, spiritual homes where beauty and art occupy a dominant place."

This limestone bust of an extraordinarily beautiful young woman is probably the most famous work of ancient Egyptian art. It embodies our contemporary ideal of beauty: a faultless, symmetrical face enhanced by make-up tastefully applied to brows, eyelids and lips, and a long, graceful neck. The Queen wears a multi-coloured floral necklace and a tall, flat-topped crown bound by a ribbon. An uraeus serpent, the prerogative of royalty, once adorned her brow. Two coils of the uraeus's body and tail are preserved, but its head has broken off. The bust never left the studio of its creator, the sculptor Tuthmosis. It was the master portrait of the queen that served as a model for all other representations of her. When the next generation deserted the city of Tel El Amarna, the bust was left on a shelf in Tuthmosis's model chamber. The small room eventually caved in, burying and protecting the colourful sculpture for more than three thousand years.

When Nefertiti was first shown to the world in the Berlin exhibition of 1924, a major scandal broke out among Egyptologists. Accusations of theft, tales of disguise, smuggling, deliberate concealment – some more fantastic than others – flew in all directions.

What was this Egyptian treasure doing in Germany? The story started in the early nineteenth century, when a German archaeological expedition to Egypt discovered the sculpture in the course of excavations at Tel el Amarna. To throw light upon the modern history and mystery of this distant face, I turn now to the most eminent of French Egyptologists, Professor Jean Leclant. He is the leading figure and Permanent Secretary of the *Académie des Inscriptions et Belles Lettres*,[1] one of the five academies that constitute the *Institut de France*.

My friendship with Jean Leclant is a long-standing one. His wife, Marie-France Hatvany, a pretty, elegant woman always at the height of fashion, has also been a faithful friend over the years. Although we often meet during my frequent visits to Paris, it was only recently that I had the opportunity to interview Jean Leclant at the Academy. Knowing from our past conversations that I was very interested in the Nefertiti mystery he brought up the subject straightaway.

"To start with, let us look at the Nefertiti affair. Ludwig Borchardt, a German scholar of considerable distinction, discovered Nefertiti's bust at the Tel El Amarna site in Egypt in 1912. The important thing to bear in mind is the matter of the licence to dig. It was not an official German organisation that granted this licence, nor was it the museum. The licence was made out to James Simon, a wealthy Berlin businessman. He was the co-founder of the Deutsche Orient-Gesellschaft (German Middle-East Company) and it was he who put up the money for the expedition."

"So it was a private expedition?"

Leclant smiled ironically and replied, "In fact it was supported by the Germans behind the scenes. At the time we are talking about, the Director of the Egyptian department of Antiquities was Pierre Lacau, who had succeeded Gaston Maspero[2] in the post. It had been agreed between the two powers that then governed Egypt – Britain and France – that responsibility for antiquities should lie with the French."

---

1 'Belles Lettres' – Humanities. Colbert, the Chief Minister of Lonis XV founded this Academy in 1663 to encourage historical and archaeological research and provide suitable mottoes for use as inscriptions on royal buildings, .
2 Gaston Maspero, 1846-1916. Director-General of Excavations and Antiquities for the Egyptian Government. He cleared the sites of the Pyramid at Guizeh and the Temple at Luxor. Regulated excavations and tried to prevent illicit trade in antiquities.

"Are you saying this arrangement was a clear agreement between the French and the British?"

"Absolutely. The British were not interested in the subject. In 1909, they had even given Maspero a knighthood to indicate that all was well between Britain and France in Egypt – at least in archaeological matters. The Egyptians themselves had no trained archaeologists. They knew perfectly well that they had treasures, but they had full confidence in the integrity of the French archaeologists. Indeed, a previous French Conservator of Monuments for the Egyptian Government, Auguste Mariette[1] had blocked the Khedive's wish to give precious jewels to the Empress Eugénie, Napoleon III's wife, saying that they were too important. Napoleon took action against Mariette and that is why he did not receive the *Légion d'Honneur* at that time. Anyway, in 1912 Pierre Lacau was in charge with, under him, several French scholars brought up in the disciplines and methods of Maspero, in particular a scholar called Gustave Lefebvre."

"I understand he was the arbitrator in the matter of the eventual ownership of any finds that were made," I said. "Why should he have been involved?"

"It was not a question of arbitration. Lefebvre was acting in his capacity as an Inspector in the Antiquities' Department. Also there was the representative of the Deutsche Orient Gesellschaft, Ludwig Borchardt. When it came to dividing up the finds at Tel el Amarna, the entire responsibility rested with Lefebvre. The problem was that everything happened in such a hurry. When the dig came to an end in January 1913, a certain number of discoveries were presented for sharing out, but naturally some of the finds had not been cleaned, because there had not been time to clean them all. That was how the bust of Nefertiti slipped through. There were ten baskets of heads. 'A head, a head, another head' – amongst them Nefertiti's."

At this point I asked, "Is it true or possible that Lefebvre did not know that amongst all these heads there was the head of Nefertiti?"

Leclant replied, "He was absolutely unaware of the fact. Like many others, Nefertiti's head was covered in dirt and grime. It was simply a matter of saying, 'five on the right, five on the left, these for the Germans and these for the Egyptians'."

"And that's what they called division?"

"Naturally it was part of the agreement governing share-outs that if there was an object of exceptional interest, the Egyptians would have first choice, and if they wanted it, give something else in exchange. Anyway, that is the story of what happened."

I commented, "It has often been alleged that the Germans stole the bust and tried to hide the fact."

Leclant replied, "They did not steal it. That is wrong. It was just a matter of the circumstances in which the share-out took place."

---

1 *Auguste Mariette, 1821-1881. Cleared and protected many important sites in Egypt and Nubia. As Conservator, he eliminated unauthorised excavations and restricted the sale and export of antiquities.*

"Yes, but they hid this important bust all the same!"

"I understand what you are saying, but it was covered in grime. Lefebvre ought to have said, 'All these heads have to be cleaned.' Only when the heads had been cleaned should the share-out have taken place. Lefebvre spent the rest of his life biting his nails over it."

Leclant continued, "What happened took place between scholars who were supposed to be honest people. Lefebvre could not have thought that the Germans were acting in bad faith. That is why the head went through. The share-out took place officially. It was lot number so-and-so, lot number so-and-so, this for the Germans, and this for the Egyptians. Then 'Baraka'![1] There were hundreds of objects to be shared out. That's the way it happened."

I insisted, "But they hid it. Wasn't it lot No. 18?"

"Well, we can say they hid it. They can say they didn't. I don't know about lot No. 18, but there is one interesting point. During the proceedings, Borchardt is supposed to have said, 'I am interested in this particular bust,' and marked the basket. If he did say this, he had no need to do so. The surprising thing, of course, is that none of this came out until the 1920s."

I asked, "Why? What happened?"

"The consignments of discoveries were back in Berlin but of course, the First World War broke out in 1914, and for the four years of its duration, nobody was interested in the objects from the share-out of Tel El Amarna. Everybody had other preoccupations. Then, in July 1920, James Simon announced that he was donating to the Prussian State everything that had been discovered during the dig. In 1920, Borchardt began to publish articles on Nefertiti. In 1924, the bust of Nefertiti went on display for the first time, twelve years after its discovery. Public interest was immediate and worldwide. There was also widespread anger – from the Egyptians, from the French, from everybody. But there it was. The bust was in Germany. Press campaigns were launched for Nefertiti to be returned to Egypt. The Egyptians demanded the return of their 'stolen' treasure, but all their attempts failed. Hitler came to power in 1933. He admired the sculpture, so it stayed where it was."

"And then came the Second World War in 1939," I remarked.

"Yes, and Nefertiti was on the move again. The order was given for the contents of the Berlin Museum to be sent to safety in provincial towns. Part of the collection ended up in what after the war became East Germany, and part in West Germany. After the fall of Hitler, American troops recovered Nefertiti from her place of safety in a salt mine. That was in 1945. They gave her back to the Germans at Wiesbaden, in West Germany. She went on display there in February 1946. Then she returned to Berlin in July 1956 and found a temporary home in the Dahlem Museum.

"That is where I saw her," I interrupted.

"Yes, she was the museum's star exhibit. There she stayed until 1967, when

1 *'Baraka!' is Egyptian and means 'it is finished; a blessing on it!'*

she was moved to the Egyptian Museum at Charlottenburg. She now resides in the Berlin Museum.

"Of course," continued Leclant, "Nefertiti is just one item, albeit the most famous, brought back by that 1912 expedition. What you have to remember is that in the 1920s, only a few of the Tel El Amarna finds went on display. There was not room in the existing museum; so many crates were left unopened until a new museum could be built. But Hitler would not entertain the idea. He said, 'If I am to reorganise the German Museum I will do it with works of art, not with the collection of James Simon that will take ages to sort out.' So nothing was done. The crates remained unopened. They were dispersed during the Second World War and most ended up in the hands of the East Germans. They had by far the greater part of the collection. Some items were exhibited in East Berlin, but in very poor condition because East Germany was short of money to house them properly and would not hand anything over to the West. Only after the Berlin wall came down, leading to the re-unification of East and West Germany in 1990, did the archaeologists of both sides start talking to each other. Eventually, all the Egyptian antiquities were brought together in a reunited Berlin Museum. There were scores and scores of crates and baskets, a vast number of objects. We know now because we can see them; nobody could have known before 1995. For eighty years everything had remained untouched, in the original crates. To get to the bottom of it all, you will need to see and study all the documentation and records that the museum possesses. Even then, who knows?"

So all these crates came from the division made in 1913!" I commented.

"Nobody really knows. Were they all part of the share-out process?? All I can tell you is that the museum has many masterpieces originating from the Tel El Amarna site. It is all politics. You are not going to start a campaign to get Nefertiti back, are you? That's all over. We live in Europe now."

I said, "The Queen's story is a tragic one. She was stolen, taken from her native land, never to return."

Jean Leclant replied, "By 1951 the Egyptians had realised they would never succeed. What did they do? I saw in their newspapers a headline spread over five columns – 'You can keep her, your Marie-Antoinette'."

It was time to ask a few questions about the real Nefertiti. In the fourteenth century BC She was the Queen of King Akhenaton, the first pharaoh to establish the worship of one God –the Sun God. Nefertiti supported her husband's religious reforms and may have acted as a priestly officer, a position normally reserved exclusively for kings.

I asked, "Is it true that Nefertiti fell out of favour in the twelfth year of the King's reign?"

"No," replied Leclant, "It is not true at all. It's wrong, all rubbish. Nefertiti is in all the inscriptions and reliefs of Akhenaton's reign."

"And where do the mortal remains of the Queen lie?"

"Nefertiti's tomb was in the Eastern desert. It has been pillaged; nothing remains. It's a mystery."

"What about her name? Explain its meaning." This was my last question.

Leclant wrote down the following for me; Nfrt - ity. "The beautiful one has come." He added, "In Arabic, there are no vowels. So you can call her Nefret, or Neferet, or Nofret. For me, I say Neferet-ity."

I often reflect on Jean Leclant's account of Nefertiti, her famous bust andthe following text that frequently comes to mind: "Buried for over three thousand years in utter darkness beneath the ruins of her creator's studio, condemned once more in modern times to yet more darkness, and again once more after that, she now turns her penetrating gaze upon the admirers who come to contemplate her, as they no doubt once did, in real life, the queen she represents. What is she thinking of, this Pharaonic Mona Lisa, this beautiful mystery of mysteries?"

The Rosetta Stone

"Now that we have concluded with Nefertiti," said Jean Leclant, "there are other cases of ownership of archaeological finds passing from one country to another. An interesting example of this is the Rosetta Stone.[1] This was taken from us at the time of the French defeat in Egypt by the British in 1801. The Stone became a spoil of war. It would be pointless to demand its return. We would be reminded that the French army in Egypt was defeated and signed the Treaty of Capitulation, one of the articles of which specified that all large, important Egyptian antiquities were to be handed over to the British. However, when the British Commander-in-Chief demanded possession of all the papers produced by our scholars relating to the study of their finds, the French refused. The French scholars said that if the British army came to seize the papers by force, all they would find would be a pile of ashes.

The French would have burned them rather than hand them over. They argued that knowledge accumulated by their scholars was intellectual property. Eventually, the British General agreed that the surrender of documents was not included in the treaty terms, which related only to the objects themselves.

As everyone knows, the Rosetta Stone is in the British Museum. In 1990 I went to London to see the curator of the Museum. I was organising director of an exhibition to be shown in Strasbourg and Paris later in the year called *Memories of Egypt*. The curator was a young man, new to me, called Dr. Vivian Davies. I explained we would like to borrow several items from the British Museum. I handed him a list. Dr. Davies went white. "The Rosetta Stone! Never! It's impossible!"

"Everything is possible," I commented.

"No, definitely not. The Stone has never left London; here it will remain!'

"You are a young man," I replied. "I can tell you that the Rosetta Stone has already been to France!'"

---

1 *The Rosetta Stone. The Stone was found by chance in 1799 in the Nile Delta region of Egypt, not far from the town of Rashid, which was known as Rosetta by Europeans. The finder was Lieutenant Xavier Boucharda, a French officer on Napoleon's 1798 military expedition to Egypt.*

"Impossible!" exclaimed Davies.

"My dear friend, allow me to explain. In 1972, France intended to celebrate the one hundred and fiftieth anniversary of the decipherment by the French scholar Jean-François Champollion of the inscriptions on the Stone, and I was chosen to organise the event. I wrote to your predecessor, Professor I.E.S. Edwards, to ask him to allow us to borrow the Stone for our ceremonies. We knew each other well. But, back came the reply, 'You are asking the impossible. The Stone will never leave England.' I consulted the French authorities concerned. We wrote another letter to Professor Edwards. With his reply, Edwards enclosed extracts from the British press which expressed hostility to the idea of a loan, also stating that it would be in summer, a time when thousands of people on holiday visited the Museum to see the Stone – and so on. Seeing that the Museum authorities were against us, we now informed our government – to be precise, the Foreign Ministry and the Ministry of Education – of our lack of success. The matter was taken up at the highest level with H.R.H. the Duke of Edinburgh. Finally, as a result of an appeal made to Queen Elizabeth II herself, the Rosetta Stone did come to Paris."

"So that is the real story, Dr. Davies. In view of the present circumstances, perhaps I could ask instead to borrow one of the Museum's two magnificent lion sculptures from Soleb.[1] You know, I worked there for twenty-five years."

"Dr. Davies agreed and one of the lions featured in our exhibition."

Jean Leclant then explained to me the deciphering of the Rosetta Stone.

"In July 1999 the British Museum celebrated the two hundredth anniversary of the discovery of the Rosetta Stone. For a long time there were differing opinions as to who really did decipher the hieroglyphics. A traditional British view attributed it to the English scientist Thomas Young. Now Young may have been an eminent scientist who made important discoveries about the properties of light, but he certainly did not succeed in deciphering the inscriptions on the Rosetta Stone. I will admit that he made some progress towards it, but it was the French scholar Champollion who in 1822 published the first and correct list giving values and meaning to the hieroglyphics. At the present time, the authority of the British Museum recognise the contributions of both men, but there is no doubt that it was Champollion's work that has provided the foundation for the work of all Egyptologists since his day."

The Life and Career of Jean Leclant

I had known Jean Leclant for many years when I finally decided that it was time to ask him to tell me about his early days as a scholar and what prompted him to follow the subject that had made him famous as one of the most respected and knowledgeable persons in the field of archaeology throughout the world. This is what he told me.

1 *Soleb is a village in the North of Sudan where many interesting antiquities were discovered.*

"When the time came to consider what subjects I should study in the sixth form at the Lycée Henri IV in Paris, my parents said that since I was a very bright pupil I should take mathematics and science, which were the required subjects for entry at the age of eighteen to the Ecole Polytechnique.[1] This was the usual progression for those who were good at mathematics, but I was good at other subjects as well. I said I wanted to become an historian. From the age of eleven or twelve I had been very interested in Egyptian history and had spent a lot of time in the Egyptology Department of the Louvre Museum studying the exhibits. Tibet too appealed to me; it was a country of mystery. When I was sixteen years old I entered the humanities and philosophy section. My parents were not very pleased. However, the headmaster summoned them and explained that I had a vocation for archaeology and the best course of action for me would be to study for the Ecole Normale Supérieure.[2] There I would be able to study archaeology, take my degree and after that the *agrégation*.[3] My parents accepted his advice and so in 1938 I found myself in the *Hypokhâgne* the class for pupils aiming to enter the *Ecole Normale Supérieure*."

"In 1939, war broke out and the Khâgne was evacuated to Rennes in Brittany. This is where I took the written examination in the summer of 1940. In October I learned that I had passed and was therefore eligible to take later in the month the second part of the exam, the very difficult oral. Few candidates pass both parts of the exam at the first attempt but I was lucky enough to satisfy the examiners first time round, and began my university studies at the Ecole Normale Supérieure right away".

"On arrival at the college the Head, Jérôme Carcopino,[4] interviewed me. I was told he was an imposing figure, always dressed in striped trousers and black jacket, with a pearl in his cravate. "Look out when you go to his office," I was told, "there is a long corridor with a floor polished like glass. Mind you don't fall flat on your face. It will be a bad start if you turn up with a bloodied nose!" Treading very carefully, I arrived safely in his presence."

"Young man, sit down in that chair. I see in you the student destined to be the philosopher of your year"

"Sir, I replied, 'I am not particularly interested in philosophy.'"

"What? I see that you have excellent marks in philosophy."

---

1 *The Ecole Polytechnique is one of France's most celebrated State Colleges. After training, students either take a commission in the army artillery or engineering corps, or embark on careers in the public services or other occupations that call for very high standards of engineering, mathematical and scientific knowledge.*

2 *Ecole normale supérieure: a famous college, founded to supply university teachers, though many of the students do not make teaching their career. It is affiliated to the Sorbonne where the college students, all of whom are the pick of France's secondary schools, follow university courses. After graduating, many students go on to take the concours d'agrégation. The School has produced many of France's greatest writers and thinkers.*

3 *'Le concours d'agrégation' is a highly competitive State-conducted examination open to graduates for admission to a carefully limited number of posts on the teaching staff of universities and senior posts in the Lycées.*

4 *Jérôme Carcopino, French historian (1881-1970) whose field of study was Antiquities, especially Roman history. The author of many learned works, well known to a wider public for his popular "Daily Life in Ancient Rome" (1939).*

"Sir, I don't want to study philosophy. I want to be an historian, an archae-ologist."

He looked at me and said, "Young man, you are saying that just to please me. I was just like you. When I came here as a student I was interviewed by the great scholar Georges Perott. I told him I wanted to be a Graeco-Roman archaeolo-gist just like him. You are not saying that just to please me, are you?"

Carcopino started to tell me the story of his life. He was very pleasant, but I had not come to hear him talk about himself. He went on and on asking ques-tions and answering them himself. Eventually he said, "Right let's get back to you. What exactly do you have in mind? If it is classical archaeology, that means Athens and Rome for you."

"Sir, I would like to go to Egypt, or Tibet."

"Young man, that is two different things. If it's Egypt, I shall give you letters of introduction to the Professor of Egyptology. If it's Tibet, you will need to see the Professor of Tibetan Studies."

I settled for Egypt.

"In that case, you need to see Professor Jean Sainte-Fare Garnot. He is a young Professor, every one is talking about him."

And that is how I took my first steps in my chosen profession."

During the course of a long and distinguished career, Professor Leclant's main interest has been the Valley of the Nile. He directed excavations in Egypt, Sudan and Ethiopia. He created the Antiquities Department of Ethiopia. He has been a Professor at Strasbourg University (1953-63), at the Sorbonne (1963-79), the Ecole des Hautes Etudes and at the Collège de France (1979-90). For many years he was President of the Society for Nubian Studies, General Secretary of the French Egyptological Society and Vice President of the French Committee for Unesco. He is a member of many foreign Academies, including the British, Italian, Belgian, Danish, Swedish, American and Russian.

He has over a thousand publications to his name, including books and arti-cles for the wider public who know him from his frequent radio and television broadcasts. He has played an important rôle in the organisation of international exhibitions, especially *The Kingdom of the Nile, which travelled* throughout Europe in 1996-99.

In addition, Jean Leclant has been awarded many medals and decorations from all over the world in recognition of his services to archaeology. He became a member of the *Académie des Inscriptions et Belles-Lettres* in 1974 and in 1983 was elected its Permanent Secretary (*Secrétaire perpétuel*), which is the supreme office in French Humanities.

Ex-Queen Farida of Egypt, Madame Simone del Duca with Isis on the left at the exhibition of Queen Farida's paintings organised by Isis at L'Hôtel in Paris in 1978.

SIMONE AND CINO DEL DUCA

The first time that I met Mrs Cino del Duca was during a weekend spent with the Duchess de La Rochefoucauld at her château de Montmirail. She was elegantly dressed, entirely in black. The Duchess told me, "The lady you see over there has worn nothing but black since her husband died and intends to wear it to the end of her days." Then she added, "Perhaps you would like to show her around the grounds if she is interested." That was how Simone and I first came into friendly contact with each other. I met her again several times at receptions given by the Duchess, but what gave me a better understanding of her was brought about by an exhibition of paintings which took place later that year.

Farida, the ex-Queen of Egypt (Farouk's first wife) was a keen painter. In the cellars of the famous 'Hôtel' on the left bank of the then fashionable St. Germain des Prés district of Paris she organised an exhibition of her own paintings. For the most part these were portraits of Egyptian peasants, but there were also some of Egyptian personalities famous at the time. Special lighting effects enabled each portrait to be highlighted individually, an original touch that added life and vigour to the paintings. The exhibition attracted many visitors, but no buyers. By the end of the first week Farida was in a state of some despair and turned to me for help. "Isis, you know everybody. Do something! Invite your friends to come and see the paintings."

I spent a long evening going through my address book and writing invitation cards. When I came to the name Madame Cino del Duca, I hesitated. I really did not know her well enough, but then I thought, "Well, why not? If she wants to come she will."

The big day arrived. My friends rallied round, turning up in good numbers, including Simone who asked for me and invited me to walk round the exhibition with her. Seeing that she appeared to be quite interested in the folklore art around her, I left her side after a short while, thinking that it would be more discreet to let her contemplate the paintings on her own. She called me back, however, and said quite simply, "Please make a note of the ones I want." She indeed bought several paintings, the most expensive ones – very highly priced. This was a generous and helpful gesture towards a distressed Queen in exile. Simone's kind-hearted generosity, her humanity if you will, is indeed one of her most marked characteristics.

Simone Cino del Duca is one of France's most remarkable women and has for many years been a subject of conversation in French social circles. She has a very strong personality and found herself, upon her husband's death, in possession of a very large business in the management of which she had no experience or knowledge. Yet she resolved to carry on her husband's work – and add to it. It was a long, hard task; the responsibilities she assumed were onerous, but she bore them with dignity and success to become the first woman publisher.

Who is Simone? She came from a bourgeois family living at La Varenne St. Hilaire in the Marne valley near Paris. Not far from where she lived, there was a printing works. One day Simone, then a young woman, knocked on the office door of the firm's owner, carrying the manuscripts of some short stories she had written, in the hope of having them published. That was how in 1939 she met the man who was to become her husband, Cino del Duca. But it was 25th January 1947 that the couple married. It was a true love-match. Cino's business prospered. On his sudden death in 1967 Simone decided in his memory to take over what had become a major enterprise.

She had great admiration for her late husband and wanted to measure up to him. Telling herself she would just have to roll up her sleeves and get on with it, she went into his office and sat down in his chair. She had the intelligence and wisdom to listen to her husband's business collaborators. He had chosen his associates well and Simone did the same. She carried on the business for several years, working long hard hours.

Eventually she started to sell one part of the business after another, at a time when economic conditions were at their most favourable and her enterprises were prospering. Having done this, she asked herself, "What am I going to do now?" Simone had developed a taste for work and she has never since lost it.

It had been a wish of her husband to build and endow a hospital. Anxious to turn his wishes into reality, she was cautioned not to do so by Maurice Schumann, a former government minister who had been a friend for many years. "Hospitals are bottomless pits," she was advised. "On the other hand, helping in areas of medical research not being funded by the government and desperate for long term finance would be a much more worthwhile thing to do, if not quite so gratifying for the donor."

Bearing these words in mind, Simone conceived the idea of creating a medical foundation, which she named The Cino del Duca Foundation; this has now been in existence for twenty-five years. For the foundation premises she bought a splendid mansion in the eighth arrondissement of Paris – 10 rue Alfred de Vigny. Income was provided by rents from properties, which Simone bought for the purpose, and by a portfolio of investments. The Foundation has specialised in research in the important fields of cardio-vascular problems and diseases of the nervous system.

Through her foundation, Simone came to know many professors of medicine, especially the humanist doctor Jean Bernard and Jean Hamburger. Such contacts inspired her to create The Cino del Duca World Prize. This prize, worth 50,000 francs, is awarded annually to someone who in the literary, medical or scientific world has made important contributions to modern humanism. Recipients are often those who have already achieved pre-eminence in their field, for example Nobel Prize winners and members of the Institut de France.

A jury appointed by Simone and composed of professors of medicine, members of the French Academy and the Academy of Medicine awards the prize.

Through the management council of her Foundation and the panel for the World Prize, Simone gathered round her the nucleus of her salon.[1] When it was suggested to her that the Foundation could be a venue for lectures, Simone put the idea into practice, inviting eminent figures to give lectures in their specialist fields. Her friends are invited as guests. Simone often gives lunches at which she entertains leading literary and scientific thinkers. There is an art in presiding over a successful salon, and Simone possesses it. She listens, directs the subjects and course of conversation, involving the various guests in such a way that nobody monopolises the discussion or feels left out.

Many people have cause to be grateful to Simone. Her donations now embrace several fields. She created annual prizes for painting, music and sculpture and made scholarships and grants available for young authors.

A dominating feature of Simone is her faithfulness in friendship. She always keeps her word and treats others with respect. She has no time for those who lack these standards of behaviour. Never devious or calculating, she bestows her friendship with generosity and an open heart, even to those who are unable to reciprocate. Sometimes, though, she can be hard and aloof, as if to protect herself from the spontaneity of her kindness and from daily appeals to her benevolence.

When Simone formally placed the Cino del Duca Foundation under the aegis of the Institut de France, a marble plaque in her honour was placed near that of Mazarin who founded in 1643 the public library housed in the Institut.

Simone is a Commander of the Légion d'Honneur, France's highest civilian decoration and one that is rarely awarded to women. She is also a corresponding member of the Académie des Beaux-Arts and holds over thirty foreign decorations. In a public announcement Simone has stated that on her death the major part of her fortune will go to the Cino Del Duca Foundation.

Besides all her activities in connection with her charitable foundations, she finds the time to lead a busy social life. She loves entertaining, which she does out of sheer pleasure and in her own individual way. She does not rely on her many assistants and secretaries to organise the receptions and dinners for her, but takes upon herself all the arrangements down to the last detail. At weekends she goes back to her country house where she entertains her friends who can relax in the swimming pool and the extensive grounds. When Simone is in Paris she gives frequent dinners. I have been a guest at many of them, but two stand out as exceptional occasions.

The first took place in May 1994 when Simone gave an extraordinary soirée beneath the Louvre Pyramid to mark the arrival of a magnificent tapestry which she had bought from an English antique dealer in London to present as a gift to the Louvre. It is a tapestry of Asian origin measuring seven metres by six metres

1 Salon: in a historical and literary sense, a regular assembly held in a private house, presided over by the lady of the house. At 'literary' salons, those interested in literature, the arts, science and philosophy would gather for conversation and discussion.

and depicting a little princess riding on an elephant against an exotic background of plants, flowers and monkeys. The tapestry is in the museum, displayed in its own special room. It happened that the dinner was held two weeks after Jacques Chirac had been elected President of France. Madame Chirac was one of the guests and stood by her hostess's side to welcome the guests, who numbered some four hundred. Many prominent figures were present, including the Minister of Culture, Douste Blazy. In his speech he recalled that as a student he had been able to pursue his education from the age of fourteen thanks to a scholarship made available by Simone's husband. Dinner was served under the illuminated glass vault of the Pyramid. The guests were seated at round tables of eight; each table had two waiters, one to serve the champagne and wine, the other to serve the exquisite dishes. The orchestra playing gypsy music greeted the arrival of the dessert. It was truly an extraordinary event that we thoroughly enjoyed and will never forget.

Five years later, on 29th September 1999, Simone gave another special dinner, which I attended with my husband, this time in the superb setting of the Armenonville Pavilion in the Bois de Boulogne. On this occasion the dinner was in honour of the hundredth anniversary of her husband's birth. It was a touching idea. Although Cino died thirty-six years ago, Simone still thinks about him every day and often goes to visit his magnificent tomb in the Père-Lachaise cemetery. She invited all her friends to this fabulous anniversary dinner. Virtually all Paris was there.

After greeting the hostess and her chief guests – Maurice Druon, at that time was the Permanent Secretary of the Académie Française, Jacques Chancel, the popular television journalist and interviewer and Yuri Boukoff, the famous pianist – we were served with champagne in one of the reception rooms. We then moved into a lecture room where Maurice Druon and Jacques Chancel spoke to recall memories of Simone's husband whom they had both known well. Maurice Druon reminded his audience that it was Cino who had published his historic novel *Les Rois Maudits*[1] forty years previously. Simone has an inborn gift for organisation and for choosing the seating arrangements of the diners so they all have a pleasant, interesting evening. The refinement of the dinner, accompanied by the best wines would have delighted any gourmet. Rarely in Paris today are there soirées that match those given by Simone del Duca.

Just how big was the business concern which Simone inherited and what were its origins? The answers lie in the story of her husband's life.

Cino del Duca

One sometimes hears people say just how much they would like to be able to change places with some rich and famous personality. That has never been my attitude. I admire and am happy to know those who by their genius, intellect and determination have succeeded in reaching the heights in their chosen field.

1 '*The Accursed Kings*.'

I admire them all the more if they have done so honestly, while remaining simple and unpretentious, preserving their human side and always mindful of their often humble past. Such a person was Cino del Duca.

He was Italian, born on 25th July 1899 in Montedinove, a small village on the Adriatic coast. His father was a poet, a hero from the days of Garibaldi and unfortunately an unlucky businessman. In 1914 he lost everything; the family, now living in Ancona, had to move into a hovel without even mattresses for their younger children. The eldest of the four sons was Cino, then sixteen. The disastrous change in the family circumstances saw the beginning of Cino's unlikely career. Neither his father nor his mother had the will to adapt and to seek ways out of poverty. Cino left school, determined to find work at a time when jobs were few and far between in order to do what became an obsession with him – feeding and looking after his family.

There were no job centres. Cino went round the streets, knocking on doors asking for work, glad to do anything that would earn some money, however little. On his rounds he chanced to meet a travelling salesman who was also going from door to door, trying to sell to housewives the popular, if often bloodthirsty, weekly instalments of serialised novels produced by the firm for which he worked, Hiermann Publications. The salesman took a liking to Cino and as the two walked the streets together he explained his job so enthusiastically to the sixteen-year-old that Cino thought he would like to do the same. His friend introduced him to Hiermann Publications. He was taken on. For two years he sold 'blood and thunder' novelettes and kept the wolf from the family door.

By 1917 Italy had become embroiled in the First World War. Cino was called up for military service. It was three years before he was demobilised. When he came out of the army it was with a much wiser head on his shoulders. He looked for a job that would pay more regular wages than he could earn selling magazines door to door and found one as a telegraph operator with Italian railways.

In his army days Cino had become keenly interested in politics. He now actively expounded Socialist ideas and openly opposed the Fascist movement that was taking hold in Italy under its leader Mussolini who seized power in 1922.

Cino's politics cost him his job and not only that. He was arrested and imprisoned in Naples without trial for four months. Whilst in prison he managed to write in secret his first novel *Prince Charming*. Released without charge but jobless, he turned once more to Hiermann Publications. For three years he travelled throughout Italy selling their stories. In 1929 he decided to use his savings to become his own boss. He set up his own small publishing firm in a basement in Milan but realised he needed an author and by advertising found a young woman who could write stories round his own plots. During his time as a salesman, Cino had listened carefully to what the young housewives who were his best customers had to say. Time and time again he heard the same remarks. There was too much violence and murder. What the women really wanted was tender romance, passionate love stories, and the chance to dream their dreams. So Cino would give customers what they wanted. In his basement he wrote the first instalment of a romantic story; he had it printed and went round selling it whilst his collaborator carried on with the tale. His readers were delighted; word quickly passed round and within months Cino was employing ten salesmen to cope with the demand. For three years his business grew; he was able to buy a printing works and establish a distribution network throughout Italy.

Trouble lay ahead. Cino continued to give voice to his Socialist ideals and his hatred of Fascism. He was on the black list of Mussolini's thugs and a victim of reprisals and persecution from the Black Shirts. Mussolini had his eye on Cino's printing press for his own propaganda. The pressure became too great, even for a man of Cino's courage. In 1932, he left his business behind and moved to France and freedom taking with him only what little capital he had been able to salvage (2,000,000 Italian lira).

Once again he set up his business in a basement, this time in Paris, and formed the company that was to become his life's work, Les Editions Mondiales (World-Wide Publications). His formula was the same – door-to-door selling. The results were also the same – phenomenal success. Not content with women's magazines, he launched highly successful children's comics including *Hurrah, L'Aventureux* and *Tarzan*. By 1938 he had become a prosperous businessman and was able to transfer his offices to the very centre of Paris, to the rue des Italiens near the Opera House. But again, war and Fascism were to intervene.

In 1939 France was at war with Hitler's Germany. Cino volunteered to join the French army. A year later France fell and Paris was occupied. Cino joined the French Resistance. With his publishing experience he was able to organise the printing and distribution of fiercely worded anti-Hitler pamphlets. Hitler was not amused and gave orders for the Gestapo to find him and shoot him on the spot. Cino avoided capture, working with the Resistance until the Allied liberation of France in 1944 and the final defeat of Hitler. He was awarded two medals, the *Croix de Guerre* and the *Médaille de Vermeil de la Ville de Paris*.

His business like many in Europe was in ruins. Cino started all over again. With Italy, Hitler's ally, now free from Mussolini and Fascist dictatorship, Cino returned to Milan and set to work to revive his old publishing business there. By 1946 he was in business again. There was no shortage of readers, but the war had devastated industry and paper was scarce. Cino coaxed his business along. The year 1947 saw the start of better times for his affairs in France. He received his first allocation of newsprint, an event that was to mark his real and final return to business. From this time on there appeared no limit to the success that his tireless energy and enterprising genius created. Not only did he resume publication of his pre-war titles. He launched new titles aimed mainly at a female readership, titles that became famous, such as *Nous Deux, Intimité* and *Modes de Paris*. By the early 1950s he was printing and distributing half a million children's comics and four million women's magazines weekly. He built three new ultra-modern printing works. One alone employed over a thousand workers. Sometimes accused of being interested in publishing only light, easy, popular works for a mass readership, Cino's answer was to publish new editions of the works of prestigious writers such as Pirandello, Kessel, Vialar and Maurice Druon. As if this was not enough, Cino turned in 1953 to film production, forming his own company, Del Duca Films. His touch was sure. Success followed success at the box-office with films still fondly remembered such as *Touchez pas au Grisbi*, *L'Air de Paris*, *Le Ballon Rouge* and Antonioni's *L'Avventura,* which won first prize at the Cannes Film Festival. The year 1959 saw the appearance of *Paris-Jour*, France's first daily newspaper in tabloid form, another Cino del Duca production. In 1967 there was another new venture, *Télé Poche*, the first French television magazine. Lavishly illustrated, it was an instant success. More than a million copies were sold in its first week.

On 24th May 1967, during a visit to his Italian publishing house in Milan, a cerebral haemorrhage brought his sixty-seven year life to a sudden end.

And what about the man himself?

No account of Cino's career would be complete if it did not indicate his honesty, integrity, warmth and generosity. Throughout his life he strove to bring popular education within the reach of millions, to give a taste for reading to those who did not possess it, and to point the way towards an appreciation of more serious works of literature. He published romances and love stories to bring happiness and, where possible, beauty into workaday lives. His rule never changed, "Every one of my stories has a moral, no evil shall go unpunished, no virtue shall be unrewarded." As an employer he was much loved. For him it was important that the workplace should have a pleasant and happy atmosphere. The wellbeing of his workers was one of his primary concerns and showed itself in many personal acts of kindness to his staff. Nor did he forget struggling young authors. As early as 1952 he was giving financial help to aspiring writers. Among the early beneficiaries were Félicien Marceau and Alain Robbe-Grillet.

On 28th May, four days after his death, Paris paid tribute to Cino del Duca with a solemn funeral. The daily newspaper *Le Figaro* in its obituary provided a fitting epitaph, 'Cino del Duca, the King of Hearts of the publishing world.'

A talk with the Count of Paris, Duke of France, in 1999.

A TALK WITH THE COUNT OF PARIS, DUKE OF FRANCE

During dinner, one evening in December 1998, I was fortunate enough to be able to meet His Grace the Count de Clermont, who would become the Count of Paris on his father's death. Some months later, on 14th June 1999, I visited him, accompanied by my husband Peter. As chance would have it, this meeting took place just three days before the death of his father. During our meeting we touched on a whole range of subjects concerning political, social, cultural and humanitarian matters. But first I asked the Count to tell me a little about his early life, his childhood and upbringing.

His early days were in accordance with the strict traditions of other members of his family, a royal family but one in exile.

Count Henri de Clermont began, "I was born on 14th June, 1933. Today is my birthday! I am 66 years old. I was born in Brussels. We were all born in exile but in 1947, at the age of fourteen, I was granted special permission by the President of the Republic, Vincent Auriol, to set foot on French soil. This permission was granted solely to me and not to other members of my family. It was so that I might continue my education in France.

My father made his return to France in 1950. This was a great change for us and the cause of overwhelming happiness. In exile we moved from country to country, staying in Brazil, Morocco, Spain and Portugal.

Perhaps as a result of my travels, I have a love of languages. I can speak Portuguese, Spanish, a little Arabic; I understand German and I can also speak English. I learnt Ancient Greek at one time but I was always better at reading out the letters and words than I was at understanding what exactly they meant! It was not an entirely useful exercise, just a hobby."

"Where did you study?" I asked.

"At a secondary school in Bordeaux where I stayed with friends in the town. I have always kept in touch. They are good friends; one is President Chaban-Delmas. I then moved to Paris to study Political Science. My tutor was a certain Jacques Chirac! After that, I spent eleven years serving in the army..."

"By choice?"

"No. My father had really pushed me into it and it was General de Gaulle who found me a post in his secretariat at the National Defence in Paris. I became *Chargé de Mission* for General de Gaulle."

"Can you tell me any interesting stories about that time?" I enquired.

"No, I'm sorry. I can't do that. I was in charge of a top-secret office!"

"But, surely, all that is a long time ago now?"

"It was interesting. I was the go-between for General de Gaulle and my father. It was the General's wish that my father succeed him in office. The discussions had begun in 1957 and were still a talking-point in 1962."

I replied saying, "I was aware that there had been a great deal of gossip about who would succeed General de Gaulle and that de Gaulle's followers were taking secret soundings as to the suitability of possible successors."

"Other events were attracting a great deal of attention at that time: events such as the popular referendum on the future status of Algeria; the referendum in the Senate; and then General de Gaulle was gone, gone for good."

"During the period of my life when I was in the army,   I spent five years in the Foreign Legion. It was a very special time in my army career and one that I hold dear, especially as so many countries have now abandoned their military service as the army has become more and more specialised in its deployment, employment and necessary skills. The more wars are fought in a worldwide arena, the more it seems that military service, as many knew it, is a waste of time."

"Was it not good personally for those who were conscripted?" I asked.

"No. What we have to realise is that the army of today must be professional. I agree that there is good to be gained by having some form of service. However, it is 'national' service and not 'military' service that we really ought to be organising. Service to the country should be organised in such a way that the youth of today grows in social and civil awareness. How about national service in various industries, trading and commercial organisations?"

"After my service in the Foreign Legion, I returned to civilian life and joined the National Bank of Geneva at the Rhône-Inter branch. It was quite a small bank but I was in charge of a department seeking to attract customers with large fortunes! As a result I was regularly in contact with the Vatican, the Shah of Iran, the King of Morocco, the Emirates, and so on."

"So have you a love for the world of finance?" I asked.

"Money in itself did not interest me. What did, was having contact with a wide range of people through their finances."

Turning to another topic, the Count continued, "I married very young, you know. I was only twenty-four when I married the Duchess de Württemberg at Dreux in 1957. We divorced in 1974. Since then I have thrown myself into the export trade, principally assisting French businesses to develop their export trade with Argentina, Morocco, Egypt and most other countries in the Middle East. It has been a great help, of course, to be able to speak and understand many of the languages of the countries with which I am dealing. It has also been of great benefit – oiling the wheels so to speak – that I know a country's President, or King, or a Minister of State. These are contacts that I have built up over many years. Such friendly relations assisted my work in developing our overseas trade."

"Have you also had contact with all the Presidents of the French Republic?"

"All of them, apart from Giscard d'Estaing. But I was invited to meet him on one occasion."

"Was that because he was anti-royalist?" I said.

"No, not exactly. Giscard d'Estaing was always pro Giscard d'Estaing."

"I then set about making my name through the creation of a perfume business. My first perfume was Blue Lily; the second one is Royalissime. Another of my interests is painting and, fortunately, a number of people seem to enjoy what I paint. Creating beautiful scents and creating beautiful pictures are, to me, two sides of the same coin. One pleases the nose; one pleases the eye; and both please the spirit, I hope! The first exhibition of my paintings was held in London at the studio of Nicholas Harding. Since then, I have also had exhibitions in Spain, the United States and frequently in France. I aim for one exhibition a year. I also like to write and have had three books published. The first was something of an autobiography with a political slant to it entitled *A Mes Fils* (To my Children); the second was in the form of an open letter to the French Head of State at the time of the 1996 general election when Chirac was elected. I completed my third book, last year. It is entitled *Will France survive the Year 2000?*"

"Was Chirac's election to your advantage?" I asked.

"No. It was to the advantage of France. I have never taken a stand politically. I have not supported the left and I have not supported those with right-wing convictions. My allegiance is to my country, France.

"My latest project is a rather special association and one that is close to my heart. I intend to found the 'Institute of the Royal House of France.'"

I was surprised to hear this, especially in modern day republican France. I asked the Count, "Given our growing multicultural environment in France, have your background and education prepared you to re-establish the traditions and observances of a Royal Family within the France we know today?"

"The traditions into which I was born and which my family has continued have never been so strict that they could not be adapted. Tradition has its place. However, too much tradition can lead to rigidity and one is then rooted to one spot. Nothing would change and we would never make any progress, would we? For me, tradition is something that forms the core, the axis of my life. I feel that it is a royal axis, a regal core. Therefore, it is not so much a case of going along with the rules and notions of the moment that interests me, as having the inner conviction and continuity of a royal inheritance. What I could call this royal inheritance is both easy and difficult to continue. It is easy in the sense that it is a matter of conscience that one has a duty to listen to others and continue the family line. It is difficult from the point of view that one is trying to achieve a fair balance between forces of chaos on the one hand and forces of over-regulation on the other. If one follows the path of too much order and regulation, one arrives at a state of fascism. If one follows the path of too much chaos, one arrives at a state of anarchy. Therefore, it is important to know how to achieve a state of equilibrium to balance these forces. It is as important to achieve this balance in planning one's personal life, as it is in planning society. This is the role of our family, as a royal family. It is our duty to maintain this equilibrium from year to year and from one generation to the next. We take a longer perspective. We are concerned with building for the future, rather than being caught up in the matters of the instant. That is what I have learned."

"Regarding your own close family ties and the international role of the Orléans family, have these close bonds of friendship extended to other sovereign rulers and their families? When I interviewed your father, back in 1962, he told me, "It is a waste of time dealing with royalty. They live in a dream world. They do not live in the reality of today. Actually, I am a socialist."

Count Henri replied, "Human beings, whether they are of royal line or not, cannot escape from the times in which they live. None of us is protected from the advance of time and the course of history. I believe that every Prince and every King has found this to be true. For example, take the experiences of Prince Charles. I admire what he has tried to achieve within a modern context. He is a most interesting person to meet and get to know. Equally, I find it fascinating to learn the thoughts of such people as the King of Spain, Prince Jean of Luxembourg and the Archduke Otto von Habsburg. I have gained greatly from my personal contact with such people, people who are not run of the mill. I dislike the social whirl but personal friendships are another matter. I believe that if, at some future date, we are called upon, as a royal family, to take on public responsibilities in France, then it will be essential to know the thoughts and feelings of France at that time."

"Are you related to the King of Spain?" I asked.

"Yes. He is a cousin as our grandmothers were sisters; and the King of Belgium's family are also cousins through the line of King Louis-Philippe; also the Italian royal family, and part of the German family. However, we are not related to the English royals."

"Yet I was given to understand that the Queen of England could lay claim to the throne of France through her ancestry?"

"No, that is false. In France Salic Law prevails, which means that the entitlement to the throne passes down the male line." Smiling, he added, "Since the Hundred Years War it has been so."

"Do you know Prince Charles?" I asked.

"We have exchanged letters and met twice. He is a Prince for modern times. He is modest and intelligent. I admire his social, political and ecological ideas. He has had to deal with great unhappiness in his life. Overall, I would have to say that I like the King of Spain the most.   We got to know each other when we were both very young and have remained firm friends ever since."

"Have you drawn up an action programme covering your social, cultural and political ideas?" I enquired.

"It could be dangerous to prepare such a programme too far in advance. The world can change very quickly these days. A programme for three months can be obsolete in four. I believe it is important, above all, to have a personal philosophy and core values. That's why I can relate so easily to Prince Charles and the things that he believes in. Having high aspirations and core beliefs draws together political decision-making and humanitarian concerns, so as to improve people's lives. Moreover, we must pay special attention to the environment and take charge of what we are doing to it so that our lives in future really will be more liberated."

"Don't you think that we have sufficient freedom already?" I asked.

"We do not have any real freedom... not at all."

"Do you have any particular preferences in party politics?"

"Definitely not. I am in contact with all political parties."

"Even the Communist Party?" I added.

"Why not? Even with the Trotskyists!"

"And what about Le Pen?" I asked.

"No. He does not do anything for me. Le Pen is on the whole a destructive force. The others at least try to be constructive some of the time. Alain Krivine is a man who, from time to time, has interesting things to say. The same is true of Robert Hué and also, perhaps, Cohn-Bendit... Each has his place in the order of things. Each plays his part in building something new and worthwhile. However, if you are a destructive person, like Le Pen, nothing new or good remains. You must appreciate that my party, my political party, is France herself."

"Are you for the movement towards a unified Europe?" I added.

"I am for one Europe, so long as each member country is able to protect its own sovereignty. I support the notion that countries will come together in union, as in an agreed marriage. However, within that marriage, it is vital that the bride retains her own identity and, similarly, that the bridegroom keeps his identity. However, if you study the results of European elections, they are not too encouraging. Look at how few actually vote. Turning to the debate over monetary union, I can see difficulties with the proposed single currency. Surely, in the European economic plan, we are all heading towards, what I might term 'electronic money.' Transactions will, in large part, be cashless... perhaps. However, that may well leave many people out in the cold. People who, for one reason or another, will not have access to 'electronic money.' There could be as many as 12 per cent of Europeans who would not have the means to have access to electronic money. There will always be the poor and those on the margins. Furthermore, I am concerned about the effects on small businesses who trade in tiny amounts of cash. There is a danger of creating a European economic plan to suit large multinational companies. It could be that although they would like monetary union and gain from it, the social and economic lives of the 'little man' would be made poorer by it."

I then enquired, "Regarding international political planning, what is your view concerning the intervention of NATO in the Balkans?"

"Firstly, I must tell you that all war is stupid. It is a form of madness. However much war is presented as a 'moral' war, it is always, fundamentally, a conflict about politics and economics. The economic aspect is always concealed. I see France being sucked into this masquerade and that hurts me a lot."

"To close our fascinating discussion, may I ask you the classic question, 'What advice do you have for the young?'"

Henri, Count of Paris, thought for a moment and replied, clearly and with passion, "That they will, above all, have hope in this world that is full of despair."

THE VARIS

I have met many interesting people in the embassies and salons of capital cities, but none more so than Helen Vari and Georges, her husband, both Hungarians by birth who chose to take Canadian nationality. Our paths crossed in 1981 at a diplomatic lunch given at the Netherlands Embassy in Paris by the wife of the Ambassador Mrs. Jean Tammenoms-Bekker. At this lunch Helen came in contact for the first time with the Duchess de La Rochefoucauld, who was the guest of honour. Helen had a Canadian friend, Zena Chery, who was also a friend of the Duchess. During lunch, Helen passed on a message from their mutual friend advising the Duchess to take certain vitamins, the latter replied, "Thank you. Please tell Zena that I do not need them. My health is perfectly good." Feeling sorry for Helen, I took her to one side and explained that the Duchess does not take kindly to being given advice. Despite this little episode, Helen and her husband became for several years members of the Duchess's circle of friends and were often invited to her salons.

From being penniless refugees, Georges and his wife had become billion-aires, with Georges controlling a hugely successful business empire. Their story started in Hungary. Georges was born in 1924, the only son of a Hungarian lawyer and small landowner who was fortunate to be still alive. In 1920 the communists had seized power in Hungary. Georges told me, "My father was a fanatical nationalist. As an opponent of the communist government, he was arrested, tried and sentenced to death. Thank heavens in 1921 the Communists were removed from power before the sentence was carried out. In 1936, when I was twelve, I was sent to a boarding school in Lausanne, but when war broke out in 1939 my mother insisted I should be brought back to Hungary. I continued my schooling in Sentes, the little town where we lived, not very far from Budapest. When I qualified for university, my father asked me which law school I should like to go to, since in those days only law and medicine offered careers of any standing. As my reply was non-committal my father sent me to Budapest, convinced that I would read law. When I came home for the Christmas vacation he asked me how I was getting on with my law studies. You can imagine the family scene that took place when I announced that I was doing an engineering course! Father insisted. I had to read law. I was determined to become an engineer, so I read law and engineering, and qualified in both."

In 1944 Georges's father was killed when the court in which he was conducting a case received a direct hit during a bombing raid on Budapest by the Russians, who invaded and occupied Hungary in 1946. By 1947, Georges was working as an engineer engaged in restoring old palaces and buildings of historic importance. Strongly anti-communist, he was from the time of the Russian occupation a member of the secret movement hoping one day to restore freedom to Hungary and overthrow the hated Stalinist regime of Rakosi, the prime minister, who was a puppet of the Soviets. Popular feeling came to a head in 1956. The freedom fighters took to the streets of Budapest. The Russians sent in the tanks. By November, resistance was crushed. A wanted man, Georges joined the exodus of those making their way to the Austrian border hoping to get across and find freedom in the West. After walking for four days, he and many others managed to cross through the barbed wire guarding the frontier. "I had always wanted to go to Canada," Georges recounted, "so at the Canadian Embassy in Vienna I applied for asylum in that country and was successful."

Georges arrived in Montreal in January 1957. "It was extremely cold," he continued. "A military camp near the city was being used for refugees and that is where I and others like me were taken. We were told that in Montreal there was an organisation that helped Hungarian refugees. As soon as I could, I caught a bus into the city. I well remember the temperature. It was 25 degrees below zero and I had no overcoat. The address I had been given in St. Catherine Street turned out to be the wrong one, or so it seemed. My enquiry there produced startled looks and the remark 'It's not here. This is St. Catherine's Street East. Perhaps the place you are looking for is on St. Catherine's Street West.' Eventually I arrived at the correct building. I was given shoes and clothes. The man in charge of the operation gave me five dollars. His name was Brian Mulroney; during the years to come, our paths crossed many times and he eventually became the Conservative Prime Minister of Canada from 1984 to 1993. I was able to find work in the office of an engineering firm. Quite a story really. I was doing the work of an engineer but being paid as a workman. At the end of the first week I received my tiny cheque. It was hard work and long hours for a few dollars. Same thing the second week. On the Friday of the third week, I was taken to one side and told that the manager wanted a few words with me. That's it, I thought, I'm going to be given the sack. But no. I was praised for the speed of my work and asked if I could come in on the Saturday and Sunday. There was a job that had to be done urgently. I breathed again.

For some years I had been engaged to Helen. Then, in 1963 her grandmother who lived in Austria died and Helen was able to obtain permission from the authorities to leave Hungary to attend the funeral. That is how Helen managed to escape from Hungary.[1] I travelled to Austria and brought her back with me and we were married in Montreal in March 1963.

After five years in the engineering firm, I joined Sicant, a large construction company and became their chief engineer. We had several ongoing projects building flats, hotels and churches. In 1967 Montreal staged the International World Exposition – Expo 1967 – and my firm had a large presence there. The year 1969 saw the start of a big change in our lives. I had a telephone call one

---

1 *Strict controls were in operation to prevent Hungarians from leaving their own country.*

day from an American friend who advised me to come to New York to meet the Chairman of the Morse Company. The Company had a large project coming up in Paris and needed a specialist in high-rise construction who could speak French and English. I jumped at the opportunity. Worried that I may need expert advice on the financial details of a possible deal, I took an accountant with me. We arrived at the company's offices; whilst we were waiting for the meeting to take place, my accountant had to answer to an urgent call of nature. No sooner had he left me, I was called in to meet the Chairman. During the ten minutes that my accountant was otherwise engaged, I negotiated by myself and a deal was done. A few weeks later, at the end of July, my wife and I flew to Paris.

There I met Jean-Claude Aaron, the well-known property developer and I became an associate of his company, Sefri, in the construction of the Montparnasse Tower. As technical director I was responsible for all the building work. The project was completed in 1973."

I asked Georges to tell me about the tower. "All Europe was talking about it," said Georges. "It's a huge skyscraper complex, the tallest building in Europe – a business centre with fifty-eight floors of offices. Beneath it is a five-floor car park. The tower is built over a Paris metro line which continued to operate throughout the construction period."

It should be said that Georges is an uncomplicated man, always relaxed; above all he has a sense of humour and a fund of anecdotes from years in his profession.

"You must have lots of interesting tales to tell about such a project," I prompted.

"True. For example, there was the incident of the little old lady who opened my office door one day at lunch time when the rest of the staff were out. 'Are you the person responsible for the construction of this tower?' she asked. 'How could you build such a thing? It's disgusting. A monstrosity!' There was also an amazing story concerning one of the men working on the construction of the twenty-eighth lift shaft. He stepped out through the temporary plywood door opening on to the shaft expecting a working platform to be in place. For some reason it wasn't. He just stepped straight into space. By an extraordinary reflex of self-preservation he managed to grab the two lift cables with both hands. Miraculously he lowered himself down through the twenty-eight floors until he reached the bottom. His hands were cut and bruised, but otherwise he was unhurt, apart from shock." "It was fate," I interrupted, "I believe in it." "Maybe," continued Georges, "Anyway it was definitely human intervention that gives me my last story. When the time came to dismantle all the workman's day-huts, more than one was found to contain a bed. Well, it was somewhere to entertain their girlfriends out of working hours."

Once the Montparnasse Tower was finished, Jean-Claude Aaron suggested that I take on all the other work the company had in hand. I became the vice-chairman. For three years I was involved in the construction of high-rise buildings in France. Then came the oil crisis of 1976. There was no longer any work in France and Sefri began to look for work abroad. The first big project was with the Russians. After prolonged, difficult negotiations, we won the contract to build a two thousand-room hotel in Moscow for the 1978 Olympic Games.

"Dealing with the Russians had its funny side at times," said Georges, "There were many conditions attached to the hotel contract, one of the most important being that our company, Sefri, should employ only foreign workers brought in from abroad. When I asked the reason for this, the Russians said the wages we paid were too high and they could not have Russian workers being paid amounts like that. Another contract with the Russians involved the building of new embassies in Paris and Moscow. It was agreed that Sefri would build the Russian embassy in Paris – it is a gigantic place – and the Russians would build the French embassy in Moscow. By 1978 the French embassy was finished, but I soon received a call from the officials there saying that the balconies were falling down. It was all very complicated; the point was that the new building was due to be officially inaugurated during a visit to Moscow by the French President, Valéry Giscard d'Estaing. The date of the visit could not be changed. The inauguration ceremony took place as planned, attended by the French President and his Soviet counterpart, Leonid Brezhnev. The balconies were on the ground in ruins."

Another story was that during the construction of the Hotel Cosmos in Moscow, I was having certain difficulties. So one afternoon I spoke to the Commercial Attaché at the French Embassy, explaining that I was having problems with import licences. Perhaps he could have a word with the Soviet Deputy Minister of Commerce. The attaché promised he would contact him the very next morning, but added, 'Between now and then he will already know all about it, thanks to the listening devices they have everywhere!' I found that an interesting experience. But I wasn't the only person to have one. A French colleague of mine had an encounter in Moscow with the Russians which was more like a nightmare. On the evening of the day he had flown into Moscow, we were having dinner in a restaurant. After the meal, my colleague excused himself saying that he wanted to fetch something from the car. He came back furious; his possessions – case, passport and money had been stolen from the boot. Naturally he wanted to inform the police: our interpreter warned against it, saying that the story may cause more problems. My architect friend insisted. The reaction of the police confirmed the interpreter's fears. 'What! You are accusing a citizen of our country of theft?' And they locked him up. It took two days for the French Ambassador to have him released from jail. By now, my friend had already had enough of Moscow. Armed with his new passport supplied by the French Embassy, he made straight for the airport. He didn't get any further than passport control. 'What? No Soviet entry visa?' And they locked him up again.

After Moscow in 1978, we created a new company – Sefri International – and I bought it from Jean-Claude Aaron. Over time I expanded the company, extending business operations to four continents. In 1989 I sold Sefri to one of my French collaborators and returned to Canada where I carried out major building works, including the International Hotel in Toronto."

Georges subsequently became the 'Honourable Georges Vari' on his appointment by the Canadian Prime Minister, Brian Mulroney, as one of the hundred Canadians making up the Queen of England's Privy Council in Canada.

Various causes have benefited from the generosity of the Varis. In Canada they endowed the Georges and Helen Foundation for Culture and Education, which makes grants available for students. In the students' residential quarters of the Sorbonne they subsidised the Canadian hall of residence. The cost of the long and laborious restoration of the frescoes in the Hôtel des Invalides was born by them, as was the renovation of the Cathedral of St. Thomas d'Aquin. Recently, to help make up for the heavy losses caused by the storm that did so much damage in 1999 in France, the Varis presented a thousand Canadian maple trees to the city of Paris and a further two thousand to Versailles.

The Varis support public causes out of a debt of gratitude, saying, "As far as possible we like to make donations in France and Canada, the two countries in which we have been successful."

Helen too is capable and enthusiastic; she likes to be closely involved with the causes that they take up. When in August 1998 Pope Jean-Paul II paid an official visit to Paris, he stayed at the Vatican Nunciature. Helen donated and was responsible for all the floral decorations, going daily from room to room to make sure the displays remained fresh and attractive.

DIPLOMACY

A Sorry Tale of the Overweening Diplomat

During my career as a diplomatic journalist and indeed throughout my life since the age of eighteen, I have met and known many diplomats from different countries throughout the world. Most of them I held in the highest regard, impressed by their skills, tact and impeccable manners. Others disappointed me.

One such disappointment was a certain Egyptian Ambassador to Paris, a handsome, elegant, cultivated and personable man. He appeared to possess all the qualities necessary to please ambassadorial circles. His name was Naguib Kadri. He was the personal appointee of the Egyptian president, Anwar El Saadat. With his charm and knowledge of French culture, he was very popular in French circles, especially in the salons of Parisian high society.

Unfortunately his success in these surroundings went to his head – and turned it. He became a snob, disdainful of his fellow countrymen to the extent that he became deeply unpopular with all the Egyptians in Paris. His own embassy staff hated him. I can relate the following story that illustrates his overbearing manner because I was present at the occasion.

A certain French Countess arranged a reception in honour of the Ambassador. She thought that by inviting all the Egyptians who moved in the right circles she would be giving pleasure to Kadri. I shall never forget his reaction when he arrived at the reception to find all his compatriots present. A look of complete astonishment and contempt came over his face and in a loud, haughty voice that took one's breath away he exclaimed, "What! Are you all here?" The occasion never recovered from the embarrassed silence that followed, despite the admirable composure of the hostess.

The end of Kadri's reign in Paris came in tragic fashion. Among the many embassy staff with whom he had sour relations was the Cultural Counsellor, Atef Sedky. One day, after a particularly acrimonious encounter, Sedky (who later became prime minister of Egypt) could stand it no longer. Seething with indignation, he caught the next plane to Cairo to complain in person to the Egyptian Foreign Minister. The latter was not unaware of the Ambassador's reputation. His reaction was immediate, "That's it! Enough is enough! He's out!"

Not many days afterwards the unsuspecting Kadri locked in his own self-esteem received a very nasty surprise when he picked up his copy of the daily *Figaro*. In it he read that he was no longer Egyptian Ambassador to Paris and was being recalled to Cairo. In a state of shock, he rushed round to his closest lady friend to whom he repeated bitterly, "Look what they've done to me! I can't believe it!"

Before leaving Paris, he gave a farewell cocktail party. Surprisingly – and for the first time – he invited all Egyptian society in the capital. It was a case of far too little, far too late. On his return to Egypt he retired into obscurity.

British Diplomacy – A British Ambassador in Paris

It is at the Foreign Office in London's Whitehall where the decisions are made as to who will be proposed as the next Ambassador for a particular location abroad. The choice is made after a great deal of careful study. The principal point is always that the person selected should know the language of the country to which he, or she, will be appointed. Chinese, for example, is a requirement for certain postings. Obviously this is done so that there is an ease of communication and an immediate cultural sympathy.

In the case of an important neighbouring country such as France, the choice of Ambassador has to be perfect. The British Ambassador in Paris has a hard task. He is responsible for an Embassy staff of some one hundred and sixty officials, of various grades, roughly half of them British and half of them French.

Sir Reginald Hibbert says that it is all a question of 'organisation.' I knew this eminent British diplomat and Ambassador and his wife for the thirty consecutive years that I was based in Paris. I have quite unforgettable memories of their various social gatherings that I was privileged to attend. I recall especially one very memorable occasion.

The year is 1980. Sir Reginald and Lady Hibbert have organised a grand charity ball to raise funds for the United World Colleges, a Foundation in which The Prince of Wales and Lord Mountbatten were keenly interested and in which the French participation was led by Mr. Olivier Giscard d'Estaing, the brother of the President of the Republic. Prince Charles especially supported this event, just a few days before his marriage to Lady Diana. As he was not yet married, Lady Diana did not accompany him, which caused much disappointment. It would undoubtedly have been unsuitable for her to be there in terms of diplomatic etiquette.

On this particular evening, the presence of the disco from the most famous nightclub in Paris at that time, Régine's, transformed one of the grandest of the Embassy's reception rooms into a veritable discothèque. Régine added, over the musical volume of the evening, that her presence was "especially in honour of Prince Charles!" Those of us who had visited the Embassy on other, more formal, occasions fully realised the irony of such live musical animation reigning within what was normally one of the most strictly regulated social rendez-vous in the whole of France.

Meanwhile, in one of the other neighbouring Embassy salons, there was English music played by the bandsmen of the Welsh Guards, promoting classical dance arrangements. I must admit, however, that it was not enjoying very much success for its efforts and undoubted skill. Most of the company had made tracks towards the somewhat stronger chords of Regine's disco–dance music! It was a night when rules were made to be broken, or at least, bent a little.

A whole host of Ambassadors were present that evening, along with Princess Grace of Monaco accompanied by her son Prince Albert. The decorations were superb; the women's dresses gorgeous; the buffet extraordinary; and the party went on well into the early hours of the following morning. A night to remember indeed.

In 1999, I met Sir Reginald Hibbert once again, this time in London. I asked him if he would give me one or two of his foremost impressions of his posting in Paris. He replied: "Firstly, it is important to realise that the residence of the British Ambassador in Paris is, in fact, a listed historic monument. It is a palace in which the Ambassador lives. It is a very fine building and the French attach great importance to our maintaining it and keeping it in excellent condition. Indeed, when I first went there, the Foreign Minister, in one of my first interviews with him, alluded to reports in the press that people in Britain were beginning to say that the Embassy in France was too luxurious and too expensive. He stressed that he hoped I was making it clear to people back in Whitehall that the French government really did attach great importance to our maintaining our favoured position in the rue du Faubourg Saint-Honoré, near the Elysée, where we had been installed for so long."

He added: "I could compare our Embassy residence in Paris to the best five-star hotel. One could live there very comfortably and also provide the best for our guests at the same time. Bear in mind that we were entertaining almost continuously and would have a succession of important guests staying with us, coming from London to Paris to do business of all kinds in France."

I put to the Ambassador, "Your Embassy in Paris occupies a highly significant place within the diplomatic world and high society, which particular distinguished British personalities did you entertain?"

"We received several members of the Royal Family: Her Majesty the Queen on an informal visit in which she saw something of Burgundy and the châteaux of the Loire and was entertained at the Elysée by President Giscard d' Estaing; Queen Elizabeth The Queen Mother, The Prince of Wales, Princess Anne, the Duchess of Kent, the Duke of Gloucester, and Princess Michael of Kent. Nearly every Minister in successive British governments came and stayed at some time or other, some coming many times. A large number of visitors also came from the worlds of politics, business, finance and academia."

"Do you have a particular favourite amongst the members of the British Royal Family?" I enquired.

"Well, if you forced me to make a choice, I would have to admit that it is Princess Anne."

"How many years of service did you spend in Paris?" I asked.

"To start at the beginning, I was posted to Paris at the tail end of Mr. Callaghan's, now Lord Callaghan's, Labour government when David Owen was Foreign Secretary. However, soon after I arrived in Paris, there was a British General Election and Mrs. Thatcher came to power. I spent three years in Paris, from 1979 to 1982.

During the three years, half of my service was with President Giscard d'Estaing and half was with President Mitterrand and in that sense I managed to live through the 'alternation', which was then being introduced for the first time in Paris. I can make one comment about the difference between the two regimes. Regarding President Giscard, one always had a very clear, but sometimes somewhat chilly reply to questions that arose. When I went to the Elysée Palace, I would receive an answer to questions quite clearly, crystal clear in fact, but, as I have said, so clear as to be somewhat chilly. When I went to the Quai d'Orsay, I would get exactly the same answer. Now with President Mitterrand it was not the same at all. It was certainly warmer and friendlier, but it was also more opaque. One received a reply, but it would not be so crystal clear. Sometimes I would travel to the Elysée and get what I thought was one answer and then go to the Quai d'Orsay and receive a slightly different response. So, in a sense, the latter was more humanly approachable and friendly, but it is very difficult for me to say which system proved the easier to deal with and succeed. Let us just say that there was a difference in style."

"During your service in Paris, and with regard to the political relationship between France and Britain at that time, could you tell me something of any 'difficulties' or disputes in which you were involved with the French government?" I asked.

"Now, while I was in Paris, we had a series of 'points of friction', you might say, with France, largely arising from uncertainty about Britain's proper place in the European Community. Mrs. Thatcher bargained hard; as everyone also knows, she wanted our money back. There were all sorts of tiresome disputes that arose: disputes about turkey meat, about mutton and lamb, about fishing, about the Community's budget, about the agricultural policy, and so on. I seem to recall that it was Sir Charles Petrie who once commented that the troubles between Britain and France tended to be 'SW1 troubles' that is to say, troubles between British organs of government that are all concentrated in SW1 and the French organs of government, and not really between the two peoples. I must say that was very much my own experience in France too.

During working hours, one would tend to be occupied, all too frequently, with trying to elucidate and smooth out various points of friction explaining them to London, or explaining and clarifying London's attitude to the French.

When working hours were over in Paris, or one was on tour in France, all doors were open with no difficulties after all. Certainly, outside Paris, the whole of France was open to us and there was a tremendous wave of sympathy towards and friendship for Great Britain. Thus I think it is quite wrong for people to believe that, somehow, France is a difficult, or in any way, an unfriendly country. It is simply not true. However, we do have points of friction that arise constantly, and still do to this very day, between SW1 and the Ministers in Paris; between the organs of the British government and those of the French government. Anybody who is posted to Paris is bound to feel that friction, to feel that awkwardness."

"And so, speaking at that political level, there has always been the sort of friction to which you refer and this continues to the present day. But how do you find the relationship between England and France on a cultural level?" I asked.

"What I would say is this. With France, our cultural relations are of very great importance. I think that it is sometimes thought that politically France and Britain are not quite on the same wavelength. But be that as it may, I would say that culturally we tend to be close and the French respect for British culture and the British respect for French culture are very high.

During one of my years there, I would also say that the two most important events that occurred in Anglo-French relations were the Gainsborough Exhibition at the Grand Palais and the production of *Peter Grimes* at the Paris Opera. Both made a powerful impression in France and I would say a much better and a much more useful impression than was made by the many rather more ephemeral events that were grabbing the headlines at that time in these little frictions and quarrels we had with France on political matters. In saying this, I do not mean that political matters were not of due importance. They were, of course, of very great importance to us. However, I do feel that very often the reaction, on both sides, to these small events was altogether too impatient, altogether too intolerant, and showed a lack of understanding in each country of what the other was aiming at.

People tend to say that this is the fault of the tabloids, because the tabloids rush to criticise too freely. I don't think that it is entirely that. I think that in spite of the closeness of Britain to France, both geographically and in terms of personal communication, there is a failure in Britain to have a complete understanding of what makes France 'tick', how France works, and the same is true the other way round! This is something that, in the long run, needs to be overcome and it can only be overcome by spreading the knowledge of French in England and the knowledge of English in France; progress has been made on both fronts; although I think it is true to say that Britain now tends, surprisingly in view of what has been recorded in past history, to be lagging a little behind France in learning about the language and culture of the other."

I then asked, "Mr. Ambassador, as one travel across the world, one realises that it is the English language which seems to dominate; most international business is conducted in English, or American-English. Do you think that the French, who are fiercely proud of their own language, have come to terms with that?"

"It is perfectly true that the French are now facing up, very well, to their task of knowing enough English to cope in the world as a whole, especially in the United States. When I was at school and at university the position was that French was the number one foreign language that people needed to learn. I would argue very much that that is still the case, as French is still very widely used in the world; more so than other foreign languages that one can think of, for the conduct of public business; and, of course the French language opens the door to a high culture, a fellow civilisation. I think that it is a great pity that French is no longer the number one foreign language in British schools."

"You were a principal British Ambassador during Mrs. Thatcher's 'reign'. Can you tell us your impressions of her and of any contacts you had with her? Personally, I have a strong admiration for this *'grande dame!'*

"Mrs. Thatcher has a sharp intelligence and is, above all, a determined and resolute woman. I can recall one memorable evening at the beginning of her premiership when she came to Paris for a summit, accompanied by a large team of ministers and officials. There were so many that we organised dinner at a series of tables of eight in two separate rooms. We naturally invited wives with their husbands. Mrs. Thatcher was interested only in business. So we ended up with one room full of official men with Mrs. Thatcher, and one mixed room where everybody had a party. Both before and after dinner Mrs. Thatcher held official meetings. Throughout the evening the sheep were kept well away from the goats."

"Over which group did Mrs. Thatcher preside?" I asked.

"The male-only dinner, of course! Those were the days."

"As for your daily life at the Embassy, could you have anything like private moments and personal times? How about the weekends?" I enquired.

"Serving in Paris, one could never enjoy a private lifestyle. For example, on Sundays, if we were in Paris, we would dutifully attend a service at an Anglican church in Paris; one had five to choose from. Afterwards, if it were possible, my wife and I would enjoy taking our dog for a walk. Constantly walking behind us, of course, were the security guards!"

"I remember now, Mr. Ambassador, that you were always accompanied by several bodyguards. Why was that? Why all that surveillance?"

"Yes, that's true. Two bodyguards always followed us. The reason? During the whole of my posting there we were dealing with a difficult security problem because of a possible threat from the IRA. We had one or two rather disagreeable events; disagreeable circumstances at the time of the hunger strike by Bobby Sands and various efforts by the IRA and their sympathisers in France to demonstrate against us. There were one or two untoward incidents, unpleasant ones, but we managed to deal with them. Thus, during the whole of my time in Paris, I was always accompanied by two members of the French Service 'for the Protection of VIPs in France.' This, of course, has a slightly inhibiting effect on one's movements. On the other hand, one gets very used to it and, in the end, becomes very friendly with all the different detectives one gets to know. There again, all those stories are perhaps for another day..."

"Mr. Ambassador, what final thoughts do you have on your service in France?" I asked.

"I think that during my time in France I managed to visit pretty well every corner of the country. The longer I stayed, the more I grew to admire the conduct of modern France and the way in which modern France has been developed and ruled. It is really quite extraordinary how they have recovered from the disaster of the Second World War and how well their methods of centralised government have served them."

I led our discussion towards a conclusion by reminding the Ambassador of a diplomatic dinner which we both attended and which I found to be particularly interesting at the time. It was shortly after President Mitterrand had come to power and had included communist Ministers in his government.

Sir Reginald and his wife had organised a grand dinner. Amongst those on the guest list were a French communist government Minister and two or three socialists from Ministerial Cabinets. The occasion was splendid. The arrangements were sophisticated and luxurious. The sixty-four guests were seated around one large, ancient French table, with an exquisite centrepiece. This antique silver-gilt piece of craftsmanship had been created during the early Napoleonic period, bought by an English Prince, who offered it to the British Embassy as a gift. I remember noticing that among the guests that night were several elderly aristocrats from well known old French families, as well as at least two Duchesses.

One of the Duchesses said to me "What a thing! That the Ambassador from Great Britain should be entertaining Communist Ministers!" Then the other Duchess added thoughtfully, "How interesting! It's the first time in my life that I have been in the company of a Communist – Minister or not!"

Sadly, Sir Reginald died on 5th October, 2002 at the age of 80. He had an attractive personality as well as great ability, but always remained modest. He received the highest French award, Commander of the *Légion d'honneur*.

Egyptian Diplomacy – An Egyptian Ambassador in Paris

Although I have travelled the world, it is in Paris that I have found the Egyptian Ambassador who, perhaps more than any other, epitomises the highest qualities of his position by virtue of his class and style. His name is Ali Maher and he has been Ambassador since 1993. He possesses quite remarkable international expertise and knowledge. The main principle, which is at the core of his life, is that of 'discretion'. He is discretion itself. He has an enviable ability to express himself and is also a man of action. By my definition, he is the true embodiment of a great diplomat.

It is in Paris, the city I love, that I attended a number of functions. These are, in the main, diplomatic gatherings, cultural and social occasions. Here one meets the most brilliant men and women who, as Ambassadors, bring their country's best minds to the profession. It has been my privilege over the years, as a diplomatic and social journalist, to interview many of the most interesting personalities. One such privilege was to be able to interview a Prime Minister called Ahmed Maher, the grandfather of Ali Maher. That interview was many years ago as I was just starting my career in journalism. How strange that now, so many years later, I should be interviewing his grandson Ali.

The link was made on 10th June 1999 when I had a conversation with Ali Maher at the Egyptian Embassy in Paris

"What does being a diplomat mean to you?"

"Diplomacy is, at one and the same time, a skilled art-form and a matter of

His Excellency Ali Maher, Egyptian Ambassador to France since 1993.

luck. It is the skill of being able to manage efficiently relations between one country and another while at the same time protecting the interests of one's own country. One has to employ political, peaceful means by following certain rules and protocols, which have established the nature of diplomacy over the years.

Diplomacy also seeks to find solutions to the pressing problems of the day. Here we are talking about using intellectual means and making contact, through the relevant forms of negotiation or discussions with the various parties involved; as we do, for example, when we gather different protagonists together and attempt to resolve their conflicts and seek real agreement for the future."

"Drawing upon your diplomatic experience, what are the obstacles to progress that you most frequently encounter?" I asked. "Have you had conflicts which you have had to fight to overcome?" I added.

"It is important to be clear at the outset about this fact: in order to succeed in the diplomatic arena, one must possess a certain awareness which allows one to see, feel, and to comprehend the point of view of the other party, to sense and evaluate the different elements that together make up that point of view; in addition to being aware of the needs and interests, as well as any relevant and historical events, upon which the other bases his position. One needs to know these things in order to deal with the situation efficiently and to be able to offer progress to an adversary."

"Have you had many difficult moments in your career?"

"Certainly. When I was a young diplomat, the problem we had to face was that of conflict with the State of Israel. At a certain point in this conflict, the government of Egypt did not recognise the State of Israel, nor allow its diplomats to have any contacts whatsoever with Israeli diplomats. At that time, I was young, about twenty-four years old. I remember the first occasion I met a diplomat from Israel. It was during a convention at the International Court of Justice at The Hague. During a reception held within the precincts of the court, I was introduced to Mr. X..., First Secretary to the Ambassador of Israel. It was an enormous shock to me and really opened my eyes, for it was as if I had come face to face with someone from another planet. We had become so used to demonising our opponents that I was thoroughly astonished to find that he really did have just two eyes and two good ears like the rest of the world! In spite of that, there was no change in the position that we were not to have any diplomatic relations with this official.

The point I am trying to make clear to you is that when one breaks off all contact and communication, one also makes a demon of the other person. It is as though without contact, Evil fills the vacuum that remains. It is then very difficult to carry out one's work as a diplomat. Consequently, it is also difficult to negotiate. Making and keeping human contacts is of the utmost importance and is absolutely essential if there is to be any hope of diplomatic solutions.

I am trying to explain to you how, during my thirty-five years of public service in diplomacy, in order to succeed in the diplomatic arena one must have and be willing to show strength of character; one must have studied very carefully the files, one must know one's brief and have a very good understanding of the weak points and the strong points of one's adversary."

I then enquired, "Can you tell me something about how you carried out your diplomatic role during the conflict between the Arabs and the Israelis?"

"It is the story of how my country's diplomacy evolved after the ground-breaking visit of President Saadat to Jerusalem; that is the essence of it. The gesture that he made was clearly an outstanding form of diplomacy, although it was a move which was, shall I say, quite unconventional, that departed from the traditional norms. There we had it – the Chief of the Egyptian State who took it upon himself to go to a country, to go into the Parliament of a country, with which we were at war and who, having arrived, was received by Israel with the full honours due to a Chief of State, the like of which had never been seen before. That cannot, in any way, be regarded as traditional diplomacy. However, it was a master-stroke in breaking down the barriers formed by years of suspicion, mistrust and hatred."

The Ambassador added, "Negotiations, you see, are also part of the science of human relations and are at the core of relations between men and women; and between one country and another. It is most important that diplomacy should retain a human dimension at its heart. A peace treaty, for example, is the summit of diplomatic skill and endeavour. Whereas, by contrast, a war is a sad failure of diplomacy."

"Many people, I would imagine, know little about the work of a diplomat. They think perhaps that the job is solely tied up with political protest!" I said.

"The diplomat is the man or woman whom the government sends to a country to listen and understand what is happening within that country and report back to his government all those features and elements that form the basis upon which that country will make decisions. Therefore, we follow the external policy-making of the country and the internal political, economic and social situation. Also, and equally, we are there to explain and promote our own country and its policies to the country to which we are posted. It used to be said that a diplomat was sent by his government to lie for his country. That is not true. Nobody would get away with lying nowadays. The truth emerges with great rapidity.

The modern Ambassador must be a diplomat who is credible and who speaks the truth with authority and reliability. It would take just two or three falsehoods for others to realise that he was a man not to be believed. A couple of years ago, I had to face up to a very significant crisis after the outbreak of violence and terrorism provoked by the Fundamentalists in Egypt. You will remember that, I am sure. Immediately, the Egyptian Government put into action a security plan that included very effective measures of civil control."

"I remember that all too well," I said. "I was, as luck would have it, in the middle of a private visit to Egypt when this occurred. I was followed everywhere I went. I remember it well!"

He continued, "During that time, I was being interviewed by French television, the press and so on. At no point did I try to pretend that the risk (to tourists and foreign visitors) was nil. However, I did go to some lengths to explain, as well as I could, that methods of control and extensive security measures were in place and that, considering all the protection we were offering, there was no more danger in visiting Egypt than anywhere else in the world, and probably a lot less. You know that throughout the world today and in every capital city you can name, there is always some degree of risk."

"Now I would like to touch on the day-to-day life of a diplomat. Often the impression is – but I am sure you will correct me – that diplomats spend most of their time at receptions, cocktail parties and fine dinners," I dared to suggest.

"Well, firstly, it is not correct to regard such social and fashionable outings as an end in themselves. They are not. If we entertain people or attend special events, the main purpose is to get to know, understand and follow the life of the country to which we are posted. You can see that it is not only through perusing the papers or reading books that one comes to understand the feel of a country. Personal contact is all important."

Then he added, "A diplomat must always be impeccable, be well dressed and well groomed. For he does not only represent himself, he also represents his country. However, having said that, it is not necessary to be a dandy or Mr. Super-Elegant!"

I then said to Ali Maher, "I have known many Ambassadors and diplomats who were able to make interesting political reports to their governments as a result of the information they acquired whilst attending social functions."

"Absolutely, attending dinner parties is part of the job of a diplomat."

"What I wanted to say was that many people do not understand why certain things have to be done," I continued.

"Yes. You are correct. People see nothing but superficial surface dressing. They see without depth. Perhaps you have heard the saying, 'The work of the diplomat is harder on the feet than on the brain!' It can certainly be hard on the feet. However, perhaps from a little of what I have been able to tell you today, you will realise that the work can be very tiring for the grey matter too!"

I then asked the Ambassador about his own diplomatic career.

"My first post was in London from 1964 to 1967. For me, London was a school of diplomacy. In the beginning, English people seemed to me, young as I was, cold and distant, with an almost surly disposition, but as I came to know them better I began to appreciate their positive and attractive qualities. When one works in a large capital city like London, there is always something new to learn, because political developments are frequent. Then there were the sittings of the House of Commons, at which one could observe and come to a better understanding of the process of government. My stay in London was an instructive, enriching experience that played an important part in my diplomatic career.

I had not long been back in Cairo before I was off again, this time to Paris, with a scholarship to the International Institute of Public Administration. My diplomatic studies there lasted two years and ended with a period of on-the-job training at the French Embassy in The Hague. It gave me the opportunity to observe the working practices of diplomats and to compare French and Egyptian procedures. It was an experience from which I derived great benefit.

I returned to Egypt and worked for two years in the Foreign Ministry. Then I was posted to the Egyptian Embassy in Teheran under the régime of the Shah from 1971 to 1976. Four years later I was moved to Australia. The capital, Canberra, where I lived, was a city with an interesting and varied intellectual life. Australian diplomats were uncomplicated and open-minded. It was possible to have extremely frank discussions with them in a relaxed, informal atmosphere, which I greatly appreciated.

My next move was to my favourite city, Paris, where I spent two years as First Secretary. From there I was fortunate enough to be posted back to Cairo as Chief of Cabinet to the Foreign Minister, Boutros Boutros Ghali who was in office from 1977 to 1991 before being appointed to the position in which his name became world famous – Secretary-General of the United Nations. I found my work so exciting and rewarding that I remained in the job for five years. I had a very good understanding with my boss!

My next challenge was in Tunis, as Head of Mission, representing Egyptian interests. I stress that I was not an Ambassador because, at that time, diplomatic relations had been broken off between Egypt and Tunisia. The post required a great deal of hard work and ceaseless effort. Let me come back again to the importance of human contacts. As time passed, I made friends with government ministers and officials. Everywhere I was treated as an Ambassador, but I was not a real one until the day that diplomatic relations between Egypt and Tunisia were restored. Putting modesty aside, I have to admit that this event represented a great success for me. Seeing the Egyptian flag being officially raised over our embassy building was a moment of great emotion."

Back once more in Egypt, Ali Maher had a second spell as Chief of Cabinet of the Egyptian Foreign Minister, Amr Moussa. (In theory, and usually in practice, diplomats have a home posting between foreign assignments.) Then in June 1993 came his most prestigious appointment – Egyptian Ambassador to France.

"I was very happy to be back in France with this great honour. I am lucky too, because the relations between our two countries are excellent. I am also fortunate to have experienced an extraordinary cultural event – the celebration of two hundred years of cultural relations between Egypt and France. To mark the occasion, there was a programme of events entitled *France-Egypt: A shared Horizon*. For two years, in 1997 and 1998, Egypt was promoted throughout the whole of France, from north to south, from east to west, with exhibitions, symposia, films, books and pamphlets and, of course, extensive media coverage. A similar programme to promote France ran concurrently in Egypt."

And so with this résumé of the Ambassador's career we returned to the present. There were still a few more questions I wished to ask, so I continued, "You have seen political changes in France. When political power passes from a right-wing to a left-wing government, or vice versa, surely it must make life difficult for an Ambassador?"

"Not at all. It is no part of an Ambassador's job to become drawn into a country's internal affairs. Whether the right or the left governs France, relations between France and Egypt are what is important, and we are not affected by a change of ruling party. Common interests between France and Egypt persuade Heads of State and diplomats to preserve a certain continuity."

Next I remarked, "Ambassadors play an important rôle in maintaining good relations between countries yet they are never quoted during negotiations."

"No," said the Ambassador. "The pinnacle of success for an Ambassador is to not be quoted; to be present but to blend in with the wallpaper. He does not have a starring role. He is there to ease the path, to smooth away sharp angles."

I had reached my final question, "To be a good diplomat, is it necessary to be a career diplomat, or can an outsider come in and be successful?"

His reply was, "Diplomacy is a job that requires patience and character, a job in which, even for me now, there is something new to be learned every day. And it is also an extremely interesting job."

The answer of a diplomat!

The Ambassador brought our conversation to a close with an amusing story.

"Here we are, on a plane with the Foreign Minister Boutros Boutros Ghali. Destination Central Africa. Big adventure! Bad weather, terrible storm. Plane diverted to Khartoum. Visibility nil. Landing impossible. Pilot says, 'Out of fuel, can't fly on, have to go down!' Atmosphere in plane very tense. Nerves on edge. Everyone very frightened. I said to myself 'Ali, do something, anything to relieve the tension.' I had an idea. On a sheet of paper I wrote a few words, handed it to the Minister with a pen and said, 'Sir, at this moment when perhaps we are all about to die, I should be very much obliged if you would sign this decree announcing my posthumous promotion.' It helped. Everyone laughed. Anyway we survived. I still have a souvenir of the event – that signed piece of paper!"

And so to lunch. The Ambassador kindly invited me to the famous Cercle Interallié.

A few months after my conversation with Ali Maher, he told me that he had recently received a telephone call from Cairo from Georges Zezzos my editor-in-chief when I was working for *Le Progrès Egyptien*. In his day Zezzos was noted for his lively and witty commentaries on political and social events.

"Your Excellency, I am ringing to congratulate you," said Zezzos to Maher. "My name is Georges Zezzos; I am getting old now, and retired long ago. The other day I was listening to you giving an interview on Radio France Internationale. Not since the days of Fakhry Pasha and Adly Andraos have I heard an Egyptian Ambassador speak so well."

"What was your reaction to this telephone call?" I asked the Ambassador.

"I was very proud to be compared to two such giants of diplomacy as Fakhry Pasha and Aldy Andraos," he replied.

Mahmoud Fakhry Pasha was Egypt's first Ambassador to France. He was married to Princess Fawkeya, the eldest sister of King Farouk. For more than twenty-five years he was an outstanding representative of his country in Paris.

His term of office might well have been longer had not Nasser's accession to power brought his career to an end.

By the time I was in my early twenties I knew Fakhry Pasha well. On one occasion when I had been invited to a reception he offered to come and pick me up from my flat. When he arrived, he did not send his chauffeur to ring the doorbell, but came himself. This simple polite act reflected his aristocratic upbringing and education. He was well known in Paris as one of the most refined and distinguished Ambassadors.

Memories of an Ambassador's Wife

On a visit to London in 1991, by a lucky chance I was delighted to meet once again Jean Tammenoms Bekker, the wife of a Netherlands' Ambassador who from 1980 to 1985 had represented his country with great distinction in Paris. During those years I had become friendly with this elegant couple and was invited on several occasions to wonderful social events at their residency. Jean was a skilful hostess, well versed in the art of entertaining, of knowing who to invite with whom and especially where to place the guests at table. It would be a mistake to imagine this was an easy thing to do. Long study of the guest list was needed. During my career I attended diplomatic dinners at which certain guests would be far from happy with the places allotted to them. Matters of protocol had to be observed. For example, if an Ambassador is invited as the guest of honour at a formal dinner no more than four more other ambassador's should be present, and none of these should have a higher or more senior rank than the guest of honour. In a major city there will be over a hundred ambassadors, so keeping everybody happy is a delicate and elaborate affair.

As Jean and I chatted we reminisced about past times when diplomatic social life and its traditions were still maintained. I asked her to describe the duties of an Ambassador's wife.

"The rôle of an Ambassador's wife," said Jean, "is an extension of her husband's. Whereas the Ambassador is occupied with political and commercial affairs, both bilateral and international, his wife is busy first with establishing her family and household in a foreign country and then becoming acquainted with and inviting persons of influence and of importance to the country her husband represents. In each country one will change one's rôle in line with local life and customs. In Paris it is essential to be elegant, but contrary to its reputation, Paris is not a difficult post for ambassadors. The French are wonderful guests, convivial and lively, always taking into account, of course, that they like to meet other interesting people and be well received.

I asked Jean if she could tell me one or two stories about things that had happened to them during their years in Paris. "Well, said Jean, the following experience surprised us, even after a long and varied diplomatic career. It is a tradition at the Netherlands Embassy to give a Tulip reception in the spring when the garden is in its full glory with thousands of tulips in the residence. Days before the event the chef has helpers in the kitchen preparing for the expected eight hundred guests. One year, the evening arrived and as usual my husband and I stood ready to receive our guests, together with several members of our staff. But nobody came. An hour ticked by and still nobody came. Finally a member of our staff who had been out on a reconnaissance returned to say that the road was blocked and no cars could enter. The embassy was in the same street as several government Ministries, which were the recurring targets of strikes and demonstrations; and so our tulip reception was the unfortunate casualty on this occasion. But, then, something wonderful happened. Gradually, the guests started arriving, rather exhausted and the worse for wear, for many of them had had to walk a considerable distance in party outfits, particularly the women in their high heels. The guests were eminent French men and women, no longer young and with very busy lives and after the reception they would again be faced with the long walk back to their cars. We welcomed them most warmly, thanking them for the effort they had made. Their response was invariably the same: 'We did not want our problems to inconvenience the Netherlands' Ambassador. They all came and that tulip reception was one of the most successful parties we have ever given in a career spanning forty years. Each country has its own culture and code of manners. We had great admiration for the French code.

Another memory stands out. In January 1984 a group of twenty wives of French diplomats and foreign Ambassadors made a pilgrimage to Rome. They were members of an organisation called *Bienvenue en France* which was founded by Marie-Thérèse François-Poncet, wife of a French Foreign Minister who wanted to introduce diplomatic wives in Paris to various aspects of French life, both intellectual and artistic. The organisation was a resounding success and greatly enriched the years diplomatic wives spent in Paris. The group of twenty belonged to the theological circle, which discussed comparative religion; when the opportunity presented itself to attend an audience with the Pope in the Vatican, they accepted enthusiastically. The general audience in the company of hundreds of other people was immensely impressive but one morning at breakfast, quite unexpectedly, the party was asked to prepare for a private audience with the Holy Father at one o'clock. They were also told that each in turn would have the opportunity to talk to the Pope, either to ask a question or say something. And that is what happened. Finally, the Holy Father gathered the little group around him and said, " Perhaps you wondered why I wanted to receive you today. Well, I will tell you. I consider the work of diplomats and their wives to be of the utmost importance, an elaboration and extension of my own work. I wanted you to know this." On the way out we met Cardinal Lustiger, Archbishop of Paris, who looked at us in some astonishment for he recognised some of us. In the lift going down a priest asked us why the Holy Father had received us during his lunch hour and he had obviously had to forgo his lunch.

A few years later, when we met again, I asked Jean, "What do you think about the world of the diplomat nowadays?"

"In my opinion, a diplomat's job has changed completely. They themselves come from much more varied backgrounds. Improvements in communications have revolutionised the work of embassies and the way things are done. Present day ambassadors tell us that there is no longer a diplomatic corps and that Ambassadors no longer visit each other socially.[1] Some beautiful residences still remain. But now the EEC lays down the law of the thirty-five hour working week. In our time it was twenty-four hours out of twenty-four, seven days a week." Then, after a pause, Jean added, "My dear friend, the whole world has changed. Much that was fine and beautiful has gone. Yet in other ways much has changed for the better."

Mona Chaker – A model of diplomacy

In international diplomatic circles one of the most remarkable women I knew was Mona Chaker. She was born into the world of diplomacy and lived all her life in its atmosphere. Her father, Mohammed Awad El Khoni, was an eminent Egyptian Ambassador to various countries, especially the United Kingdom.

I knew Mona from the days when she was a young student at the American University of Cairo, where she was elected the beauty queen. To this day she remains beautiful; but her looks are not all. With them go refinement and natural elegance. When I asked her what was the most important duty of an Ambassador's wife, she answered, "Knowing your guests and how to place them at the dinner table – bearing in mind that some do not know each other – so that they get on well and have an interesting evening. This is the essential element in the art of entertaining."

Recounting some details of her life, Mona continued "When I married my husband, Mohammed, in 1950, he was a member of the Egyptian Permanent Delegation to the United Nations in New York. However, we were married in Moscow, where my father was Ambassador at the time. In fact, I was living in Moscow before my marriage. There I learned to speak Russian. It was an interesting time to be in Moscow – the era of Bulganin and Khrushchev. We also enjoyed our stay in Washington from 1975 to 1980. During the Camp David talks, my husband was the Deputy to Ashraf Gorbal, who was our very popular and successful ambassador to the United States for fifteen years.

When my husband was appointed Ambassador to the United Kingdom, I returned to a residence that was already familiar to me, since my father was Ambassador in London when I was very young. We were fortunate to have a long stay in London. President Mubarak allowed us to remain there for nine years. I enjoyed everything about London; what particularly appealed to me was the English sense of humour and the delightful habit of commenting lightly even on serious matters.

The first soirée we attended at Buckingham Palace was in 1988. During the course of the evening, the Queen came over to us and told us how much her

---

1 *By long tradition, when an Ambassador arrived in a country to take up his post he first presented his credentials to the Head of State, then started on a round of visits to make contact with his counterparts. The custom survives but nowadays is becoming less and less the established practice.*

sister, Princess Margaret, had enjoyed her visit to Egypt. After we had been in London for five years we were privileged to be invited to Windsor Castle. This is not something that happens as a matter of course. It was a private invitation. During the dinner my husband was on the Queen's left, while I sat between the Duke of Edinburgh and the Prime Minister, John Major. The Queen is such a lovely hostess. After dinner, she offered us chocolates, saying, "I received them on my birthday!"

Our long posting in London was unforgettable. When it came to an end, my husband retired and we returned to Egypt where I am, at present, an assistant professor in the English department at Cairo University.

They are known as one of the most popular couples in Egyptian social life.

Their successors at the Egyptian Embassy in London are His Excellency Ambassador Adel El Gazzar and his wife Heba. In the various posts they have occupied, Heba has been very successful, especially in the entertainment of their guests. After the Ambassador had presented his credentials to Her Majesty Queen Elizabeth the return journey to the Egyptian Embassy was made in the royal carriage as tradition dictates. As my husband and I were approaching the Embassy to attend the reception we saw the Embassy butlers come out into the street bearing glasses of champagne for the coachmen, who could not leave their carriages. Other butlers arrived with magnificent silver trays laden with delicacies. It was an example of oriental hospitality that we shall always remember.

Monaco – A State on its own

In the world of diplomacy, to represent one's country, as Ambassador in Paris is to hold one of the most prestigious posts that a nation's diplomatic service has to offer. Those who are appointed are usually senior diplomats with a long record of service and achievements for whom this coveted post will often be the last before retirement.

For many years, in Paris, I have known the Ambassador of the Principality of Monaco, Christian Orsetti. Monaco is an unusual State in that it is a constitutional hereditary monarchy in which the reigning sovereign – Prince Rainier III since 1949 – holds and exercises executive powers directly but shares the legislative powers with the Principality's elected National Assembly. Consequently, it is the Prince, personally, who chooses and appoints diplomatic representatives.

In 1977, Monaco's legation in Paris was the first of the Principality's diplomatic missions to be raised to ambassadorial status. For his country's first ambassador, Prince Rainier chose Christian Orsetti. Twenty-five years on he is still Ambassador and now the *de facto* doyen of the diplomatic corps in Paris, although the doyen *de jure* is the Papal Nuncio, the Vatican Ambassador.

It is common knowledge that a successful Ambassador is helped by his wife. One such lady is Marina Orsetti who is liked for her warmth, charm and ability to be the perfect hostess. Each year they give a big official party to celebrate Prince Rainier's birthday; more than eight hundred guests are present. This grand occasion takes place in the Pavillon d'Armenonville in the Bois de Boulogne.

Marina chooses special decorations on the chosen theme, which changes every year. Champagne flows endlessly and the buffet runs the length of the huge hall. It is a moment of real enchantment that my husband and I never miss it. We always meet friends for whom this has become an annual rendez-vous.

Apart from such parties, Marina's diplomatic 'hen' lunches are famous. Each guest is given a present. I still treasure the piece of porcelain that I received at one of them many years ago.

One day, I asked Marina to describe Princess Grace for me.

"Princess Grace was very popular, one reason being that when she met people her face literally lit up. She always treated everyone in exactly the same natural way." Marina has never forgotten the day when she was sitting in the drawing-room with her grand-daughter in her arms and looked up to see the Princess arriving with her daughter, Stephanie via the service entrance in order to escape the pursuing paparazzi.

MONTGOMERY

In 1942, my uncle Kamel Sedky Pasha was the Egyptian Minister of Commerce. Britain was fighting the war against the German army in the Western Desert and had stopped the German advance towards Cairo at El Alamein. General Montgomery, the commander of the British Eighth Army, was building up his forces for an offensive to drive the Germans out of North Africa. Montgomery made it known that he would like a meeting with my uncle in the form of a private visit to my uncle's splendid Pharaonic style house in Guizeh on the banks of the Nile. This visit, scheduled to last for one hour, was duly arranged. My Aunt Blanche, in the true style of Egyptian hospitality, prepared a lavish buffet-tea and all was made ready to give Montgomery a warm and friendly welcome. At five o'clock on the dot, Montgomery arrived, accompanied by two staff officers.

That day I was staying at Aunt Blanche's, playing with my cousins Gina and Loulou. I still remember how all three of us – we were about nine years old – hid on the second floor balcony to get a secret view of the General and his staff. We saw them arrive and gazed in awe at their military uniforms that seemed covered in coloured ribbons and decorations!

In appearance, Montgomery did not match up to my expectations. The officers with him were tall and impressive; I assumed that one of them was Montgomery and was somewhat disappointed to realise that the all-important general was the short, slight figure standing between them, crisp, stylish and stern-looking, but not exactly my idea of a dashing, romantic hero.

As the group entered the house, we children all became interested in our own affairs and anticipated – correctly as it turned out – that once the visitors had left there would be plenty of delicious left-overs from the buffet for us to tuck into.

My childhood recollections of this fleeting glimpse of General (later Field Marshal) Montgomery, who, in October of the same year was to become the victor in the famous offensive of El Alamein, were brought back to me in London many years later through an American friend of mine, Carol Barcia, who recommended that I should become a member of an international cultural and social club in London called The Overseas Women's Club.[1] At present, its members are drawn from fifty-one countries throughout the world. As the number of members per country are limited, there is always a waiting list of applicants but at that time I was the only member from Egypt.

1 *Loline Reed has been Chairman of the OWC for several years and directs its activities to perfection, especially in the choice of lecturers and the variety of programmes.*

In December 1996, the members of the club and their partners were invited to a dinner given at the House of Lords by Viscount David Montgomery and it was then I learned that his wife was a member of the club. In his after-dinner speech, the Viscount revealed a personality rather different from that associated with his father. He was jovial, charming, sensitive, witty and full of good humour.

At the time of the dinner, I had not yet contemplated embarking on my memoirs, but when in the summer of 1997 I began to write about my child-hood memories, I recalled that long-past war-time visit of General Montgomery to my uncle's house. The idea of extending this tenuous contact into the present led me to mention to Tessa, David Montgomery's wife, the possibility of an interview with her husband. My request was willingly granted and so it was that in March 1998, in the Peers' lobby of the House of Commons, I had the honour of an exclusive interview at which I was able to ask the following questions.

"Sir. May I ask you first about your schooldays? When you were away at school, how did being the son of a famous General affect your relations with your contemporaries?"

"My schooldays were spent in a quite normal and natural way. I behaved and was treated like everyone else. I had many friends and no problems."

"Is there a military tradition in your family? Did a career in the army appeal to you?"

"There was no such family tradition. My father was the only one to follow a military career. I never had any ambition to follow the same course."

"Just one more question in relation to your father. Did you ever meet Clifton James, your father's double?"

"No, I never met him. Almost immediately after his task was over, he disappeared. My father wanted to meet him again to reward him in some way for the role he had played, but he just vanished. While he was doubling for my father, he was paid the same salary as my father. He 'became' a famous man, receiving all the honours due to a General. In a word, he had everything. This persona seems to have affected him and he found it very difficult to re-adjust to normal life. So he decided to disappear. And he did."

"May I ask you to say something about your own life and career?"

"We were an ordinary family. No question of wealth, inherited or otherwise. I had to study hard to get into Cambridge, where I read engineering. For several years I worked abroad in the oil industry for Shell. Later I went into business, which took me to various Latin American countries."

"I understand that you undertook work for the government in connection with South America."

"The government asked me, as one of a team of businessmen, to carry out an economic study of Latin American countries, but I was never employed by the government as such."

"Is there any truth in the view that the United States is exploiting the natural resources of Latin America to the detriment of the native population? Are countries there in need of economic aid? Cuba for instance?"

"The kind of exploration you mention is no longer the case. Countries such as Brazil, Chile and Venezuela are prosperous and do not need external aid. Cuba is rather different. I was there a couple of years ago. The Cubans work very hard. To me, the policy of economic non-cooperation practised by the United States towards Cuba seemed very short-sighted."

"The present British government is committed to reforming the House of Lords. What are your views on this?"

"I am an hereditary member of the Lords but I expect that soon I shall no longer have the right to sit there. I shall be happy to give up my place. I am in favour of change if it will lead to better government and not just be of benefit to the present administration."

"I wonder if you could tell me a little about your philosophy of life, the guiding principles you would recommend to the younger generation."

"I have always worked hard to make my own way in life and this is what I recommend that young people should do."

When our conversation was over and I was walking through the Peers' Lobby with the Viscount. He remarked, "Do you know, there are sixty million Chinese learning English? That's more than the total population of Great Britain. It makes you think!"

As we parted, I was conscious that I had been interviewing a typical English gentleman – elegant, well dressed and with impeccable manners.

The Viscount is married to the daughter of a well-known English writer Daphne du Maurier. Tessa, his wife, is tall, feminine and calm. She prefers to listen rather than to talk.

HAWAII

My uncle Kamel Mouftah (one of my mother's brothers) had two daughters, Laurence and Amira. Laurence, the elder, is a traditionalist and to this day has a passion, rather than just a duty, to keep the family around her whatever the circumstances. Amira at a young age developed a very different passion – to become a doctor. At the age of twenty-two she completed her medical studies with distinction. She emigrated to the United States where she specialised in cardiovascular anaesthesia and became a professor.

She was young and beautiful and very attractive. She had no shortage of suitors. Whereas her elder sister had made a traditional Coptic marriage, Amira was a revolutionary. She fell in love with a Moslem – Adham, the well-educated, handsome son of a Pasha. In the 1950s this was not only a scandal but also an insult to the honour of a religious family with a leading position in the Coptic Church. It was inconceivable. My brother Adib, a doctor who had studied abroad, saw a brilliant future for his cousin and took her into his private clinic, the Garden City Hospital in Cairo. Here she found refuge whilst waiting to arrange her permanent departure from Egypt. Arrangements were carried out in complete secrecy and with the utmost discretion. Having finally made her decision, Amira took a plane to Italy, narrowly escaping her uncle who had somehow heard of her precipitate departure. In his anger he said, "We would rather kill her than allow this marriage to take place."

In Rome, Amira passed the ECFMG, an examination that qualified her for an internship in an American hospital. Aged twenty-four, she flew to Washington DC where she secured an internship at Providence Hospital. In October 1967 Adham joined her and they were married in an Episcopalian Church in Washington. As Amira was a practising Christian, Adham had first to agree that any children from the marriage would be Christians. He was a freethinker and made no objections. Amira enjoyed a brilliant career in California, bought herself a flat on the large island of Hawaii, on the Kona side, and they had two sons: Adam, a brilliant lawyer and Sherif, a businessman.

And so it happened that at Christmas 1992 I was invited to spend a few weeks with her, first at her home in Davis, California, near San Francisco, then in Hawaii. A memorable stay. On New Year's Day 1993 we flew from San Francisco to Hawaii with all the passengers wishing each other a Happy New Year. Four hours later we arrived at Kona airport where Adham was waiting for us. What a wonderful change of scenery. The airport buildings were constructed of bamboo, Japanese style, surrounded by palm trees. It was summer, but not too hot. I was immediately charmed by the variety of the landscape. The extent of the Maurs, the old volcanic lava flows, came as a surprise to me. In Waikoloa, where my cousin lived, all the houses were built in the picturesque local Polynesian style. Every morning, as I had breakfast on the balcony, I watched the Americans playing golf being driven by jeep from one hole to the next. This was new to me; I thought that walking the course was an essential part of the sport.

Amira and I shared a love for swimming. Every day we went with her husband to different beaches. The number of hotels on Kona seemed countless. Situated on the wide sweep of the deserted coast each had its own beach. The lovely hotel Mauna Kea is like a city in its own right. Originally, it belonged to an American called Smart but was later bought by one of the Rockefellers who furnished it with original Polynesian items including a beautiful round marble table that stands in the hall. In former days, it was at this table that the King of Polynesia entertained his guests. Most hotels are privately owned, jointly by American and Japanese companies. One of the largest hotels in the world, of which I still have vivid memories, is the Hyatt, built originally by a rich Texan family, now the Hyatt-Hilton. In 1993 it was six years old. It had taken four years and 600 million dollars to build. Few people in Europe knew of its existence. Its owners do not advertise, believing that satisfied visitors are the best publicity. But after six years the hotel had still not recouped the 600 million dollars.

For me, a day spent there was like a dream. The area that it covers is so vast that one is taken from the hall to a lake where a boat is waiting to take you to the destination of your choice. There are several stopping points including beaches where, under the guidance of an instructor, one can swim with dolphins; a variety of restaurants each with its own national cuisine. One amusing feature is that visitors staying in the hotel have to take a train to go to their rooms. The beauty of the scenery is breathtaking – wonderful parrots imported from South America, fish of all colours in the artificial rivers and lakes.

My holiday in Hawaii was a memorable one thanks to Amira and Adham who took me around to see most places. For those in search of relaxation and especially for lovers of nature, it is wonderful.

In 1959 the Polynesian islanders, along with the Japanese population voted to become part of the United States. The government takes a firm line on the preservation of the islands. Each village has its own security guard constantly on patrol in a jeep, keeping an eye on everything.

One day we visited Parker Ranch. Parker was an Englishman who married a rich Polynesian princess. His ranch is now a museum displaying the many antiques that he acquired on his worldwide travels.

My last evening in Hawaii was spent strolling through the markets. A woman selling real pearls from Japan took my interest. For ten dollars one could choose an oyster. The stall-holder would open it and, behold, inside was a natural pearl; you might find a grey, or sometimes a pink pearl. I bought ten oysters and had the pearls mounted in a beautiful ring.

For me, Kona, the largest island of Hawaii, has remained a place of enchantment where relaxation is king. I was in a different world.

SALVADOR DALI

In Paris during the 1980s, my friends included ex-King Fuad II of Egypt and his wife Fadila. From time to time they would invite me to go out with them and on one occasion I was asked to accompany them for lunch at Maxim's.[1] Our hosts were Salvador Dali and his wife Gala. There was an interesting and unusual mixture of personalities. I was seated near Gala, who was known to be her husband's muse and right hand; she had a forceful and original personality of her own. Her first words to me were, "Oh you're Egyptian! I love to go to Egypt and walk in the streets and meet handsome boys!"

During the meal, Salvador Dali invited us all to the Hôtel Crillon for the forthcoming official unveiling to the press of one of his paintings.

One of my friends, Christiane Plantey,[2] the wife of a French ambassador, came with me and we duly arrived in the hotel lounge where the journalists were waiting for Dali. Gala recognised me and came to sit with us. Dali made an extravagant, pompous entrance complete with gold and diamond- studded walking stick to match the gold and diamond rings on his fingers.

After talking briefly to the press, he came over to me, gripped my hand firmly and said, "Come with me!" I protested but Gala interrupted, "Go with him, I will look after your friends." There was nothing I could do but obey. Feeling more than a little scared, I was led away by this mysteriously silent eccentric through the long corridors of the hotel until we arrived at his private suite. We entered a lounge; Dali let go of my hand and, without a word, turned and went into another lounge, leaving me in the company of a large number of strange guests, most of them young and none of them known to me. I observed and listened, especially to the voice of Dali coming from an adjoining room where a young man was reciting poetry. I could hear Dali correcting him, shouting at him and becoming more and more furious. That was my last impression of Dali, for he never re-appeared at the party.

Gala arrived a short while later with Christiane Plantey. As we sat talking , a girl came over and said, "Madame Gala, I would like to introduce you to my new friend." Gala looked and then asked, "Is it a man or a woman?" I felt the same way. This was the first time I had been at a gathering where I was surrounded by transvestites whose sex I was unable to determine. It was a bewildering experience just to observe this strange company in which everyone seemed perfectly at ease with everybody else in a world of their own.

---

1 *Maxim's, a luxurious Parisian restaurant patronised by the rich and famous.*
2 *Christiane Plantey was one of my dearest friends who passed away some years ago. I shall always remember her.*

A ROYAL WEDDING

When the Duchess de La Rochefoucauld took me for the first time to the Lyceum Club in Paris she introduced me to her niece Elisabeth, Marquise de Castellane, who at that time was the national President of the Lyceum Club. Eventually I became a member, with Elizabeth acting as my sponsor. As time went on, there developed a kind of communication and understanding between Elisabeth and myself. She had a striking personality and all a young woman could ask for: beauty, class, wealth, titles and honours. None of these prevented her from being involved in social work among the poor. She was also drawn to politics. In 1942 she had married Count Louis de Castellane Esparron who became a Marquis on the death of his father. In 1943 Elisabeth's father made her a present of the Château de Fleurigny, a wonderful castle situated in the Yonne region. Medieval, fortified, surrounded by a moat, Fleurigny had been fought over by the English and French in the Hundred Years' War, twice visited by King Francis in the sixteenth century and lived in by many Knights of Malta.

Several times over the years I was invited to grand occasions at the castle, especially in the 1980s when guests at the marvellous lunches included Madame Chirac and the Countess of Paris. On another occasion I was invited, with Peter my English husband, to a luncheon at which the guest of honour was the Duc d'Anjou. Peter was seated next to the wife of the Czechoslovak Ambassador, who thought that all the guests present must live in castles. During the course of the meal she asked Peter, "And where in England is you castle?" Peter thought for a moment and considered saying "which one?" but changed his mind and confessed to the humble truth!

On 25th May 1991 a Royal Wedding took place to which we were invited. This was on the occasion of the marriage of Constance, Elisabeth's grand-daughter, to Prince Charles-Emmanuel de Bourbon-Parme.[1] A more idyllic setting for the event could scarcely be imagined – the château de Dampierre is situated in the Yvelines, some 35 km to the south-west of Paris. The owner of the château, the Duc de Luynes[2] was a close friend of the Bourbon-Parme family.

---

1. *The house of Bourbon-Parme originated in 1748, when the Italian Duchy of Parme came into the possession of the Spanish branch of the French Bourbon dynasty. This Spanish branch dates from 1700, when a grandson of Louis XIV became King Philip V of Spain.*
2. *Luynes: A very old aristocratic family. Charles de Luynes came into favour, power and titles in the early years of the reign of Louis XIII. The Château de Dampierre was rebuilt for the family, some sixty years later, about 1680, by J.H.Mansart, at the time the principal architect of Louis XIV, and has remained in the family ever since. Le Nôtre, the most famous French landscape designer, laid out the grounds. It is open to the public at certain times, as is the Château de Fleurigny.*

The marriage service was held in the village church. Standing outside for a while after the ceremony, the guests, many of whom had come from different countries especially for the occasion, chatted with each other and took photographs. An English couple that we did not know came up to us and asked Peter if he would take a photograph of them. "Yes of course." Peter replied in English. The ensuing conversation rather surprised the couple, who remarked, "You speak very good English for a Frenchman!" We all laughed and enjoyed the amusing moment.

Among the five hundred guests at the reception held on the lawns of the château, were many Ambassadors, as well as young members of certain royal families, such as Prince Victor and Princess Maria Pia of Savoy and Prince Jean of Luxembourg. The dresses were of the utmost elegance. The hats, especially, were a dazzling sight, extraordinary in their originality, surpassing even Ascot. Champagne, accompanied by canapés, flowed in abundance. Standing at the far end of the lawns, a group of huntsmen dressed in red hunting costume blew their hunting horns, repeating their performance several times at intervals.

At eight in the evening, the doors of the château were opened and we were led through private rooms specially opened for the occasion, thanks to the friendship between the Princess of Bourbon-Parme and the Duc de Luynes. The evening was just beginning. In the Orangery, gaily decorated with striped hangings, dinner was served for the five hundred guests. As the fabulous meal progressed, a group of Mexican musicians circulated among the tables adding to the gaiety of the atmosphere with their traditional music. Finally came the cutting of the wedding-cake with a sabre by the happy couple.

Space was made for the dancing to begin. Peter and I decided it was getting late and we had to drive back to Paris. We asked the security guard to bring our car, which like all the others, had been driven off to a parking area by security as soon as we arrived. As we left the Orangery in the dark, the long winding path was lit on both sides by candles in the ground, a romantic departure and ending to an unforgettable event that had been a privilege for everyone to attend.

AMUSING SHORT STORIES

Vinogradov

Whilst on a journalistic visit to Paris I was invited to dinner by Nawab Ali Yavar Yung who, at that time, was the Indian Ambassador in Paris. I first met him a long time ago, when he was posted to Egypt during the Nasser era.

So I attended the dinner which was informal, intimate, interesting and amusing, with only three guests and the host. There was HRH Princess Dina, the first wife of King Hussein of Jordan, Vinogradov, the famous Russian Ambassador and myself.

At the table we were seated according to protocol as follows: Princess Dina was placed on the right of the host. Opposite, was Vinogradov and I was placed on his right. Throughout a delicious dinner consisting of a variety of Indian dishes the Soviet Ambassador discussed with me various sensitive political and social subjects then, suddenly, towards the end of the meal he turned, looked at me and said, "You are the Queen of Jordan?" With a broad smile I replied, "No, I am an Egyptian journalist and a great friend of Ali." He was embarrassed and astonished. What a shock for him! There was silence for a moment, and then I said to him, "Your Excellency, it is rare for a journalist to be discreet, but discretion is one of my main principles. Those who know me trust me. It is because of this that I am invited everywhere. You can be assured that your conversation with me will be off the record."

It is interesting to relate who Vinogradov was one of the most famous Soviet Ambassadors of his time. He remained in Paris for nine consecutive years. He lived like a Lord, gave lavish dinners and receptions, and spent his weekends at his country house on the outskirts of Paris.

A question from Uruguay

During the five years that a certain Uruguayan Ambassador represented his country in Egypt I came to know him and his wife very well. Some time after they had returned to their native country I received a charming letter from them at the end of which they asked me. "Do you still have as many enemies? If you do not it is because you have stopped being successful and are not a top journalist any more!"

Thank you kind sir!

Trouble with Flowers

Prime Minister Nehru of India, a leading figure on the world political stage at the time, was coming to pay an official visit to Egypt. As I was very sympathetic

Prime Minister Jawaharlal Nehru of India at a press conference on his arrival at Cairo military airport. Isis is sitting next to him.

to India my newspaper sent me to cover his arrival in Cairo. His plane was due to land at a military airport. Waiting to greet him there and dressed in Indian national costume were the leader and other representatives of the Indian community in Cairo. In accordance with Indian custom, the leader had a bouquet of flowers to present to Nehru on his arrival, but the flowers were wrapped in the customary Indian way in a sealed packet, which concealed its contents.

When I arrived at the airport waiting room the only empty seat was next to the Indian leader with his packet. Almost immediately, and before I could take the seat, I was approached by an Egyptian security official in plain clothes. Although he thought he knew that the packet contained nothing more deadly than flowers, he was still worried, but did not want to reveal his status. So could I perhaps investigate for him to set his mind at rest? I took my seat and gently started a conversation with my neighbour. I enquired what was in the packet cautiously leaning over to loosen the wrapping as delicately and discreetly as I could. It was an embarrassing situation, to say the least. It was just as well that I was young and bold!

The inseparable companion of Nehru on his travels was his Foreign Minister, Krishna Menon. A skilful politician, he always remained in the background, in the shadow of Nehru. I once had the opportunity to talk to him and to listen to his spiritualistic views. He rarely ate, but drank fifty cups of tea a day.

Protocol – or who sits where?
When I used to write and talk about Queen Fadila, my friends and acquaintances would often ask me why I called her a Queen, when she never reigned.

Shortly after King Ahmed Fuad II married Fadila in October 1977, he contacted me by telephone at my home in Paris. On answering the phone he introduced himself as Fuad. I said, "Who?" He repeated, "Fuad." I then enquired, whom am I speaking to, after a pause he continued by saying, "The King." You can imagine my surprise. When I finally composed myself I answered, "I am honoured your Majesty, how can I help you?" "I would like to introduce you to my wife," was the reply.

So I decided to organise a dinner in their honour, but as I was not sure how to seat the guests I rang the protocol department of the French Foreign Office. I was told that, "A king who has reigned, if only for a day, is always a king and Fadila, who married him in exile, automatically becomes a queen. Although you are receiving their majesties in your home in Paris, you are, by virtue of your Egyptian origin receiving the king in an Egyptian house. He is therefore the host and the one who receives his guests. His queen should sit on his right, with the Countess de la Baume at his left." I pointed out that we were in France and that France is a republic, so the French Ambassador's wife, Madame Jean Cazeneuve, should take precedence. The chief of protocol replied, "No, Madame, you are giving a dinner in honour of a king, so you must apply royal protocol. The Count de la Baume is a descendant of the Count de la Vallière, who was of royal blood."

A few days later I gave a reception, the King and Queen were introduced to society life in Paris. They often thanked me for 'opening the door.' My guests soon started to give dinners in their honour – with the correct protocol.

A Pharaoh's Head

When Gamal Abdel Nasser nationalised the Egyptian Press in 1953 the news-papers became State property. Anwar al-Saadat was appointed General Manager of a chain of newspapers printing in Egyptian, English and French. These included the daily *El Goumhoureya* (The Republic newspaper created at the time of the revolution). *The Egyptian Gazette* and *Le Progrès Egyptien.*

Saadat had a dual rôle. In addition to his responsibilities as manager, he was Editor-in-Chief and so wrote the political editorial every day. At this time I was a young journalist – a diplomatic correspondent. What impressed me most about Saadat was the attention and interest he showed to all the staff, great and small. People could submit ideas to him and he listened to them all irrespective of the person presenting them. For example, I summoned up courage to go and knock on his door when I was a young beginner. I told him about my invitation to Cuba because his permission had to be obtained before I could accept it. He was delighted, telling me, "I strongly encourage you to go," then added with a smile, "As long as it doesn't cost the newspaper anything."

I was also impressed by his simplicity, his skill in having ears for everything, his open-mindedness and his intellectual honesty. These attributes helped him when he became President of the Republic.

In 1953, as a young colonel, he was a well-educated, interesting person well versed in international culture. He had a passion for following international pol-itics daily. Even during the Revolution, Saadat kept up to date with what was happening elsewhere in the world. This never ceased to astonish intellectuals and journalists who came from various parts of the world to interview him. They would comment, "What is striking about him is his 'Pharaoh's head.' He looks like Ramses II and so must belong to the hereditary tradition of the Egyptian people."

AN INSIGHT INTO
THE LIFE OF A CONCERT PIANIST

Since my adolescence I have been a lover of classical music and attended concerts whenever possible. Soon after I took up residence in Paris I had the opportunity in 1957 to meet at the Egyptian Embassy a young pianist named Ramzi Yassa. As we had a common interest in classical music and I liked his style I have followed his career from his early beginnings in Paris to the present day. This young Egyptian was to attain international status and a reputation which has taken him to concert halls throughout the world. His determination to succeed included taking part in competitions, the honours he achieved included a Certificate of Honour in the Tchaikovsky Competition, the Franz Liszt Century Commentary Medal and First Prize in the Paloma O'Shea International Competition in Santander.

One day I asked Ramzi to tell me the story of his early life.

As strange as it may seem I feel convinced that even when my mother was still carrying me I could hear her playing the piano! My mother is a professional musician and she started to give me lessons when I was five years old. Three years later when it had become clear that I possessed the ability and the desire to follow a career as a pianist my mother engaged a well-known tutor for me – an Italian named Puglisi. He was a hard taskmaster and a strict disciplinarian. One day I refused to play a certain piece of music in a public place for him, saying that I felt that I was not ready for it. He did not take kindly to my attitude, and reported to my mother that I was rude and ill mannered. I owe a great debt to his teaching. Through his strictness I learnt the importance of absolute precision and developed the attitude of mind of a perfectionist.

When I was seven and a half I gave my first concert. It was in the Oriental Hall of the American University in Cairo. I played to a full house and my performance was well received! My first professional concert took place when I was fourteen, in the Cairo Royal Opera House where I played with the Egyptian Symphony Orchestra. As a matter of interest, the original Royal Opera House was built in Opera Square during the reign of the Khedive Ismail in order to receive the Empress Eugénie when she came to Egypt for the inauguration of the Suez Canal. This Opera House was demolished during Nasser's time and a new one built on a different site close to the Nile. The new Opera House opened in 1988.[1]

---

1 *The Opera performed on that particular evening was Verdi's "Aïda."*

Six years later, after I had completed my studies at the Cairo Conservatoire, the Russian School of Music attracted me; I was fortunate to receive a scholarship to study in Moscow at the Tchaikovsky Conservatoire. I was there for five years and I learnt to speak Russian. For me it was a dream comes true. The general atmosphere was austere, but I was fascinated by it. I met some of the living legends of classical music, including Richter and Rostropovitch. It was an exciting and enriching experience.

My teacher at the Tchaikovsky Conservatoire was Dorenski. He was keen to enter me for an international competition in Paris. I took part and as a result was admitted to the Margaret Long Conservatoire. At the end of my studies in Moscow I returned to Egypt. However, My early French education had given me a French cultural background and I felt drawn to Paris. In 1976, at the age of twenty-eight I settled there to develop my career."

Although Ramzi's musical studies left him with little leisure time when he was a child and an adolescent, he led a normal life at the French school in Cairo where he received his general education. He was often first in his class, being especially gifted in mathematics. At the age of twelve he was buying geometry books with his pocket money and still retains a keen interest in this subject. At school, he also enjoyed the sports periods at school running was his favourite.

I followed Ramzi's concerts in Paris and saw his reputation grow. The French newspaper Le Figaro described him as "a poet at the piano." Over the years he has played in London, Paris, Moscow, with concert tours in Morocco, Spain and Turkey including other countries. He has recorded Beethoven and Chopin for the B.B.C. and played under famous conductors including Sir Charles Groves, Zubin Mehta, Vladimir Ashkenazy and Sir Yehudi Menuhin. Besides carrying out his numerous concert engagements he is a professor at the Ecole Normale de Musique in Paris and adjudicates regularly at international piano competitions in the United States and Europe.

Concert pianists, like all professional musicians, practise daily for many hours. When I asked Ramzi how long it took him to prepare for a concert he replied, "No musician can answer that question. Different works require different preparation times. The music has to mature within the mind of the performer who must seek to penetrate the thoughts of the composer, and by researching his intentions arrive at an individual and personal interpretation of his work."

In 1988 Ramzi was invited to play at the inaugural concert of the new Cairo Opera House. When I am in Paris or Egypt with my husband we always ask if Ramzi is playing and is it possible to attend. For me these are special occasions, a reminder of a long association with an always modest, unassuming and charming master of the piano who over the years has been a reliable, helpful and true friend. Ramzi has a lovely wife, Bridgette, whom I have known since she was Ramzi's fiancée in the early days. I attended their marriage which was really fabulous and took place on a boat on the Seine in Paris. Now they have two very nice children, a son Magi and a daughter Laura.

DR. RAGHEB MOFTAH
IN THE SERVICE OF THE LORD

I end my memoirs with an account of the life of an extraordinary man who was called to his Maker in his 103rd year. He completed the book to which he had dedicated his life just two years before he died. This man was my mother's brother, hence my uncle, and this is his story.

Ragheb Moftah was born in Cairo in 1898 into a Coptic upper-class family whose ancestors included many who had been prominent in the Coptic community. During the early years of the French occupation of Egypt, Napoleon Bonaparte wrote to Moftah's great-great uncle asking him to use his prestige and influence to calm anti-French disturbances by Copts and Moslems in his quarter of Cairo. It is not known whether Napoleon received a reply.

Moftah had six brothers and three sisters. One of the latter, Farida, my mother, was to exert a great influence on his career, being a constant source of support and encouragement. Throughout her life, Moftah was in awe of her.

In 1919 Moftah left Cairo for Germany where for four years he studied agriculture in Bonn. On his return to Egypt there occurred an event which was to change the entire course of his life. In 1926, he met by chance Ernest Newlandsmith a talented, eccentric Englishman, a Fellow of the Royal Academy of Music, a composer and violinist with a keen interest in theology and philosophy. Newlandsmith was passing through Cairo on a pilgrimage to the Holy Land. The two men agreed that they should meet again in Cairo on Newlandsmith's return journey.

From an early age, Moftah had fallen under the spell of the music of the Coptic Mass. In Newlandsmith, he found someone who shared his love of religious music. He admired his superior musical scholarship and invited him to stay on his houseboat on the Nile. He suggested that they should collaborate on a great undertaking – that of notating the music of the Coptic Church, starting with the form most used in the masses, the liturgy of St. Basil.

Newlandsmith was enthusiastic. From its earliest beginnings with St. Mark in Alexandria about 45AD one of the basic traditions of the Coptic Church was that of its chants. Some chants were based on the Ancient Egyptian pharaonic melodies used in the temples of Isis and Osiris, and were passed on purely orally from one generation of blind cantors to the next. The blind were believed to have greater sensitivity of hearing than the sighted. The language of the chants is Coptic. With its origins in the language of Ancient Egypt, Coptic was widely spoken up to the eleventh century before gradually giving way to Arabic.

Every winter for nine years Moftah invited Newlandsmith to stay with him in Cairo and paid his travel expenses. Day after day without fail the two men listened to the chants. Newlandsmith wrote furiously to put all the music on paper; Moftah recorded it on paper-tape reels – the best technology then available. To obtain definitive versions Moftah brought in different cantors to perform the same music over and over again. Slowly the Arabic embellishments, which had been added over the centuries, were eliminated until the heart of the original Coptic music was revealed. Convinced of the pharaonic origin of the chants, Newlandsmith was to declare, "It seems impossible to doubt that this is Ancient Egyptian. Moreover, it is great music: grand, pathetic, noble and deeply spiritual."

In 1931, Moftah accompanied Newlandsmith on his return journey to England. There they gave lectures on the splendours of Coptic music, including speaking at the universities of Oxford and Cambridge. Back again in Cairo, they continued their painstaking work until in 1936 some sixteen volumes of music had been transcribed, though the liturgy of St. Basil remained to be completed.

Moftah continued, with other collaborators, to gather and record the hymns chanted in the Coptic masses, working apparently undisturbed through the upheavals in Egypt brought about by World War II, the 1952 Egyptian revolution, and the wars with Israel. In 1954 he founded and became head of the Music and Hymns Department at Cairo's Institute of Higher Coptic Studies.

From 1979, Moftah's niece Laurence, who was head of the reference department of the American University of Cairo, acted as her uncle's general assistant and advisor. Mindful of his trusting nature she was determined to see that his work was properly recorded and protected by copyright.

In 1995, John Billington, the Head of the Library of Congress in Washington and an admirer of Moftah's work, gave a reception in his honour at the University of Cairo (AUC). He called for Moftah's collection of recordings and the volumes he had transcribed with Newlandsmith to be kept at the University library. During the two years that followed, Moftah signed agreements with the AUC Press and the Library of Congress for the preservation of all his recordings and the music in the transcriptions, agreements that also granted him copyright of all the material. In June 1997 the liturgy of St. Basil was recorded for the first time on cassette, and the AUC Press published the complete music of the liturgy, together with the Coptic words and their English and Arabic translations.

In 1996 Moftah gave a video-taped interview to the Library of Congress. In conclusion he said, "I did what I was obliged to do and it is now finished. Praise be to God." Yet he continued to work on until two years before his death in June 2001. The preservation in permanent form of most of the musical heritage of the Coptic Church was his lifetime's achievement, the result of more than seventy years of devotion to this cause.

I wrote at the beginning that Ragheb Moftah was my uncle. My memories of him go back to my childhood. He was the favourite brother of my mother Farida, and her sister, my Aunt Blanche. When I was a little girl he often used to come to our house at Heliopolis. He was stricter with us children than our father. He had the right to comment on our behaviour. This did not go down at all well with my elder brother Mounir who was a naughty, wilful boy! My mother, deeply religious as she was, admired Ragheb greatly and was a constant source of strength to him. For his part, Ragheb had the greatest respect for my mother; it is indeed true that he went in awe of her, so much so that he never felt able to call her by her name. For him she was always 'my sister.' From those early days, I remember Newlandsmith as well. I used to curtsey to him on the several occasions he came to stay at our house during his visits to Cairo to work with uncle Ragheb.

Our cousin Laurence was only being prudent in her concern to obtain proper safeguards for the results of Ragheb's work. Uncle was too unworldly, too trusting, to see the possibility that others might seek to benefit from his work. Besides, something of the kind had already occurred in our family. When Uncle Aziz, Ragheb's brother, died, the manuscript of a large work he had written on St. Mark somehow disappeared.

The title of the head of the Egyptian Coptic Church is Patriarch of Alexandria but Copts refer to him simply as *El Baba*. He is our Pope. For many years, the present Patriarch, Shenouda III, counted Ragheb as one of his best friends. Shenouda played an important, if not decisive part in the negotiations leading to the publishing and copyright agreements made in respect of Ragheb's work. And so it was that Pope Shenouda took in hand all the arrangements for Ragheb's imposing funeral. The cathedral was overflowing. El Baba led the prayers and spoke of his friend with tears in his eyes, saying, " I shall never again go to the Institute of Higher Coptic Studies because Ragheb will not be there any more." In an exceptional gesture he ordered the coffin opened during the ceremony so that he could bless and kiss the man whose life and work had been devoted to the church. As for my cousins and myself, what can we say? In the history of our family, it is the end of a long era.

A SUCCESSFUL MAN

Now that I am coming to the end of my memoirs I find that my life continues to have unforgettable surprises – some better than others. A very recent example of the enjoyable unexpected occurred in March 2003.

Whilst on holiday in Egypt with my husband Peter I was so happy to meet again my eldest nephew Ibrahim after an interval of thirty-six years. Since 1967 his life had been spent in the North America, in Canada and the United States working in the hotel business. Peter and I were very impressed when we met him sitting behind a huge desk in his luxurious office at the Cairo Sheraton Hotel. "There's no place like home," was how Ibrahim described to me his recent appointment as Managing Director of Starwood Hotels and General Manager of the Cairo Sheraton. Ibrahim is listed in *Who's Who in the World*, but I cannot help remembering how, in my early years in journalism, he used to come and visit me, his aunt. We would discuss various options for his future career. One day he told me that he would like to work in the hotel business. "In that case I may be able to help you," I replied. "I know the manager of Sheperd's Hotel." At that time it was Cairo's greatest hotel – a legend. And that is where Ibrahim started.

After gaining experience in Egypt Ibrahim emigrated to Canada and in a few years became famous and popular in his own right, enjoying a long association with the prestigious Trusthouse Forte Hotels, for which in 1986 he became the Executive Vice-President and Managing Director of the Exclusive Division/ North American Hotels. As overall director of a group of hotels renowned for world-class elegance he met and looked after celebrities and heads of state, many of whom saw the hotels he managed as their home from home.

When I asked him to tell me about some of the people he had met he laughed and replied, "There are so many. It would take too long." Briefly he mentioned President Clinton, the King of Spain and his wife – both extremely charming – and Roger Moore, who had played James Bond. "I had always wanted to meet him. He didn't have a gun or jump through any windows! In fact, he was quietly promoting Unesco and collecting funds for children's charities. He is a good example of the way in which people's real characters so often differ from their public image."

As the aunt who helped Ibrahim when he was starting out in the world, what else can I say except that I am proud of his achievements and his fabulous career!

CULTURE AND THE GODDESS

Since I came to live in England my main interest has been the promotion of French culture. Being President of the Derby French Circle gives me the opportunity to organise cultural and social events. Having a good and effective working relationship with the London head office of L'Alliance française is useful. This is a French organisation financed by the French government who sponsor worldwide membership. It was founded in Paris in 1883 to encourage in foreign countries knowledge of the French language and culture. There are fifty-two French circles in the United Kingdom. For the first time the French governing body in Paris Alliance has appointed a woman, Chrystel Hug, as the Director General of the Alliance Française in the United Kingdom. Her impact and influence has been so impressive that at the 2003 Annual General Meeting in London the Paris Director-General told me, "We hope to keep Chrystel with us for many years, she is a first-rate person. Long live women!"

England has given me another interest – a passion for animals. When I was a girl in Egypt I had a German Shepherd dog as a pet, but here the object of my affection is my cat. She is my child, my companion. We understand each other; we love each other; and we play together. I spoil her, so does my husband. She is pure white and her name is Nephtys – the goddess of the Pharaohs of Southern Egypt and the younger sister of Isis who was the Goddess of the North. My husband says he lives with two goddesses.